IMAGES
of America

VAN BUREN

ON THE COVER: An unidentified man enjoys the view from Lee Creek Bluff (Mount Vista) overlooking the Arkansas River Valley near Van Buren around 1904. Situated on the edge of the river and Ozark Plateau in western Arkansas, Van Buren played a supporting role as the crossroads of a nation.

IMAGES
of America

VAN BUREN

Tom Wing

ARCADIA
PUBLISHING

ISBN 978-1-4671-1587-2

Published by Arcadia Publishing
Charleston, South Carolina

Printed in the United States of America

Library of Congress Control Number: 2015950073

For all general information, please contact Arcadia Publishing:
Telephone 843-853-2070
Fax 843-853-0044
E-mail sales@arcadiapublishing.com
For customer service and orders:
Toll-Free 1-888-313-2665

Visit us on the Internet at www.arcadiapublishing.com

This book is dedicated to my wife, Renee, for her encouragement along the way, but also for her constant example of sacrifice, devotion, love, and commitment.

Contents

ACKNOWLEDGMENTS

Numerous people have helped and encouraged me in the writing of this book. It would not have been possible without my wife, Renee, who simply said, "You can do it," and then sacrificed her time with me for the hours of image selection, research, and writing. I am in the debt of Dr. Henry Rinne, who helped me secure the publishing contract and encouraged me along the way. Special thanks go to Liz Gurley, title manager at Arcadia, who remained patient with me and went the extra mile to finish this book. On the technical side, Andi Cumbo Floyd changed my perspective of the writing process and helped me discover the joy of letting words flow. Caroline Bercher and brothers Scott and Drennen Bulloch are to be thanked for sharing so much of their family's story—and in turn Van Buren's history—with me. Sandra Pearson and Melissa Wick, daughters of Zoe and John Cobb, donated Ora Smith's photograph collection, preserved by the Cobbs for many years in the house built by Leonard Wilhuaf. Kenneth Fry, editor of the *Press Argus Courier*, encouraged me and helped locate images. Steven Peer was instrumental in helping me locate images at the University of Arkansas at Little Rock and shared some from his own collection. Dr. Ray Wallace allowed his work to be shown here, giving insight into the people and places of turn-of-the-century Van Buren. Larry Weir is to be commended for bringing the Cornell Railroad Historical Society images to my attention, along with John Northrip, who provided me with aerial images from before and after the Flood of 1943. Norma Jean Toothaker and Joyce Gelly Patton deserve thanks for sharing personal images and stories about their own Van Buren family's heritage. I will be forever grateful to Maryl Koeth and Rusty Myers introducing me to the incredibly rich history of Van Buren. Lastly, I want to thank Randy Smith, whose passion for Van Buren is inspiring. His help with cemetery photographs, history, and his knowledge of his hometown was crucial.

Introduction

Located between the Ozark Plateau, an area of hill country extending from northwest Arkansas into Missouri, and the Arkansas River Valley, the townsite of Van Buren has seen continued human activity from prehistoric times to the present. The bluffs at Van Buren gave Native Americans from the Archaic, Woodland, and Mississippian periods a safe overlook of the land below, as well as easy access to the bounty of the river. Prehistoric and historic Indians also enjoyed the centralized location, making trade with the four corners of the continent possible.

The first documented Europeans to visit the land that became Arkansas were part of the ill-fated DeSoto expedition. Hernando DeSoto, a conquistador from Spain, came to the future southeastern United States in search of gold. Failing to find it, DeSoto paid with his own life and the lives of many of his men. The Spaniards most likely did not visit the eventual site of Van Buren, but their time in Arkansas brought disease that decreased the Mississippian-era population.

France eventually took control of the land and used limited settlement and fur trapping to establish trade and ensure Native American dependence and support. In 1803, Napoleon sold the land that became Arkansas, but not before the French left a lasting legacy. Many geographical features have or had French names, including Van Buren's Lee Creek, which was called Pappillon Creek during French colonial times.

Passing quickly from territory towards statehood after being initially settled by David Martin and Thomas Phillips, the brothers-in-law team of David Thompson and John Drennen purchased the townsite in 1836 for $11,000. Located on the Arkansas River, Van Buren grew as settlers and Native Americans moved west, some by choice and others by force. In the early and mid-19th century, Van Buren became a gateway for those affected by the Trail of Tears. The federal government created a judicial district in 1851 to handle legal affairs in Indian Territory, headquartered until 1871 at Van Buren.

The most famous prisoner ever kept at the Van Buren Federal Jail was Wyatt Earp, who escaped and changed his ways out west. In the 1860s, two armies occupied Van Buren and skirmished there in December 1862. Both slave-holding Confederates and loyal Unionists were found in Van Buren before and during the war. Confederate forces used Van Buren as a staging area from 1861 to 1863. Van Buren's Fairview Cemetery became the final resting place for a number of soldiers who fought and died at the Battles of Pea Ridge and Prairie Grove. Federal troops raided Confederate-held Van Buren following the Battle of Prairie Grove in December 1862. An artillery duel and destruction of steamboats and warehouses by Federal forces brought the war to the front door of the town. Union troops arrived in the area in September 1863, remaining through the end of the war.

Steamboat trade continued after the war, helping the community to expand and thrive; however, the coming of the railroad in 1875–1876 started a new chapter in the city's history. The Little Rock and Fort Smith Railroad, founded in the 1850s by John Drennen and completed by his son-in-law Charles Scott, was the first of a number of railroads to benefit from Van Buren's location. To better serve and speed up delivery, the Saint Louis and San Francisco Railroad ("the Frisco") built a bridge across the Arkansas River at Van Buren in 1885.

Van Buren saw some of its sons go across the Atlantic to fight in World War I. Some of them trained in the buildings of the railroad yards. By the time of the Great Depression, Van Buren's economy was still based on farming, but not without other business enterprises. Clyde Barrow, of the famous Bonnie and Clyde gang, passed through Van Buren in the summer of 1933. With Bonnie injured from an auto accident and laid up in a Fort Smith motel, Clyde and his henchmen drove up to Fayetteville and robbed a store before being pursued by authorities back to Fort Smith. Barrow ditched a stolen car on the heights above Van Buren and crossed the Frisco Bridge on foot, eluding law enforcement and reuniting with Bonnie. They were both killed in a shoot-out the following year. About the same time, favorite son Robin "Bob" Burns found stardom in radio and movies. The inventor of the bazooka, a musical instrument that was later the name of an anti-tank weapon during World War II, Burns performed with well-known entertainers such as Rudy Vallee and Bing Crosby.

World War II affected Van Buren in a number of ways. While many residents served in the war effort, the railroad yards at Van Buren, a short distance from the newly built Army post of Camp Chaffee across the river, provided a training opportunity for soldiers to learn how to run captured railroads. These Railway Operations Battalions (ROB) practiced at Van Buren but served another need when floodwaters destroyed the Free Bridge and damaged the Frisco Bridge. The ROB troops built a pontoon bridge and reconnected Van Buren with Fort Smith. The Flood of 1943 devastated downtown, damaging homes, businesses, and government buildings. While many of the flood's effects were negative, it also eventually provoked change in the river itself to help protect the area. Within 20 years of the flood, levies, flood walls, jetties, and locks and dams helped tame the wrath of the river. The Kerr-McClellan Navigation System on the Arkansas River for the first time maintained a consistent depth from the mouth of the river to Tulsa, Oklahoma. The system of locks and dams, built in the 1960s, also encouraged a revival in river traffic, as barges brought freight and commodities in and out of the region, once again by water.

While not completely abandoned, rail service has declined in Van Buren, largely due to another federal expansion project. Taking note of the German highway system during World War II, future President Eisenhower pushed for a nationwide highway system. The third-longest highway of that system, Interstate 40, passes through Van Buren. A traveler can go east from Van Buren to North Carolina or west to California. Through travel on the highways and interstates, trucks haul much of the freight previously moved by rail. Today, numerous trucking companies and terminals call Van Buren home for this reason.

From prehistoric times to the present, the site of Van Buren has seen a constant flow of goods, services, raw materials, and agricultural products move in every direction. In earlier times, people have traveled by foot, horse, boat, and rail, but more recently, cars and trucks testify to the value and significance of the interstate system. All the movement and economic activity described here and chronicled in these photographs tell the story of Van Buren: survivor of war, floods, and tornados that is river town, rail junction, and crossroads of a nation.

One

Predecessors, Pioneers, and People of Interest

The earliest European contact in the region was the DeSoto expedition in 1541. The Spaniards likely did not make it to present-day Van Buren and gave way to the French in the 17th and 18th centuries. The French explored the land that became Arkansas and established trade with the indigenous Quapaw tribe. When the Louisiana Territory became a part of the United States, Pres. Thomas Jefferson designated Arkansas as Indian Territory. Quickly settled by whites, Jefferson's plan gave way to a new territory and eventual state. Around 1818, the earliest settlers at the future site of Van Buren were Thomas Martin and David Boyd, who were both squatters. Around 1829, James Phillips, with sons Thomas and Daniel, bought the rights to the riverfront, and the site became Phillips Landing. In 1831, a post office was established and named for Secretary of State Martin Van Buren. By 1836, brothers-in-law David Thompson and John Drennen, who owned a woodlot of their own a few miles downstream at Columbus, bought out Thomas and Daniel Phillips. Thompson and Drennen platted streets and advertised residential and business lots for sale at the new town of Van Buren. Thompson died in 1837 before the family partnership and fledging city reached full potential. Drennen, followed by his son-in-law Charles Scott, invested in the new town of Van Buren and shaped the future of the community for many years. Legacies of the Drennen-Scott family remain today. Fairview Cemetery, the Crawford County Courthouse, the railroad tracks and bridge still in use today, and the family home that has been passed down by five generations of Drennen-Scott descendants exist because of the family.

Van Buren attracted a diverse group of pioneers from numerous states and foreign countries seeking fortune and opportunity. The states of Connecticut, Pennsylvania, Virginia, Georgia, Tennessee, Mississippi, and Missouri provided most of the transplants to the new town. The countries of Germany and France provided settlers as well. By 1836, Van Buren had already served as a gateway during the voluntary and forced removals of the southeastern Indians. Choctaw, Chickasaw, Muscogee/Creek, Cherokee, and Seminole groups passed by Van Buren on the Arkansas River or came overland through the town before arriving at assigned lands in Indian Territory to the west. From 1851 to 1871, the Federal Court for the Western District of Arkansas was created and convened at Van Buren to handle the numerous jurisdictional issues coming from the sovereign Indian Nations tangled in an uneasy relationship with the government.

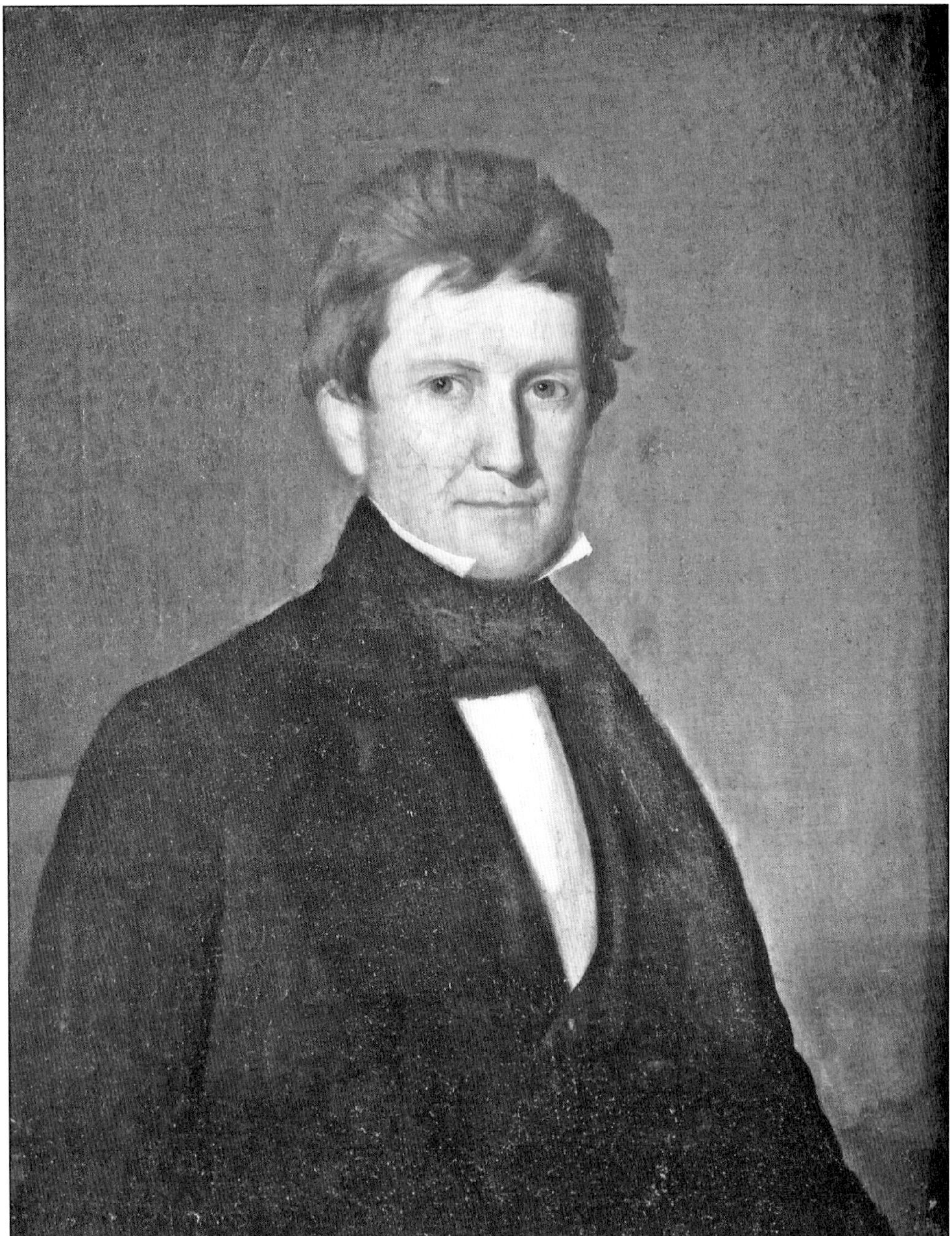

Born in Elizabeth, Pennsylvania, John Drennen was the son of an Irish immigrant and Revolutionary War veteran. Drennen married Emily Dederick Stuart and set up a mercantile business in Nashville, Tennessee. Coming to Little Rock in the late 1820s, Drennen and brother-in-law David Thompson became Van Buren's founders in 1836. This 1837 portrait is attributed to American artist George Catlin. (Courtesy of the Historic Arkansas Museum.)

Originally from Potosi, Missouri, Emily Drennen, John Drennen's first wife, had three daughters with him before dying of unspecified causes in 1844. At the time of her marriage to John, Emily was a widow and had a son named James Stuart. This 1837 portrait is attributed to George Catlin. (Courtesy of the Historic Arkansas Museum.)

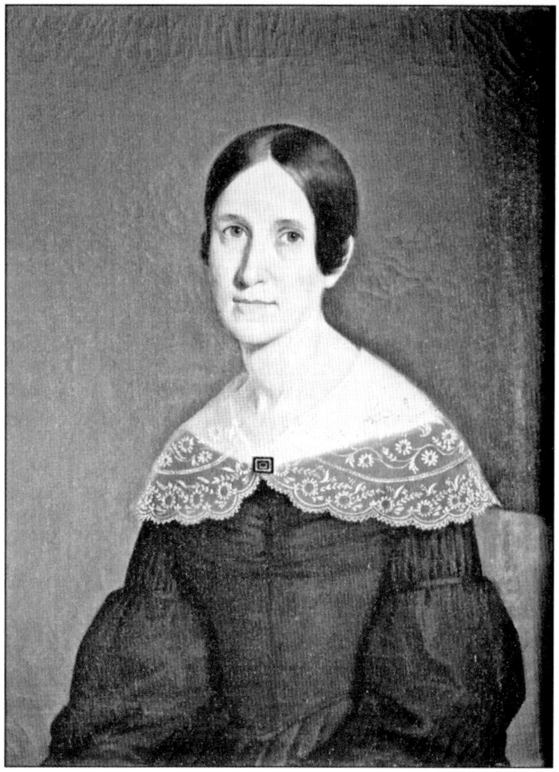

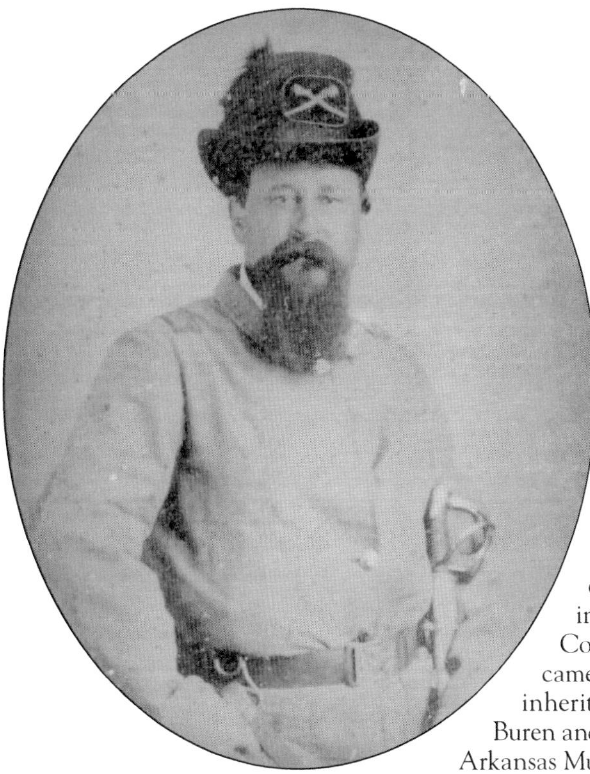

James Stuart, John Drennen's stepson, served in the 3rd Battalion Arkansas Infantry for the Confederate forces at the battle of Wilson's Creek in 1861. The unit disbanded and Stuart joined the 1st Cherokee Mounted Rifles and served as a lieutenant and captain under Brig. Gen. Stand Watie for the duration of the war. Stuart was present in June 1865 when Watie became the last Confederate general to surrender. Stuart came home to Van Buren after the war and inherited his stepfather's ferry between Van Buren and Fort Smith. (Courtesy of the Historic Arkansas Museum.)

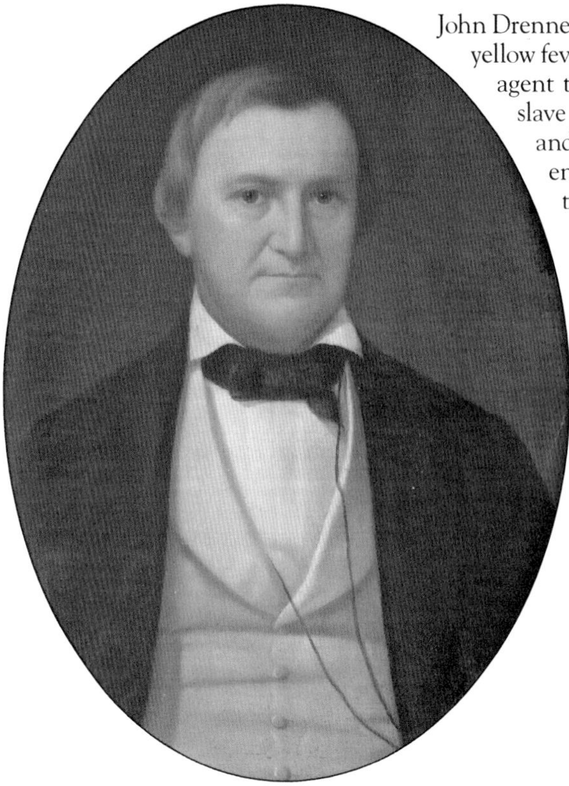

John Drennen, seen here shortly before his death from yellow fever in 1855, was a cofounder of Van Buren, agent to the Choctaw Nation, plantation and slave owner, bank trustee, real estate developer, and railroad stockholder. His tenacity as an entrepreneur helped shape the riverfront town of Van Buren in its early years. The artist who painted this portrait is unknown. (Courtesy of the Historic Arkansas Museum.)

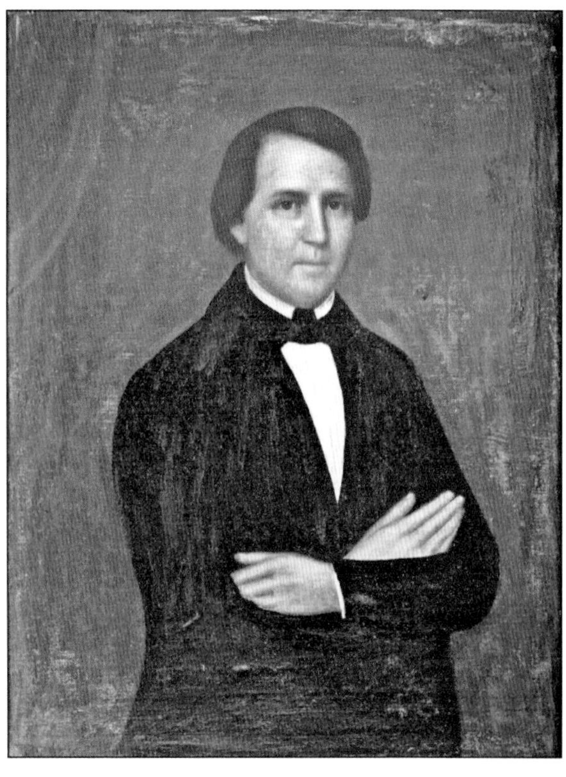

Charles Gordon Scott was born in Maryland and immigrated to Arkansas in the 1830s. He partnered with John Drennen in business ventures before marrying Drennen's eldest daughter, Caroline. Upon the death of John in 1855, Charles and Caroline inherited the estate and for a number of years paid family members from the profits gained by family-held businesses. The Scotts helped the family interests survive the Civil War. Following the conflict, Charles and Caroline sold the family's 1,000-acre plantation in southeast Arkansas. Charles was also instrumental in guiding the Little Rock and Fort Smith Railroad to completion after his father-in-law John had laid the financial foundation for it in the 1850s. Edward Payson Washburn painted this portrait. (Courtesy of the Historic Arkansas Museum.)

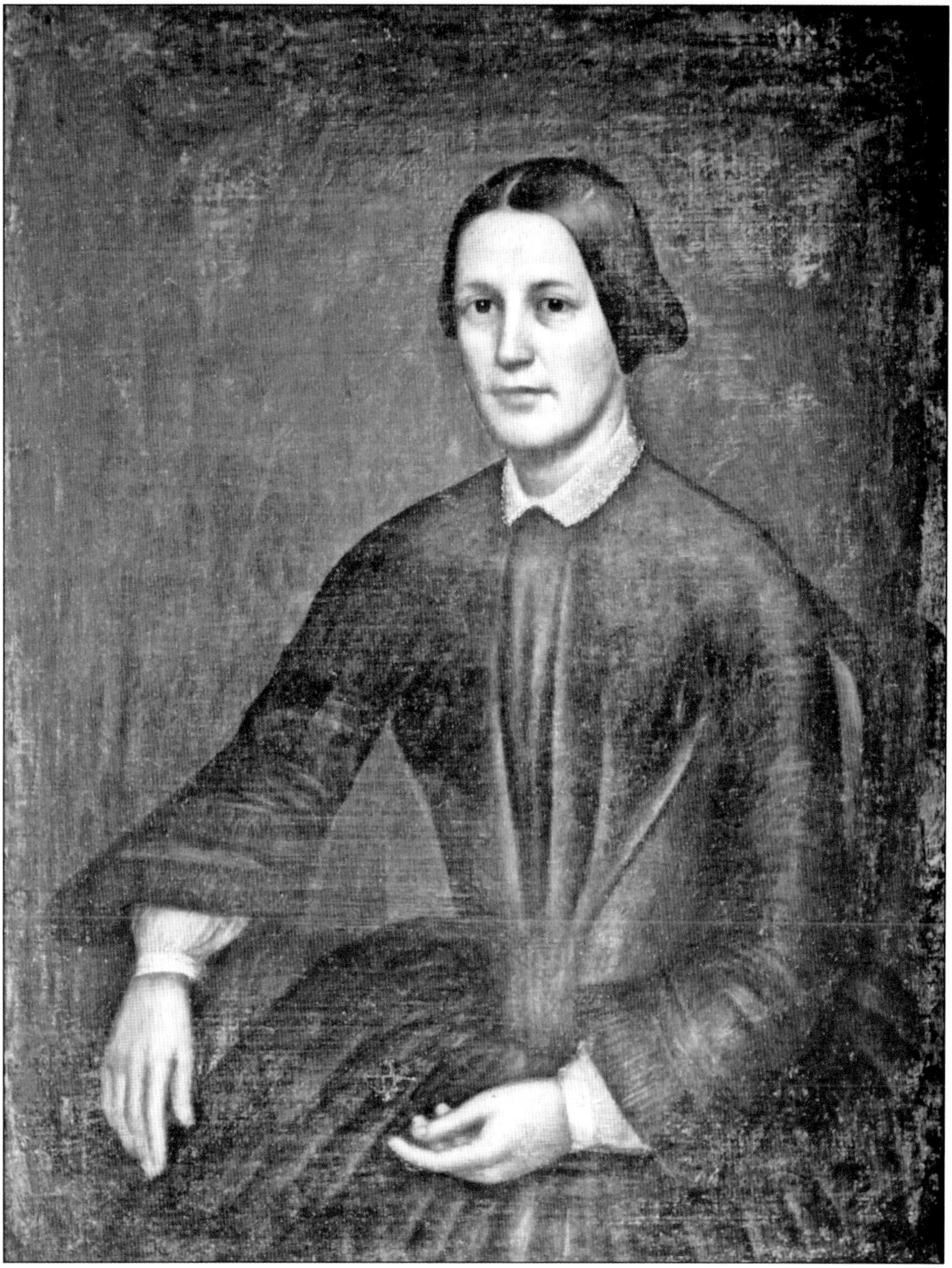

The eldest daughter of John Drennen, Caroline Scott inherited her father's financial interests with her husband in 1855. While a woman of the 19th century and essentially a second-class citizen, Caroline's name appears on many deeds and financial transactions that demonstrate an active role in the family business. The Scotts became the second of five generations to live in the house built by John Drennen. Caroline and her husband, Charles, enjoyed the power and influence of her father and continued to promote Van Buren through economic development. Edward Payson Washburn painted this portrait. (Courtesy of the Historic Arkansas Museum.)

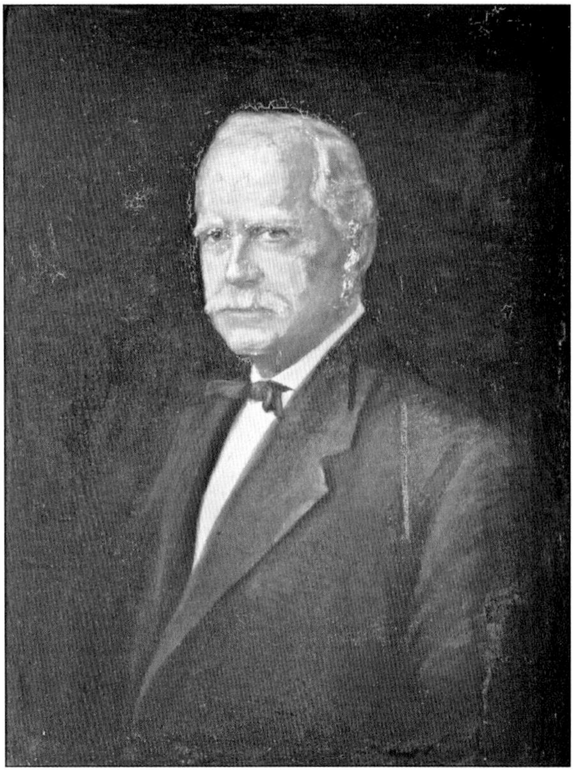

After Charles and Caroline passed in 1882 and 1910, respectively, control of the estate was placed in the capable hands of their son Phillip Drennen Scott (left). Born in 1855, "P.D.," as he was called, continued the prosperity of the family. An able businessman from a reputable family, P.D. also served as a commissioner to the 1904 World's Fair in Saint Louis. He passed in 1922, leaving the estate to his daughter Caroline Mary Scott. Caroline took care of her mother until her death in 1931. P.D.'s wife, Frances "Fanny" Dunham Scott (below), was the daughter of Van Buren newspaper editor Joseph Dunham. (Both, courtesy of the Historic Arkansas Museum.)

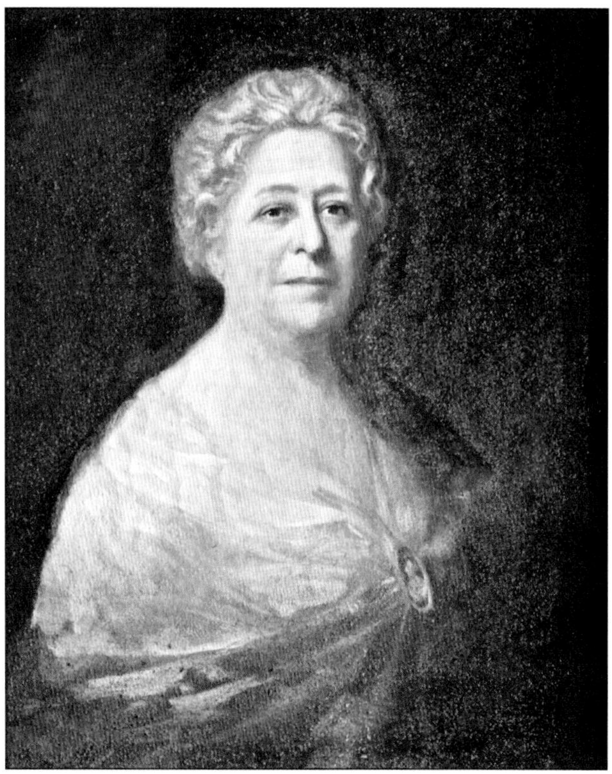

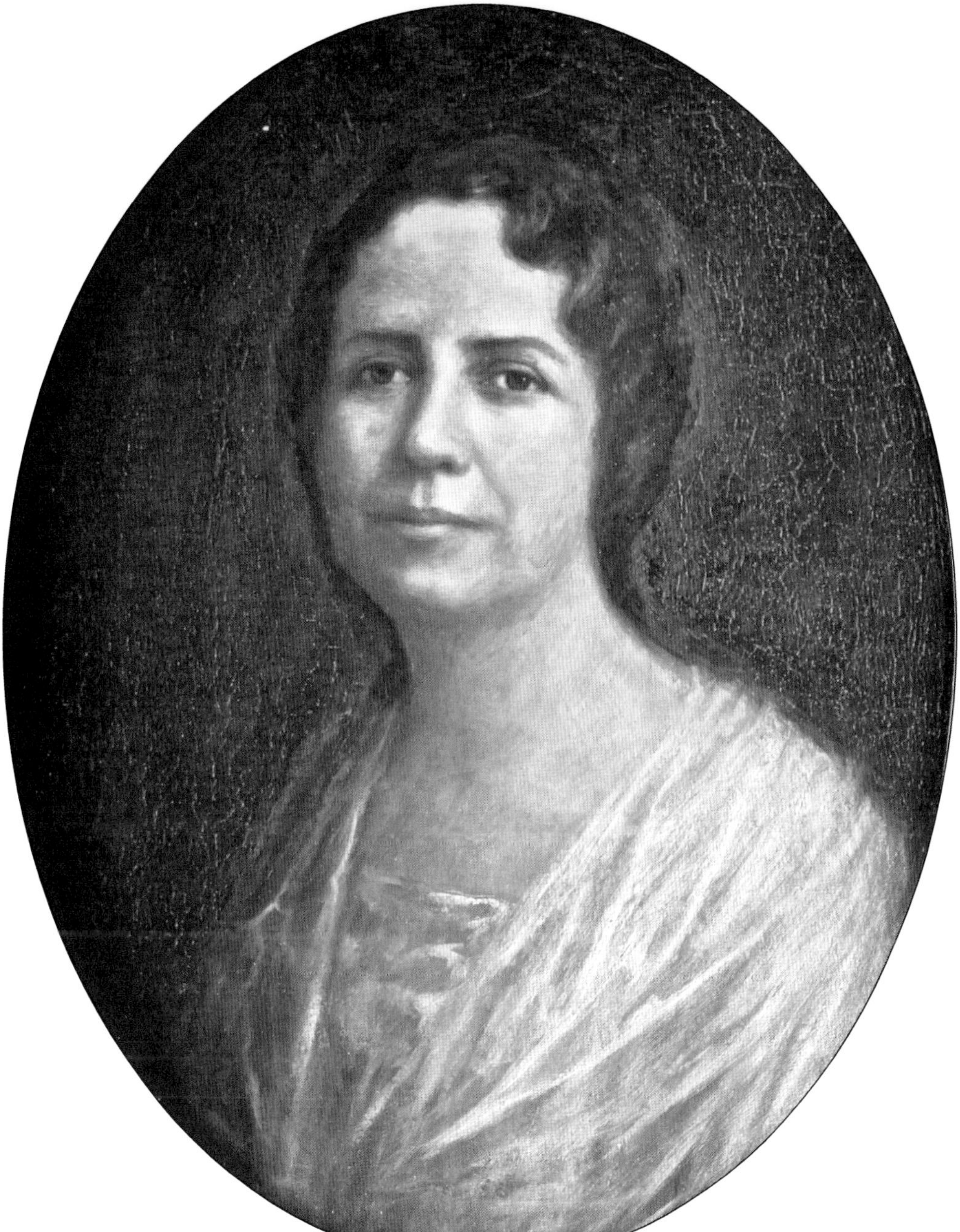

Caroline Mary Scott was born in 1892 to P.D. and Fanny Scott. Born into a life of wealth and influence, Caroline attended the Ogontz School, an exclusive finishing school for young ladies near Philadelphia. The school's most famous alumnus was Amelia Earhart. Aunt Caroline, as she was called by her family since she never married, saw her idyllic life take a turn around the time of the death of her mother. The Great Depression had taken a toll on the agriculture-related businesses of her family. Faced with property taxes, she entertained the idea of selling off the estate but chose to work instead and passed the house to the next generation upon her death in 1976. (Courtesy of the Historic Arkansas Museum.)

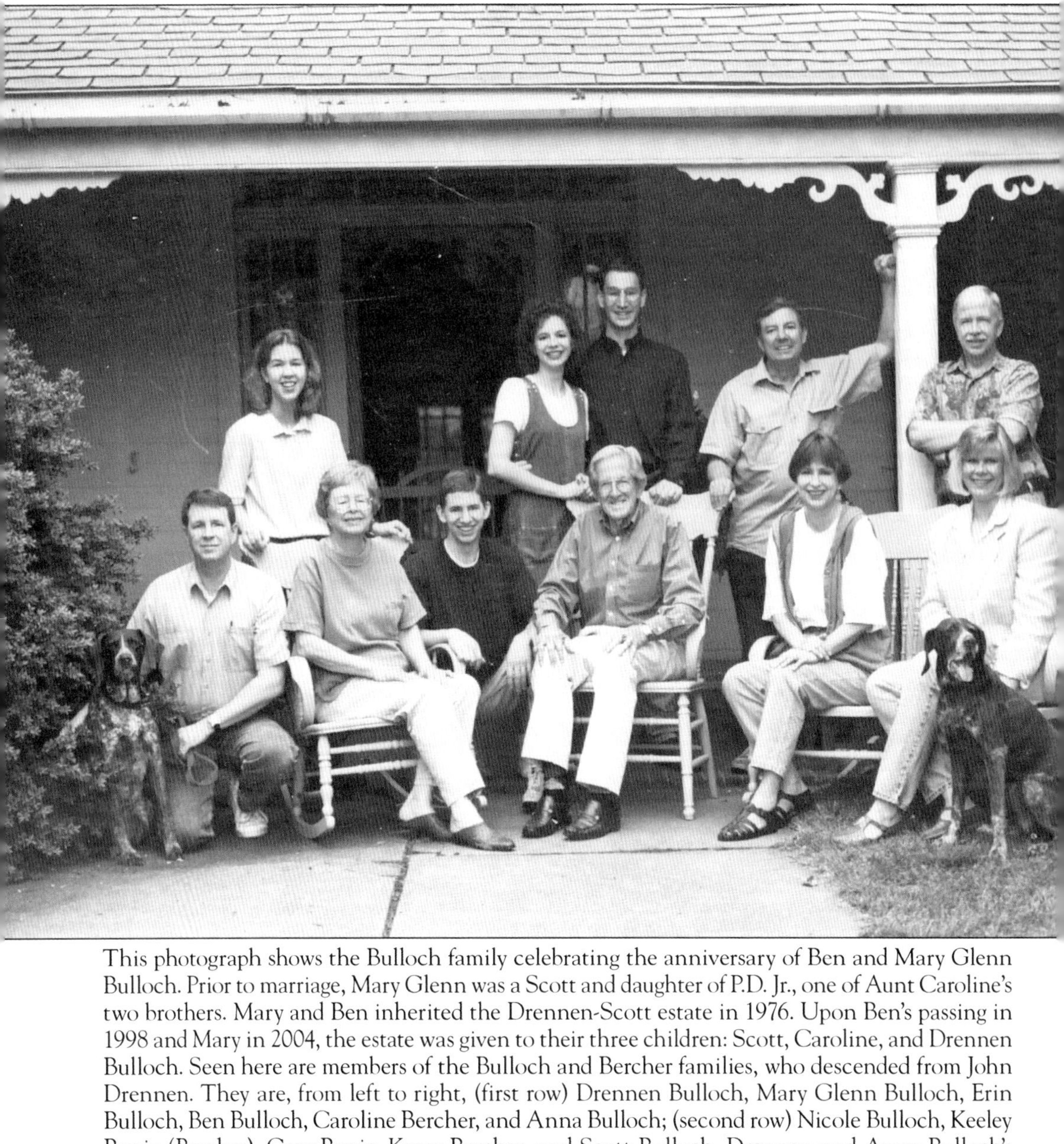

This photograph shows the Bulloch family celebrating the anniversary of Ben and Mary Glenn Bulloch. Prior to marriage, Mary Glenn was a Scott and daughter of P.D. Jr., one of Aunt Caroline's two brothers. Mary and Ben inherited the Drennen-Scott estate in 1976. Upon Ben's passing in 1998 and Mary in 2004, the estate was given to their three children: Scott, Caroline, and Drennen Bulloch. Seen here are members of the Bulloch and Bercher families, who descended from John Drennen. They are, from left to right, (first row) Drennen Bulloch, Mary Glenn Bulloch, Erin Bulloch, Ben Bulloch, Caroline Bercher, and Anna Bulloch; (second row) Nicole Bulloch, Keeley Banic (Bercher), Greg Banic, Kerry Bercher, and Scott Bulloch. Drennen and Anna Bulloch's dogs, Maggie (left) and Abby are also pictured. (Courtesy of UA-Fort Smith.)

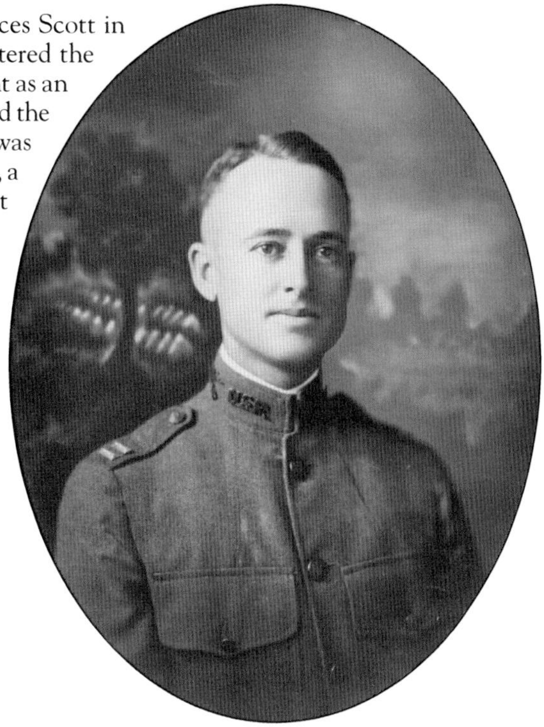

Dunham Scott was born to P.D. and Frances Scott in 1885. After attending school, Dunham entered the Army and in 1918 was sent to France to fight as an infantry captain. He was sent to France aboard the SS *Persic*, a White Star Line cargo ship that was refitted to carry troops. On September 7, 1918, a German U-boat damaged the ship but did not sink it. None of the soldiers were injured, but their guns and equipment were lost. While awaiting new supplies, the war ended on November 11, 1918, without Captain Scott reporting to the trenches, where his life expectancy would have been mere minutes. Dunham Scott was sent home and lived in Van Buren until his death on January 21, 1941. (Courtesy of UA-Fort Smith.)

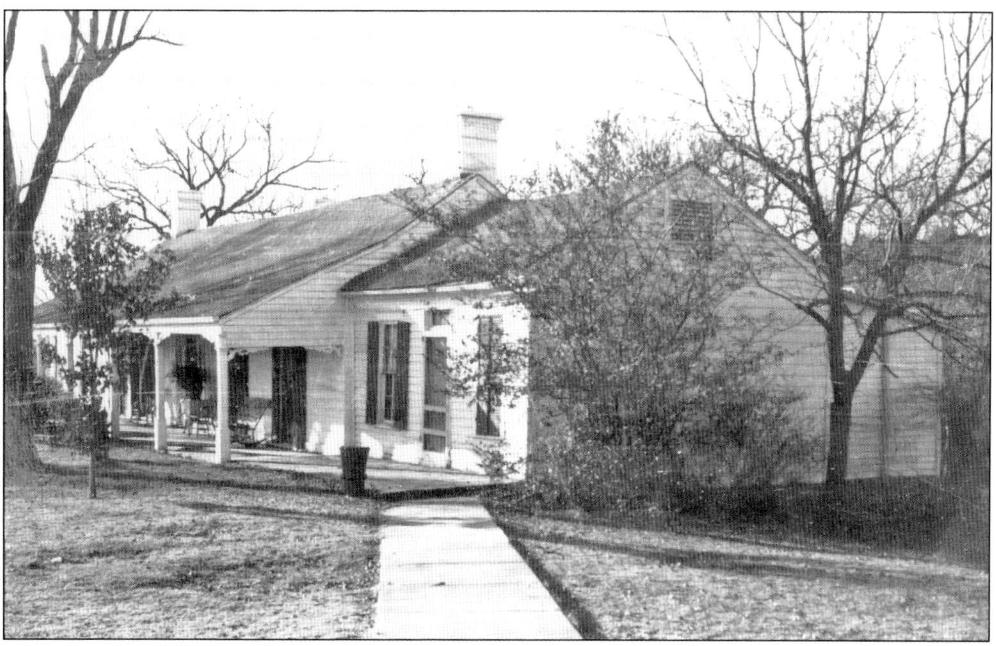

This photograph shows the Drennen-Scott House as it looked in the 1920s. Starting in 1838 as a one-room structure, the house was added to over time as the family grew and needed additional space. Built all on the same level in the Southern "dogtrot" style, the house has a central hallway, formal parlor and dining room, five bedrooms, and an office. At the time of this picture, kitchen and toilet facilities were in the backyard, separate from the house. (Courtesy of the Historic Arkansas Museum.)

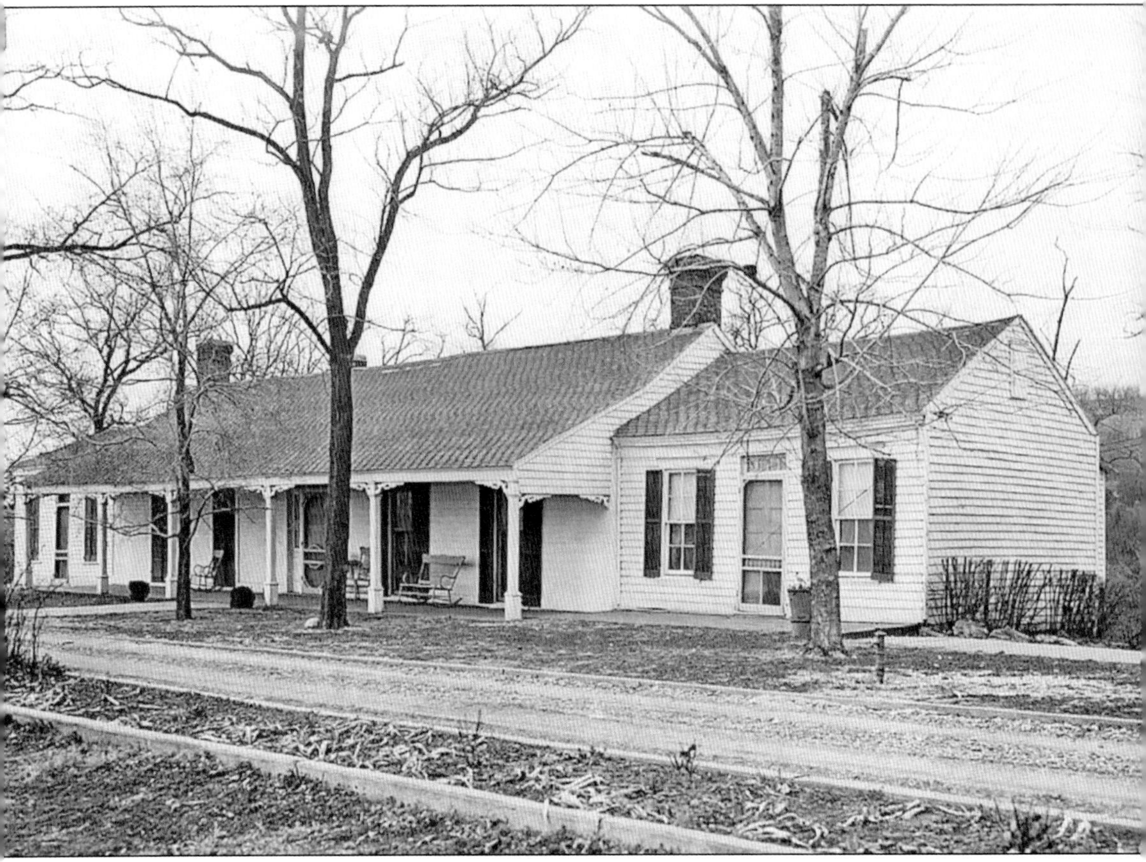

The Drennen-Scott House was photographed by the National Park Service as part of the Historic American Building Survey, a New Deal initiative to document important historic structures across the United States. The Drennen-Scott House became the 11th property in the state of Arkansas listed in the National Register of Historic Places. The site is considered nationally significant due to John Drennen's role as Indian agent and superintendent of the Southern Region of Indian Affairs. (Courtesy of Library of Congress.)

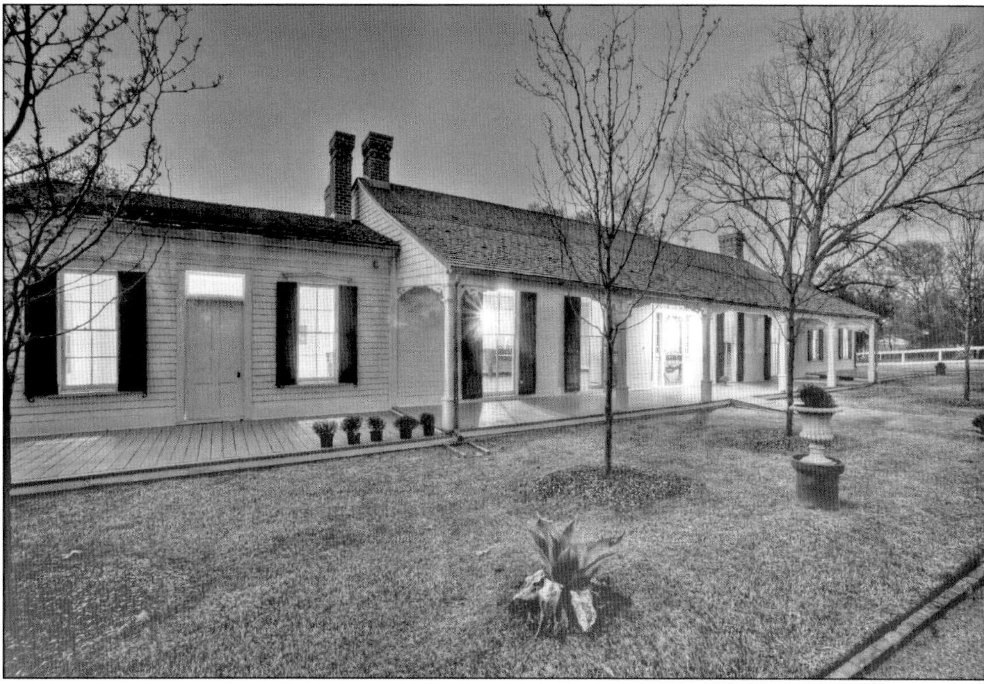

Seen here in 2011, the Drennen-Scott House is now owned by the University of Arkansas–Fort Smith. Operated as a teaching laboratory, history and archeology students conduct hands-on work at the site, contributing to the knowledge base while interacting with the public who visit. A working museum, the site includes 31 acres of John Drennen's original estate, his preserved home full of family heirloom furnishings, and a visitor center with exhibits. (Courtesy of UA-Fort Smith.)

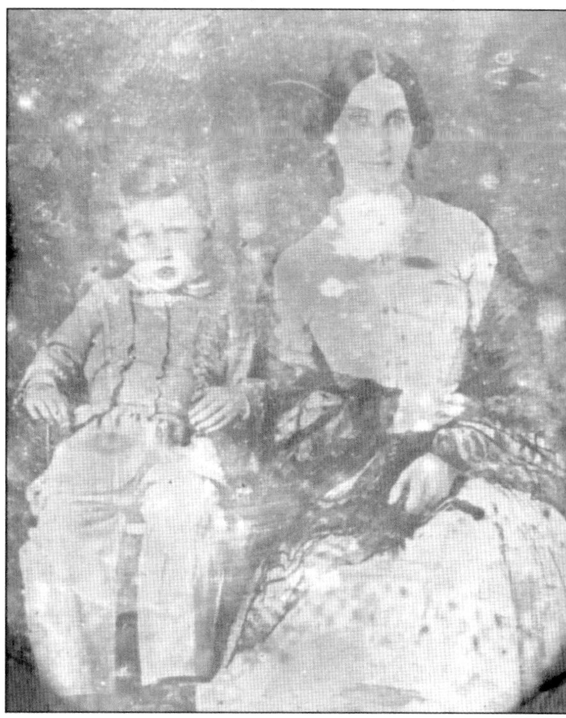

John Drennen's second wife, Catherine (Kate), is pictured here with one of their three sons, Charles Holden Drennen. He was the only one of his brothers to live into adulthood. Brothers Henry and William died before reaching 21 years of age. (Courtesy of the Historic Arkansas Museum.)

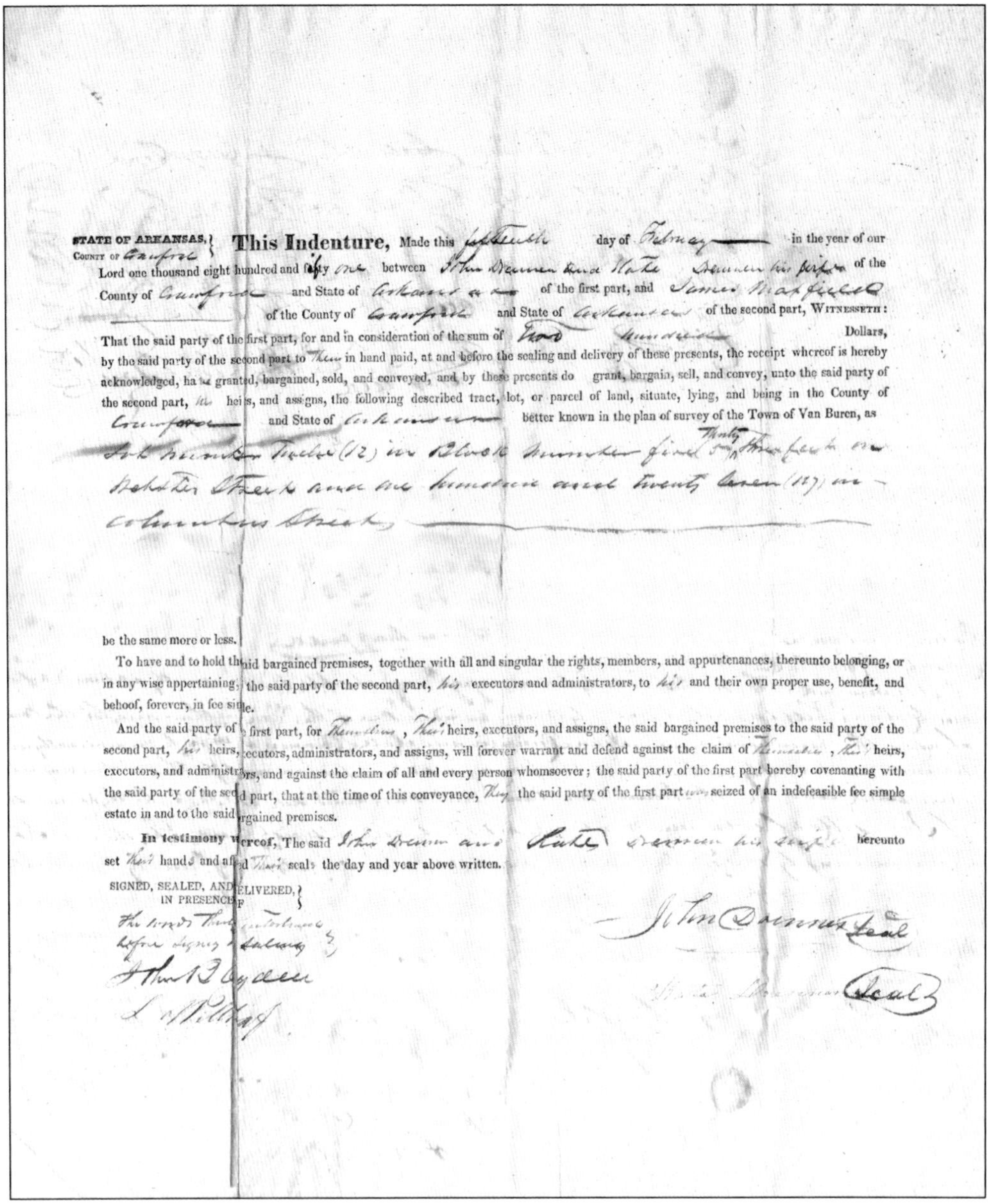
STATE OF ARKANSAS, County of Crawford }
This Indenture, Made this fifteenth day of February in the year of our Lord one thousand eight hundred and fifty one between John Drennen and Kate Drennen his wife of the County of Crawford and State of Arkansas of the first part, and James Maxfield of the County of Crawford and State of Arkansas of the second part, WITNESSETH:

That the said party of the first part, for and in consideration of the sum of Two Hundred Dollars, by the said party of the second part to them in hand paid, at and before the sealing and delivery of these presents, the receipt whereof is hereby acknowledged, have granted, bargained, sold, and conveyed, and by these presents do grant, bargain, sell, and convey, unto the said party of the second part, his heirs, and assigns, the following described tract, lot, or parcel of land, situate, lying, and being in the County of Crawford and State of Arkansas better known in the plan of survey of the Town of Van Buren, as Lot number Twelve (12) in Block number five 5, Thirty three feet on Webster Street and one hundred and twenty seven (127) on Columbus Street,

be the same more or less.

To have and to hold the said bargained premises, together with all and singular the rights, members, and appurtenances, thereunto belonging, or in any wise appertaining, the said party of the second part, his executors and administrators, to his and their own proper use, benefit, and behoof, forever, in fee simple.

And the said party of the first part, for themselves, their heirs, executors, and assigns, the said bargained premises to the said party of the second part, his heirs, executors, administrators, and assigns, will forever warrant and defend against the claim of themselves, their heirs, executors, and administrators, and against the claim of all and every person whomsoever; the said party of the first part hereby covenanting with the said party of the second part, that at the time of this conveyance, they the said party of the first part are seized of an indefeasible fee simple estate in and to the said bargained premises.

In testimony whereof, The said John Drennen and Kate Drennen his wife hereunto set their hands and affixed their seals the day and year above written.

SIGNED, SEALED, AND DELIVERED, IN PRESENCE OF }

The words Thirty [illegible] before signing & sealing

John B. Ogden

L. Nilliray

John Drennen (Seal)

Kate Drennen (Seal)

As a partner with brother-in-law David Thompson, John Drennen became a cofounder of the city of Van Buren by purchasing the townsite, selling off commercial and residential lots, and promoting economic development. This deed, dated February 15, 1851, conveys a parcel of land from John Drennen and his second wife, Kate, to James Maxfield for the sum of $200. (Courtesy of the UAFS Cobb Collection.)

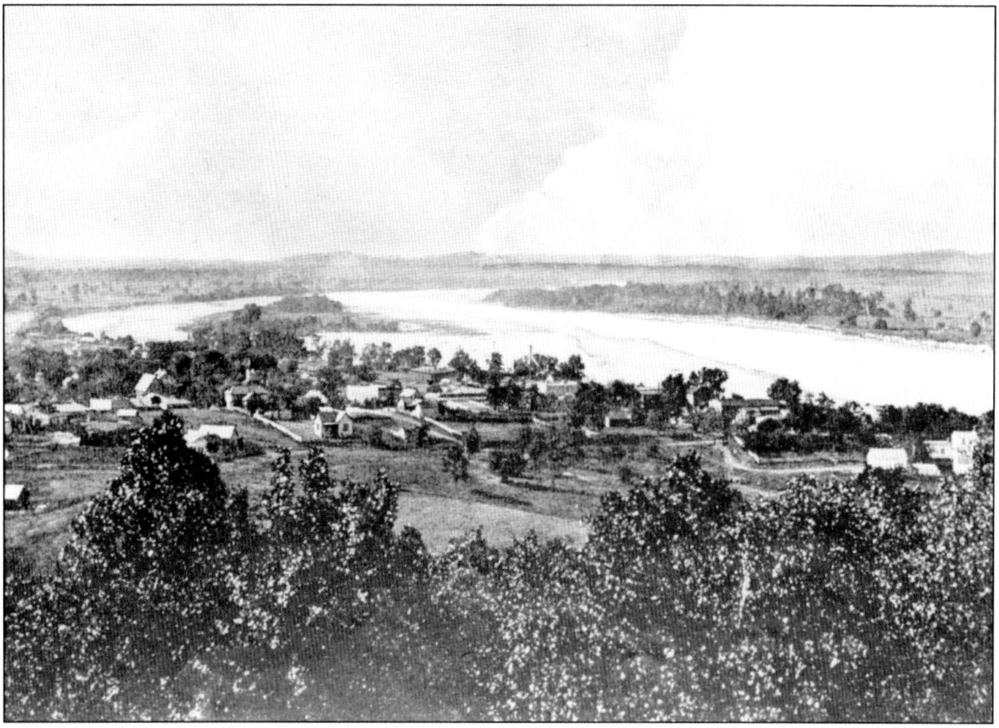

Likely the earliest townscape photograph of Van Buren, this pre-1870 image shows a town oriented along the river. On the far right, some white structures of the Drennen-Scott estate are visible. Ferries moved people, goods, and agricultural products across the river before the bridges allowed pedestrian and rail traffic. The Crawford County Courthouse can be seen at left center. (Courtesy of the UAFS Cobb Collection.)

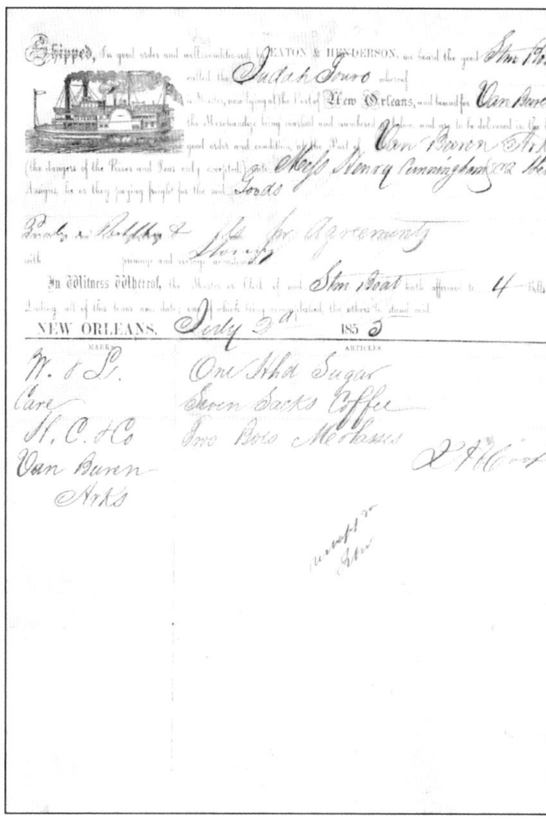

Shipped, In good order and well conditioned, by EATON & HENDERSON, on board the good Stm Boat called the Judah Touro whereof [illegible] is Master, now lying at the Port of New Orleans, and bound for Van Buren the Merchandize being marked and numbered as below, and are to be delivered in the like good order and condition, at the Port of Van Buren Ark (the dangers of the River and Seas only excepted,) unto Messrs Henry Cunningham & Co their Assigns, he or they paying freight for the said Goods [illegible] for Agreement [illegible] with primage and average accustomed.

In Witness Whereof, the Master or Clerk of said Stm Boat hath affirmed to 4 Bills Lading, all of this tenor and date; one of which being accomplished, the others to stand void.

NEW ORLEANS, July 2d 1855

MARKS	ARTICLES
W. & L. Care H. C. & Co Van Buren Arks	One Hhd Sugar Seven Sacks Coffee Two Bbls Molasses

On July 2, 1855, sugar, coffee, and molasses were loaded on the *Judah Touro* steamboat in New Orleans bound for Van Buren. Named for a successful merchant and pillar of the New Orleans Jewish community, the boat made regular runs up the Arkansas and Red Rivers from New Orleans, bringing finished goods and taking on cotton and other agricultural products for the return trip. Henry Cunningham, the consignee, ran a mercantile business on Main Street in Van Buren. (Courtesy of the UAFS Cobb Collection.)

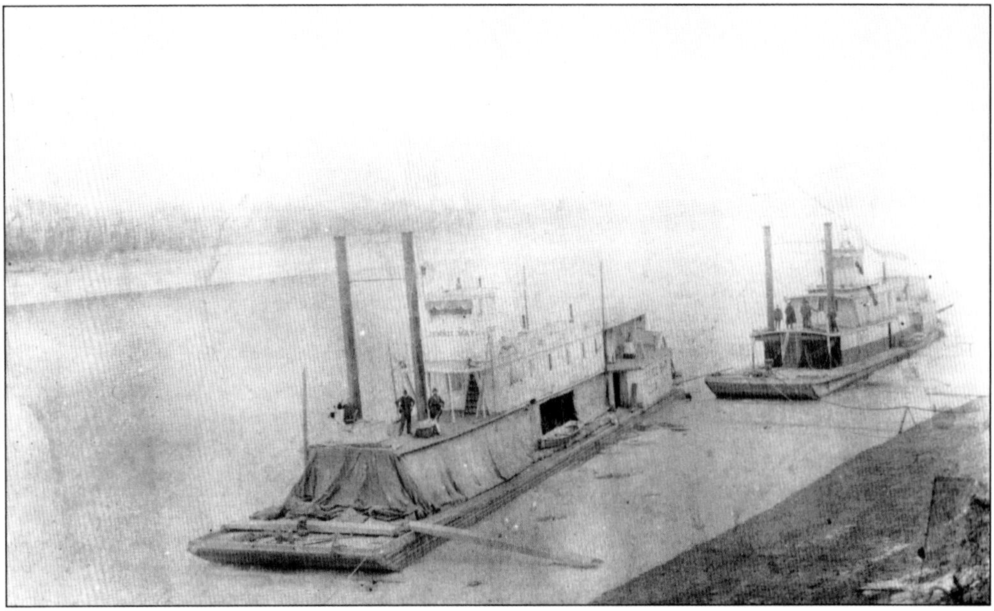

The *Jenny May*, seen here tied to the wharf at Van Buren around 1880, made regular runs on the Arkansas River to Fort Gibson in Indian Territory. Walter Huff captained the boat until about 1890, when the railroads finally took the freight business off the river. (Courtesy of the UAFS Cobb Collection.)

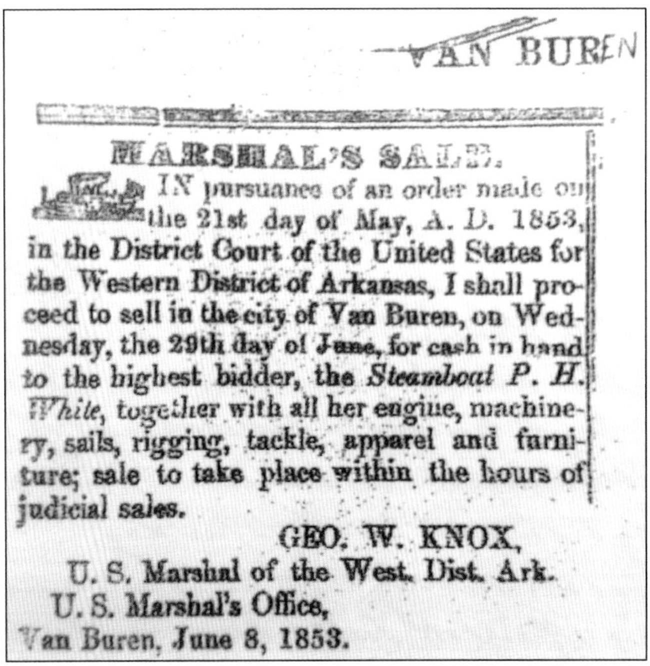

VAN BUREN

MARSHAL'S SALE.

IN pursuance of an order made on the 21st day of May, A. D. 1853, in the District Court of the United States for the Western District of Arkansas, I shall proceed to sell in the city of Van Buren, on Wednesday, the 29th day of June, for cash in hand to the highest bidder, the *Steamboat P. H. White*, together with all her engine, machinery, sails, rigging, tackle, apparel and furniture; sale to take place within the hours of judicial sales.

GEO. W. KNOX,
U. S. Marshal of the West. Dist. Ark.
U. S. Marshal's Office,
Van Buren, June 8, 1853.

George Washington Knox owned a plantation in Crawford County and in 1851 became the first US marshal for the newly created Federal Court for the Western District of Arkansas. The court had jurisdiction over Indian Territory (present-day Oklahoma) and handled a myriad of cases, from murder and robbery to illegal liquor trade violations. This advertisement from the *Van Buren Press* describes a confiscated steamboat available for sale by the marshal's office. Knox Street in Van Buren today honors George's service to the community. (Author's collection.)

This photograph of Caroline Scott, eldest daughter of John Drennen and wife of Charles G. Scott, dates to the 1850s. Nicknamed "the Queen" by family and friends, Caroline lived until 1910 and was known, like her father, for her determination. (Courtesy of the Historic Arkansas Museum.)

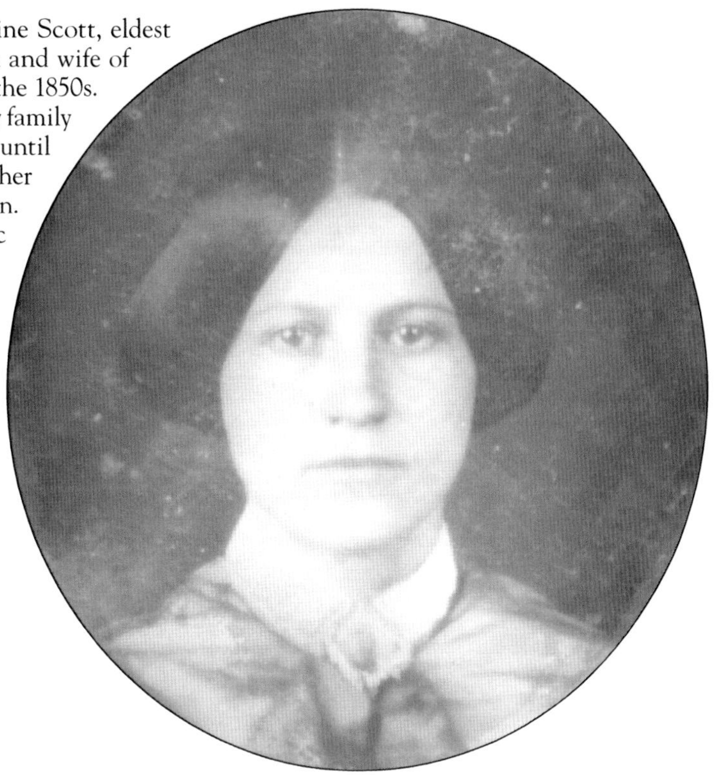

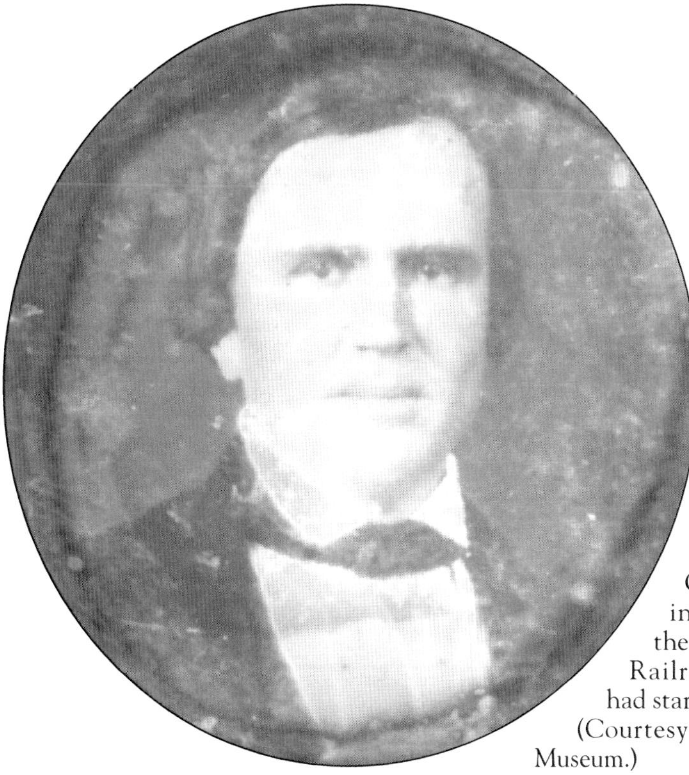

Charles G. Scott, seen here around 1850, worked with John Drennen as a partner before courting and eventually marrying Drennen's oldest daughter. Originally from Kent County, Maryland, Scott was a good businessman who ably led the Drennen-Scott family through the financial difficulties of the Civil War. Scott was also instrumental in completing the Little Rock and Fort Smith Railroad that his father-in-law had started before his death in 1855. (Courtesy of the Historic Arkansas Museum.)

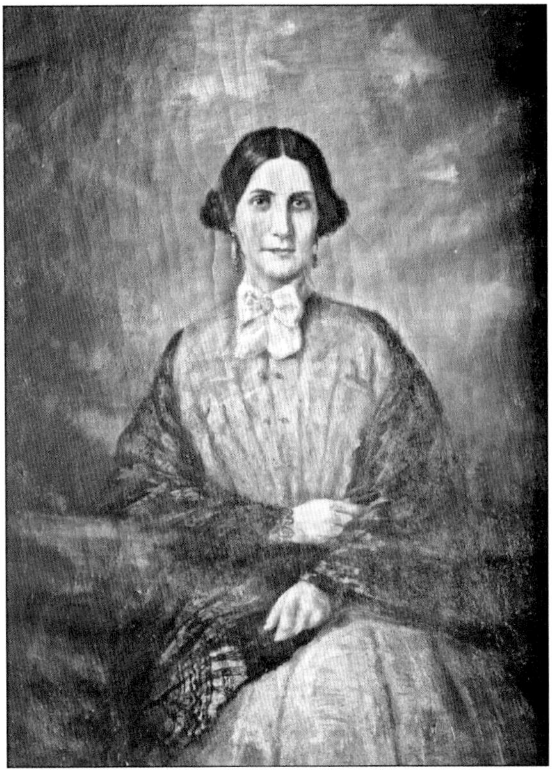

While the artist of this painting is unknown, the skill and talent are evident. Kate Drennen, John Drennen's second wife, sat for this portrait around 1850. John's first wife, Emily, died in 1844, but not before having three daughters. Kate and John had three sons, but only one, Charles, lived past the age of 21. With her husband's sudden death in 1855 due to yellow fever, Kate was only a widow for a short time. She herself died in 1858 of unspecified causes. (Courtesy of the Historic Arkansas Museum.)

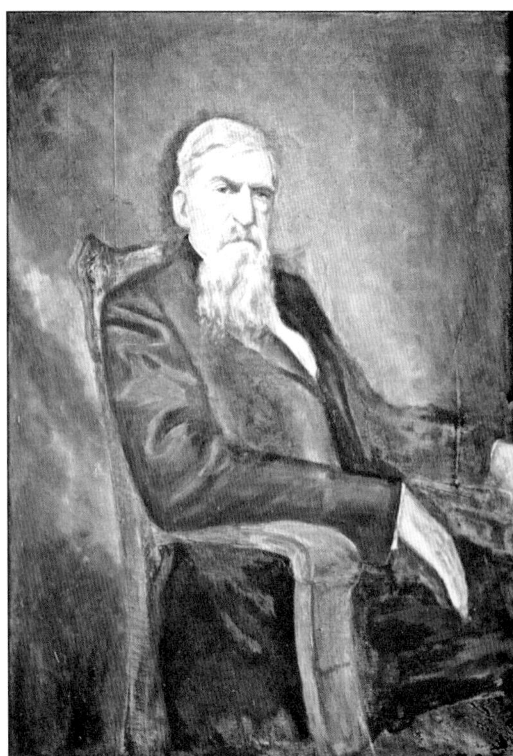

This portrait was painted in 1926 from a photograph of Charles Holden Drennen shortly after his death. Charles, the son of John Drennen, remained a bachelor throughout his life and lived continually at the Drennen-Scott House. Charles lost both of his brothers, Henry and William, in 1871 and 1875, respectively. Charles was known as an avid fisherman in family lore. (Courtesy of the Historic Arkansas Museum.)

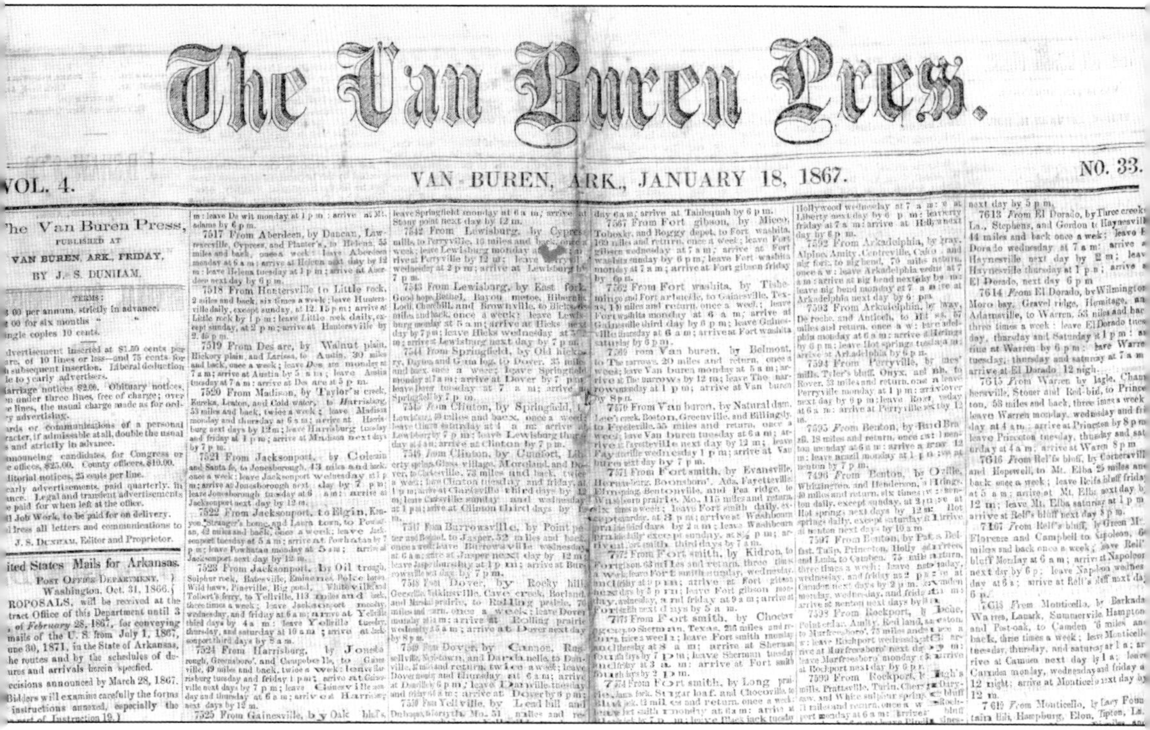

The Van Buren Press.

VOL. 4. VAN BUREN, ARK., JANUARY 18, 1867. NO. 33.

The Van Buren Press,
PUBLISHED AT
VAN BUREN, ARK., FRIDAY,
BY J. S. DUNHAM.

TERMS:
$3 00 per annum, strictly in advance.
$2 00 for six months.
Single copies 10 cents.

United States Mails for Arkansas.

POST OFFICE DEPARTMENT,
Washington, Oct. 31, 1866.

PROPOSALS will be received at the Contract Office of this Department until 3 p.m. of February 28, 1867, for conveying the mails of the U. S. from July 1, 1867, to June 30, 1871, in the State of Arkansas, on the routes and by the schedules of departures and arrivals herein specified.

Decisions announced by March 28, 1867.

First printed in the 1830s, the *Van Buren Press* has endured a number of owners and changes and is still in print today as a bi-weekly newspaper. Joseph Starr Dunham served as the first editor. (Courtesy of UA-Fort Smith.)

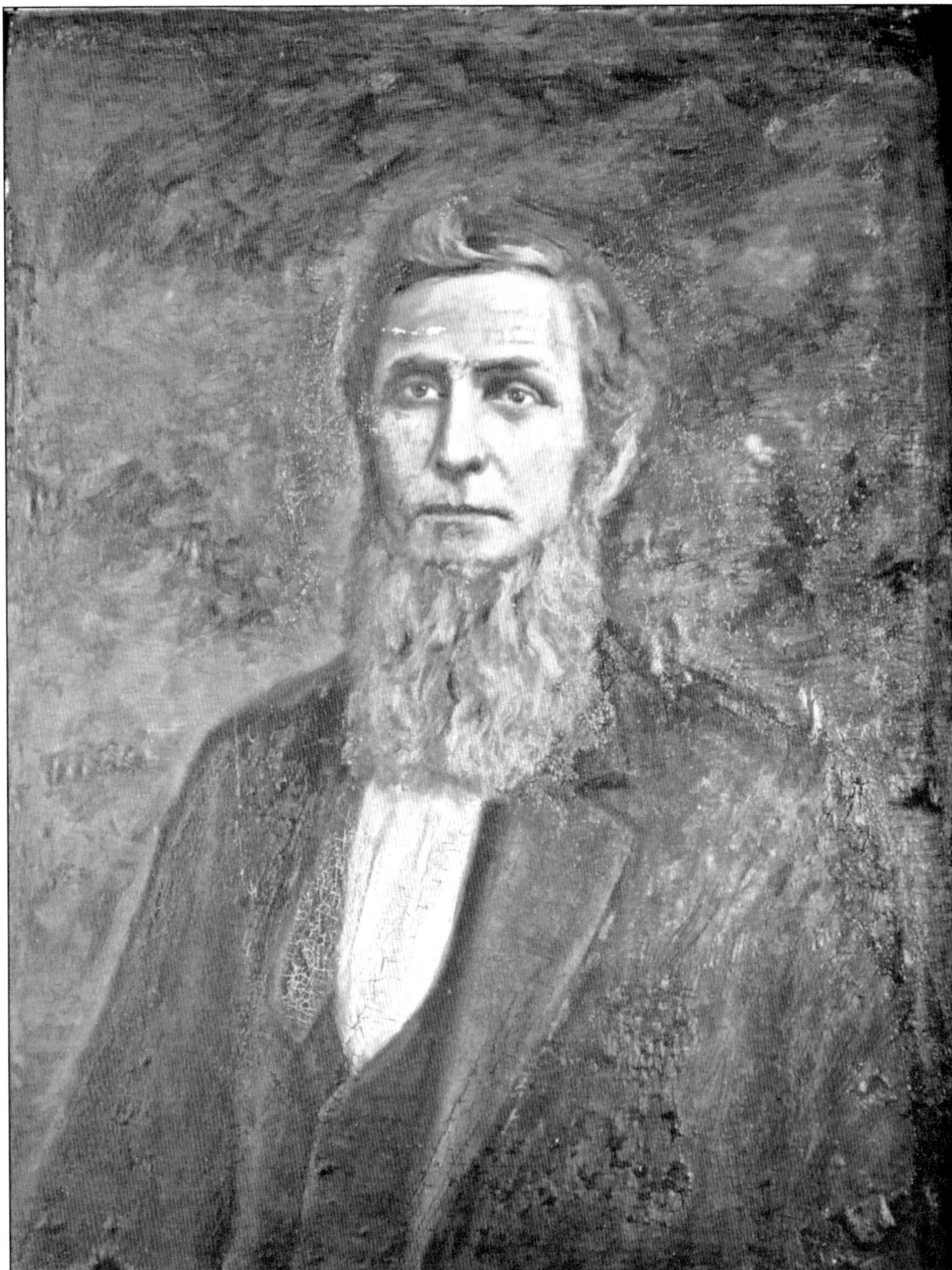

Newspaperman Joseph Starr Dunham, seen in this portrait, lived at the Drennen-Scott estate for the last 11 years of his life. His daughter Francis ("Fanny") Dunham-Scott married John Drennen's grandson Phillip. (Courtesy of the Historic Arkansas Museum.)

Mary Glenn Scott (Bulloch) is seen standing between her mother and aunt in front of the Joseph Starr Dunham house. Dunham was Mary Glenn's great grandfather and was a newspaper editor in Van Buren in the 1800s. His home, seen in the background, is listed in the National Register of Historic Places for its 1870s Carpenter Gothic style. (Courtesy of UAFS.)

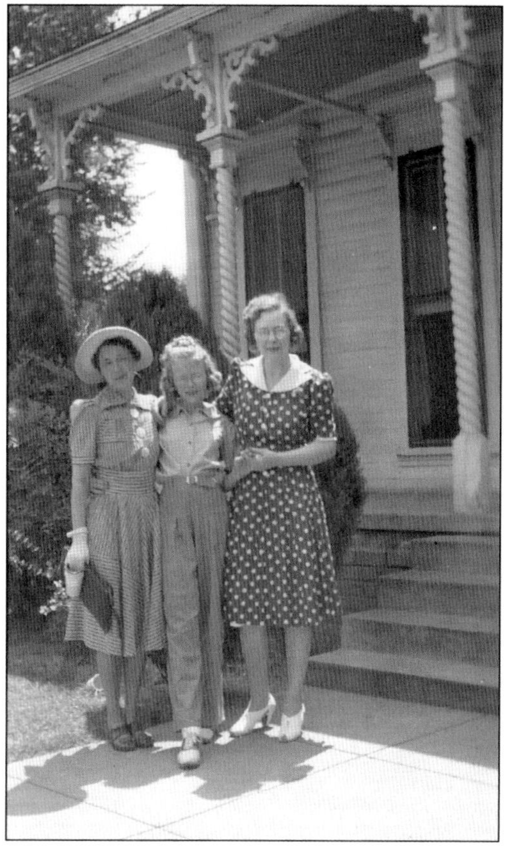

This 1880 view of the Drennen-Scott House offers subtle clues of the founding family's wealth. The ornamental plants near the driveway and the urn-styled pots, in addition to the well-manicured yard, attest to a higher standard of living. (Courtesy of the Historic Arkansas Museum.)

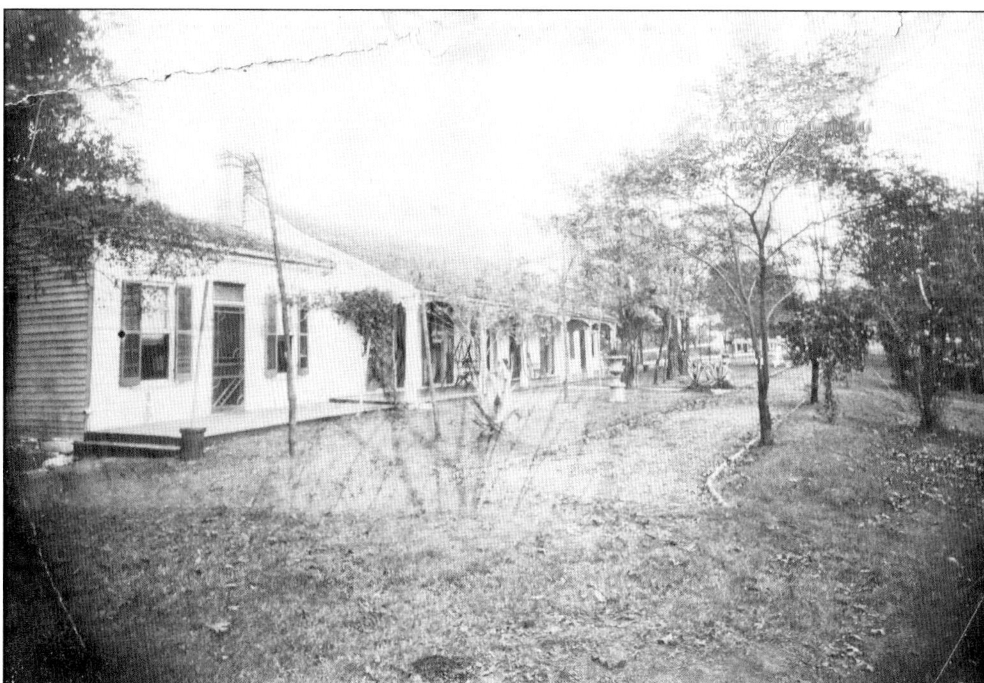

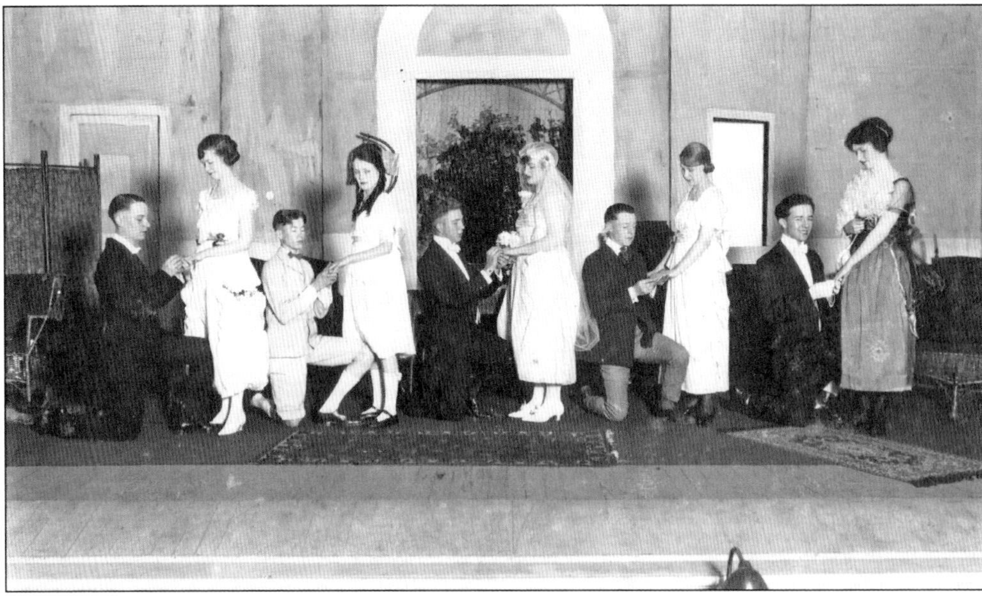

With theaters and opera houses dating back to early Van Buren, it is not surprising to find a photograph of the May 14, 1920, Van Buren High School junior class play *Whose Little Bride Are You?* Pictured from left to right are Joe Adkins and Esther Allen, Bob Ed Covey and Bessie Doyle, Ashton Sadler and Ora Smith, Clyde Randall and Anna Kibler, and Perry Shauer and Edna Hardgraves. (Courtesy of the UAFS Cobb Collection.)

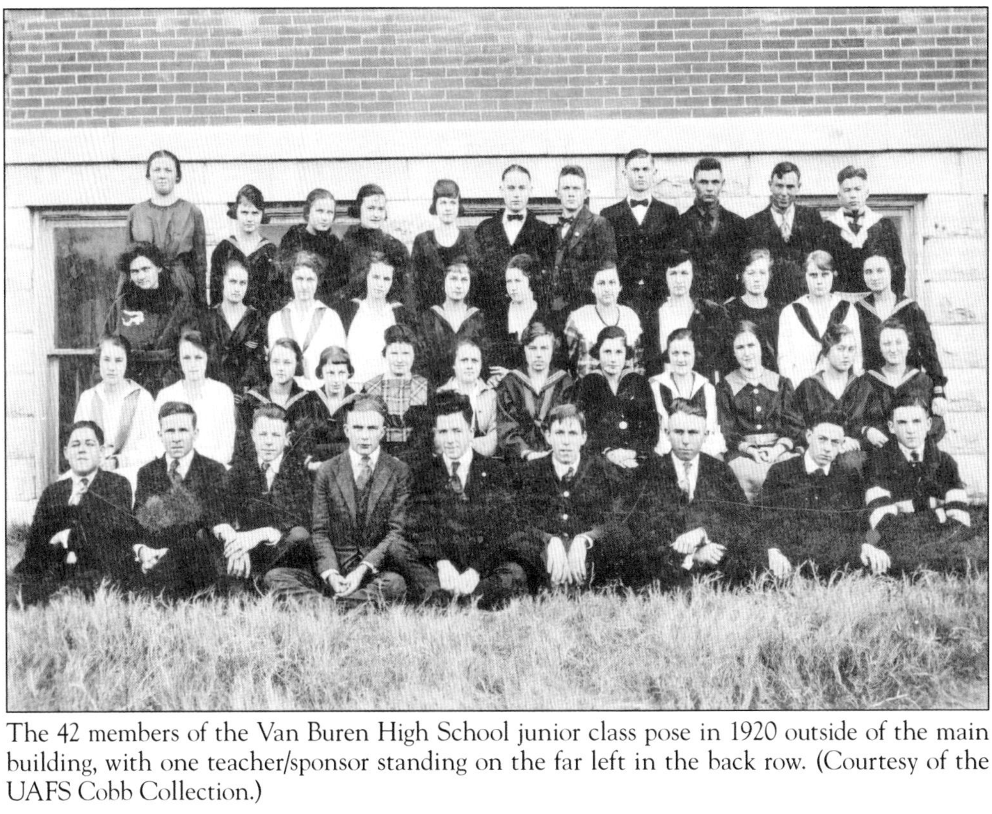

The 42 members of the Van Buren High School junior class pose in 1920 outside of the main building, with one teacher/sponsor standing on the far left in the back row. (Courtesy of the UAFS Cobb Collection.)

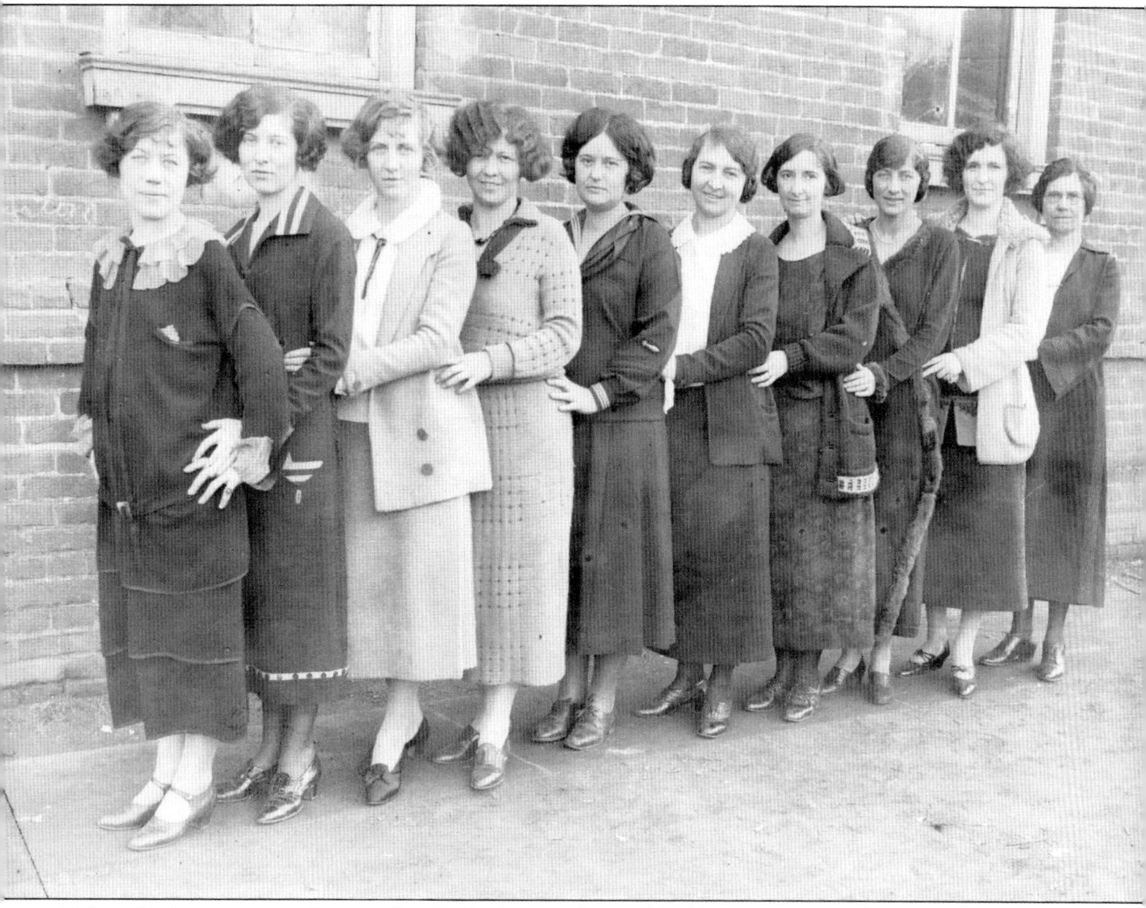

Although this photograph is undated, the hair styles and fashions appear to date to the 1920s. The young ladies are, from left to right, Alvern Clark, Louise Williams, Mary Sadler, Nell Arnold, Ora Smith, Grace Sadler, Juanita Graves, Grace Shipley, Edna Hardgraves, and Mrs. J.H. Burton. (Courtesy of the UAFS Cobb Collection.)

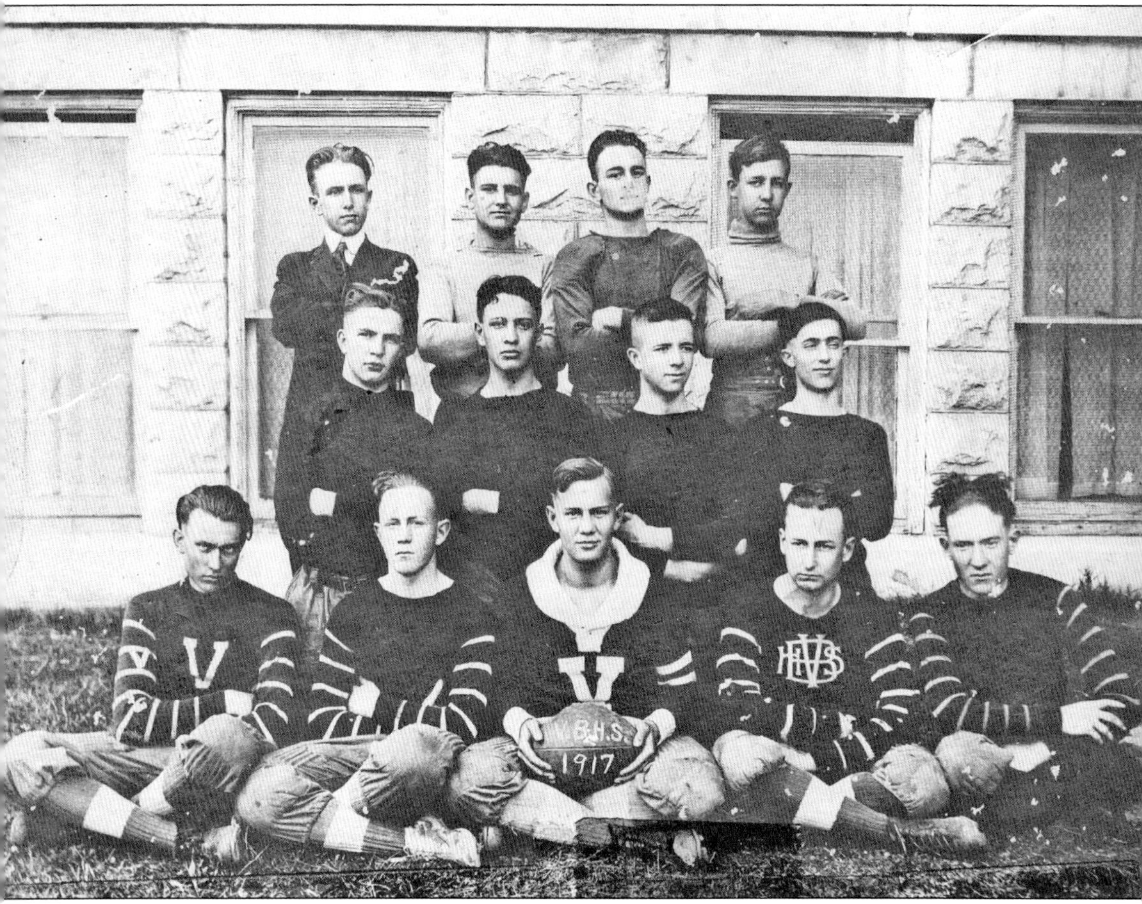

Although they only number 13, the 1917 Van Buren High School varsity football team appears to be confident and capable. Little Rock won the state championship that year, but Van Buren won it just five years before in 1912. Van Buren has won the Arkansas state championship four times: 1912, 1930, 1977, and 1996. Girls' basketball is the only sport where the school has seen more success, with five state championships. (Courtesy of the UAFS Cobb Collection.)

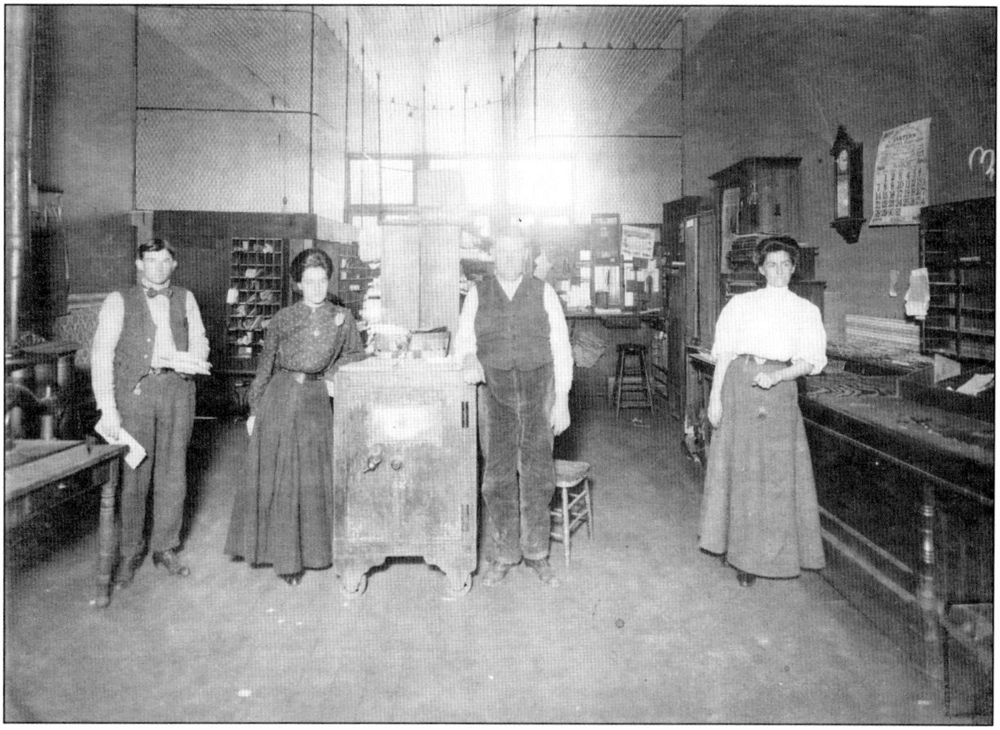

From the calendar on the wall at far right, this photograph of the Van Buren Post Office was taken in March 1909. Postal service was offered from the southeast corner of Main and Fifth Streets until a new building was constructed in 1936. (Courtesy of the UAFS Cobb Collection.)

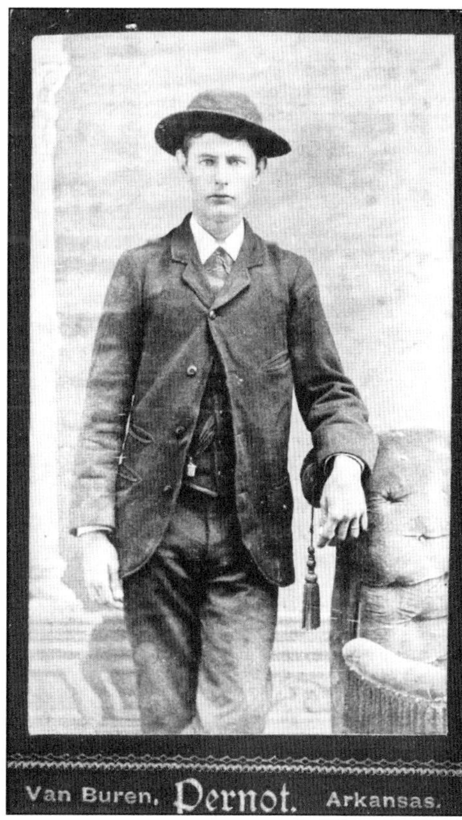

While the identity of the subject and exact date of this photograph are a mystery, the photographer, Harry Pernot, was the son of well-known Van Buren physician Dr. Henry Pernot, who immigrated to the United States from France. Dr. Pernot served as a surgeon for the Confederate army during the Civil War and came home at the end of hostilities to establish a practice and raise his family. Harry had three brothers and a sister. (Courtesy of the UAFS Cobb Collection.)

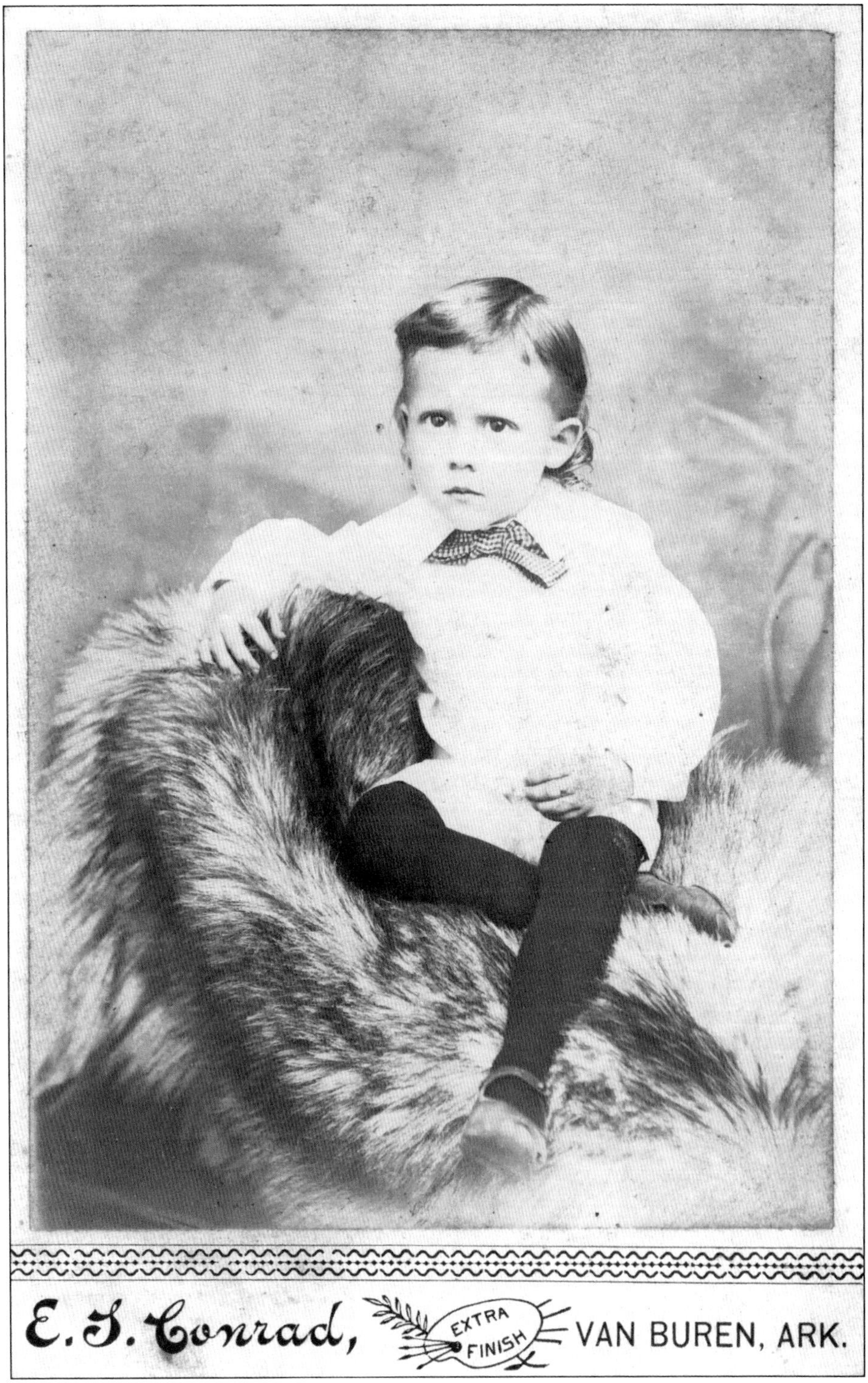

The little boy in this photograph is unidentified. From the style of his clothing, the image dates to around the turn of the 20th century. Little is known today about the photographer, E.S. Conrad. (Courtesy of the UAFS Cobb Collection.)

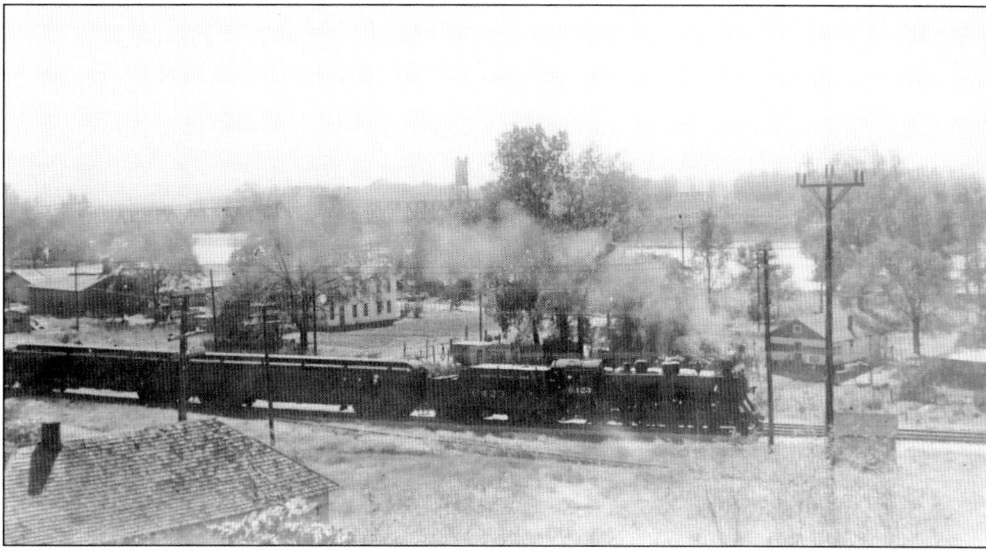

Photographed sometime in the 1940s, this steam engine and passenger cars are headed towards the west of town and eventually Oklahoma. Seen behind the train is the old waterfront of Van Buren, where the town thrived and grew during the steamboat era. The Free Bridge connecting Van Buren and Fort Smith appears at center, and the Arkansas River channel is also clearly visible. (Courtesy of the Historic Arkansas Museum.)

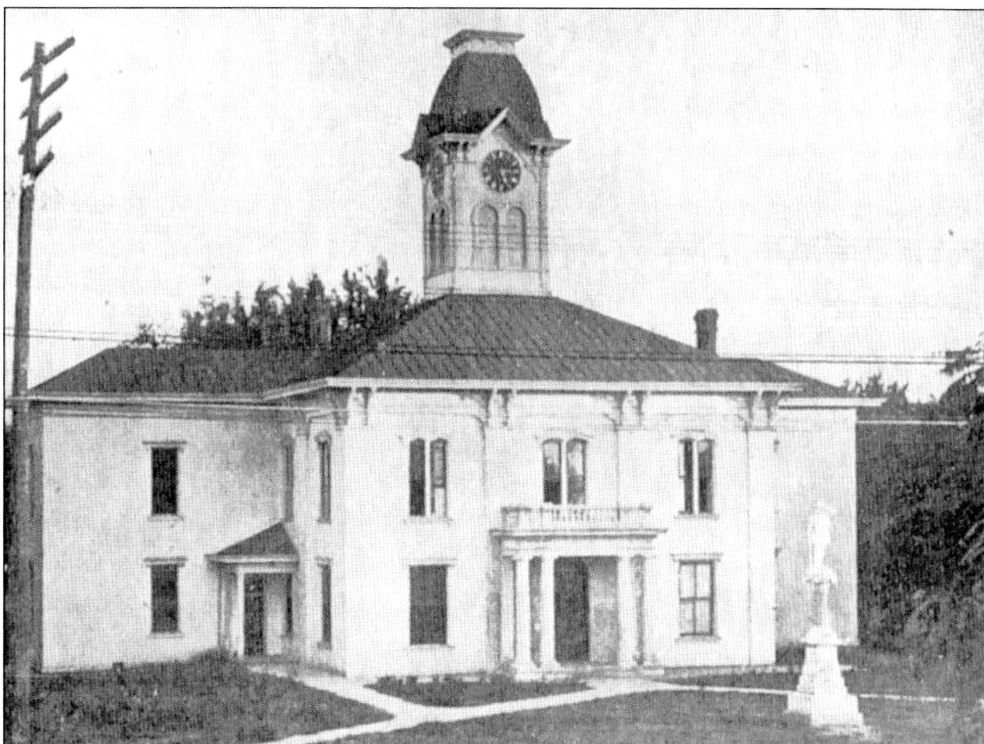

Taken in the 1920s, this photograph of the Crawford County Courthouse shows the Confederate Monument on the west side of the building. The monument was originally located in Fairview Cemetery but later moved to the courthouse. (Courtesy of the UAFS Cobb Collection.)

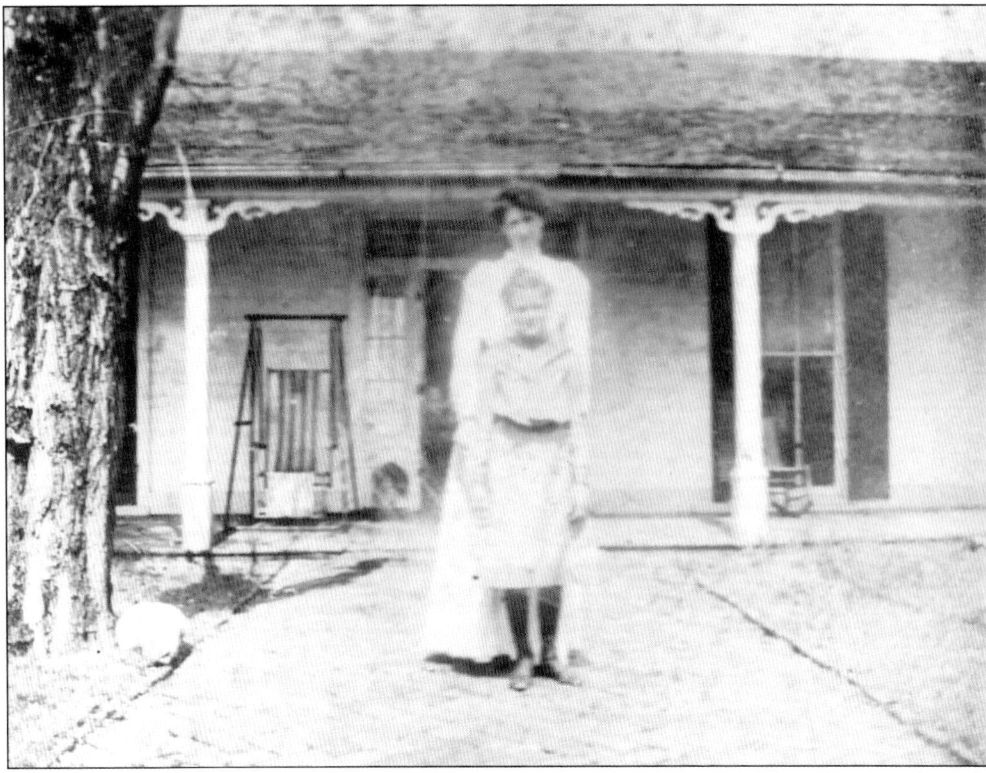

Taken in front of the Drennen-Scott House, the description on the back of this photograph reads, "I took this one of Sarah and Nannie, Caroline Scott age 9." Born in 1892, Caroline, the great-granddaughter of Van Buren cofounder John Drennen, snapped this shot in 1901. Who Sarah and Nannie were has been lost to time. (Courtesy of the Historic Arkansas Museum.)

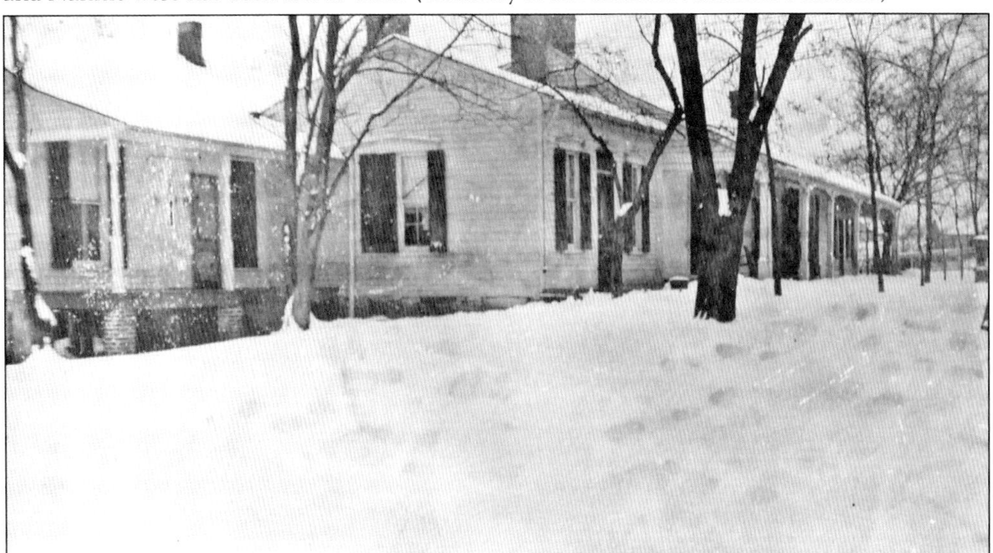

While considered firmly in the South, Van Buren does see its share of snow from time to time. This photograph of the Drennen-Scott House was taken after a snowfall in February 1905. (Courtesy of the Historic Arkansas Museum.)

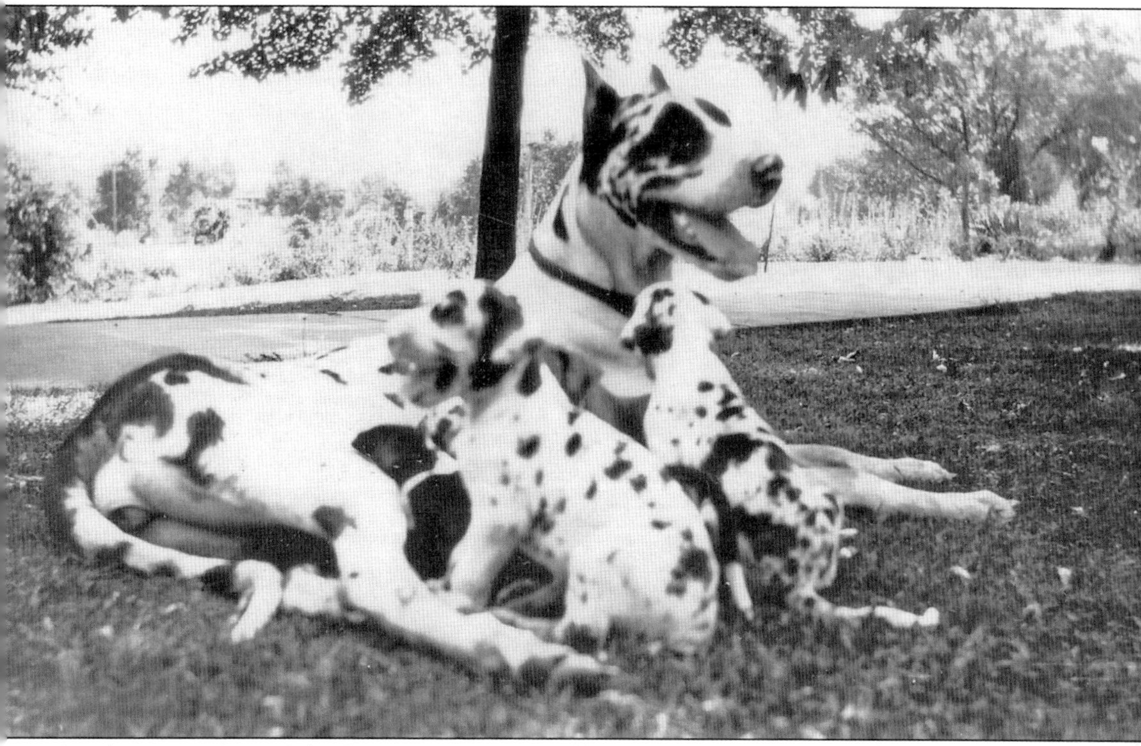

Caroline Mary Scott, John Drennen's great-granddaughter, was a dog lover and is remembered to this day for her Great Danes and Airedale terriers. Lady Polka Dot, one of her Great Danes, is seen here with her puppies at the home in Van Buren in 1931. (Courtesy of the Historic Arkansas Museum.)

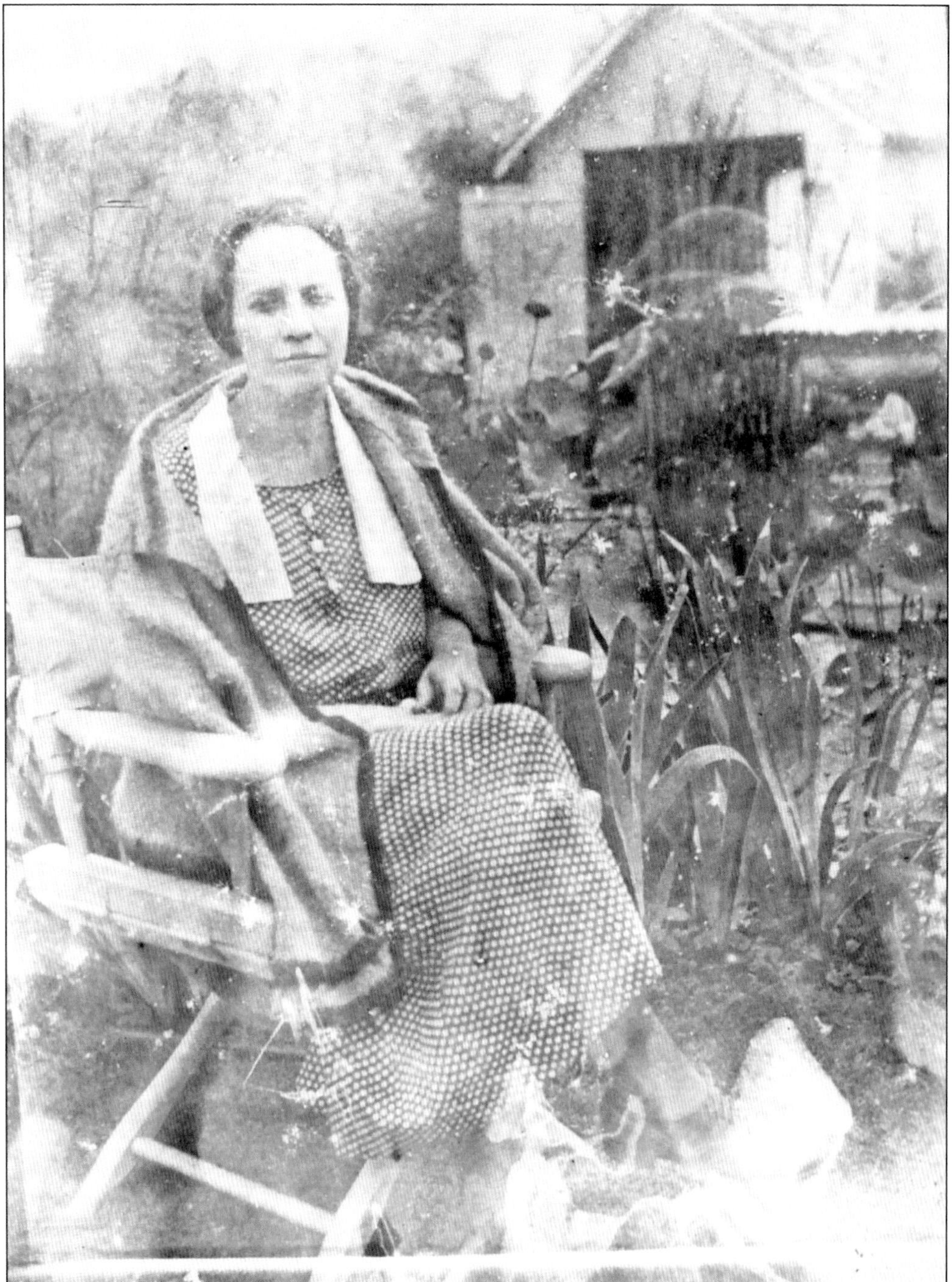

Dogs were not the only interest that held Caroline Scott's attention. She was also an avid gardener and maintained beautiful flowers and ornamental plants for many years around her ancestral home. Seen here around 1925, she is enjoying some time sitting by the goldfish pond in the middle of the circular driveway at Drennen-Scott. (Courtesy of the Historic Arkansas Museum.)

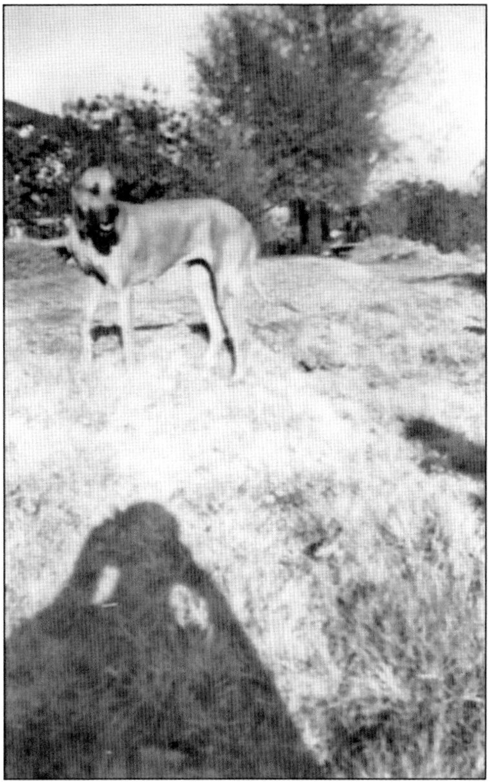

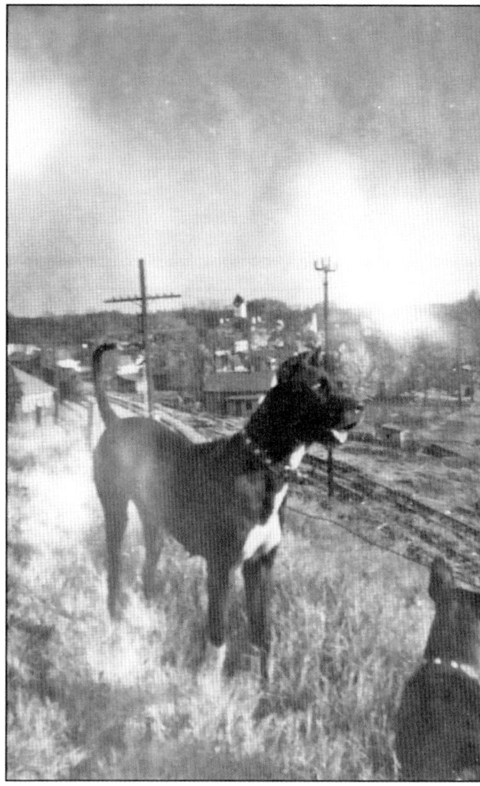

The Drennen-Scott House sits on a bluff overlooking the Arkansas River and downtown Van Buren. These undated photographs of family pets reveal the cityscape of Van Buren in the distance below the bluffs. (All, courtesy of the Historic Arkansas Museum.)

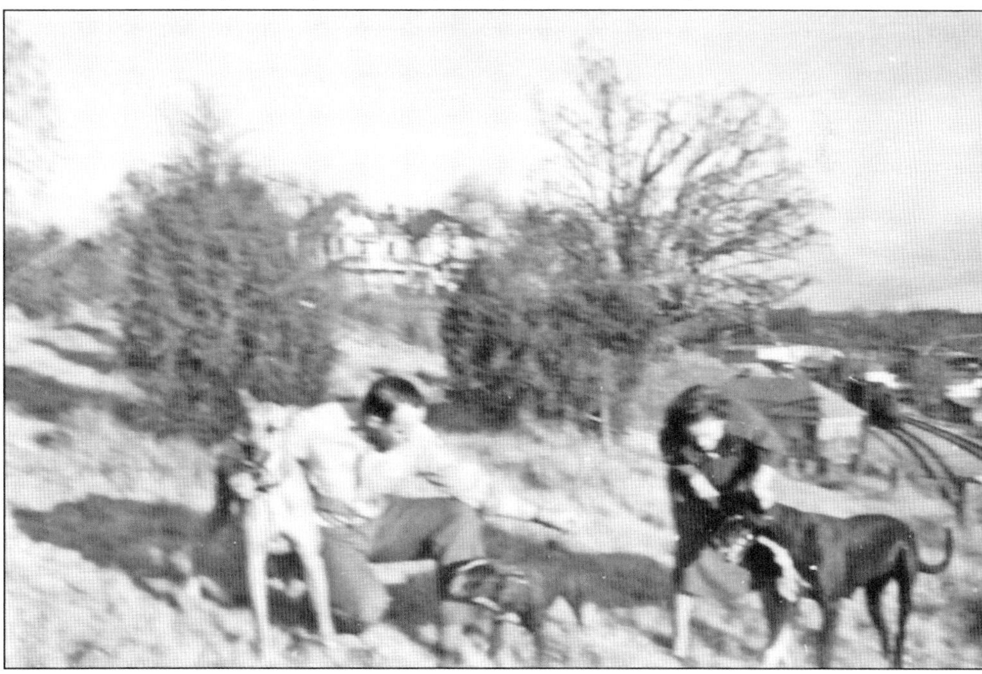

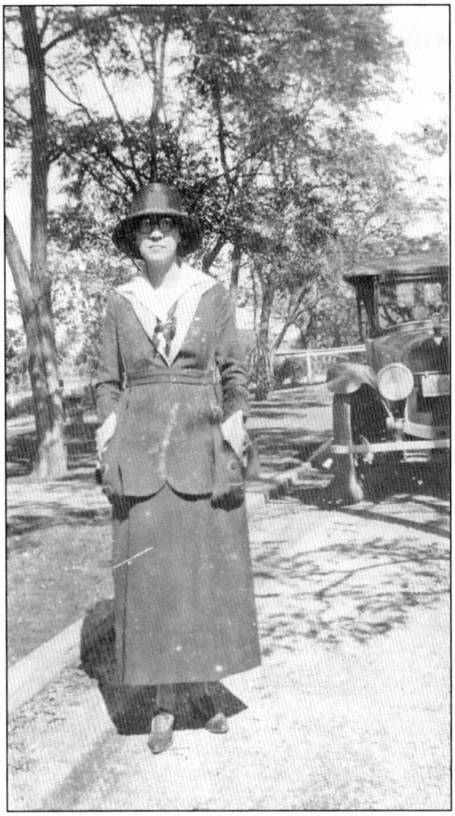

These 1920s images have women and cars as their subjects in front of the Drennen-Scott House. Caroline Mary Scott is seen with the hat and glasses at left, while the identity of the woman below is not known. (Both, courtesy of the Historic Arkansas Museum.)

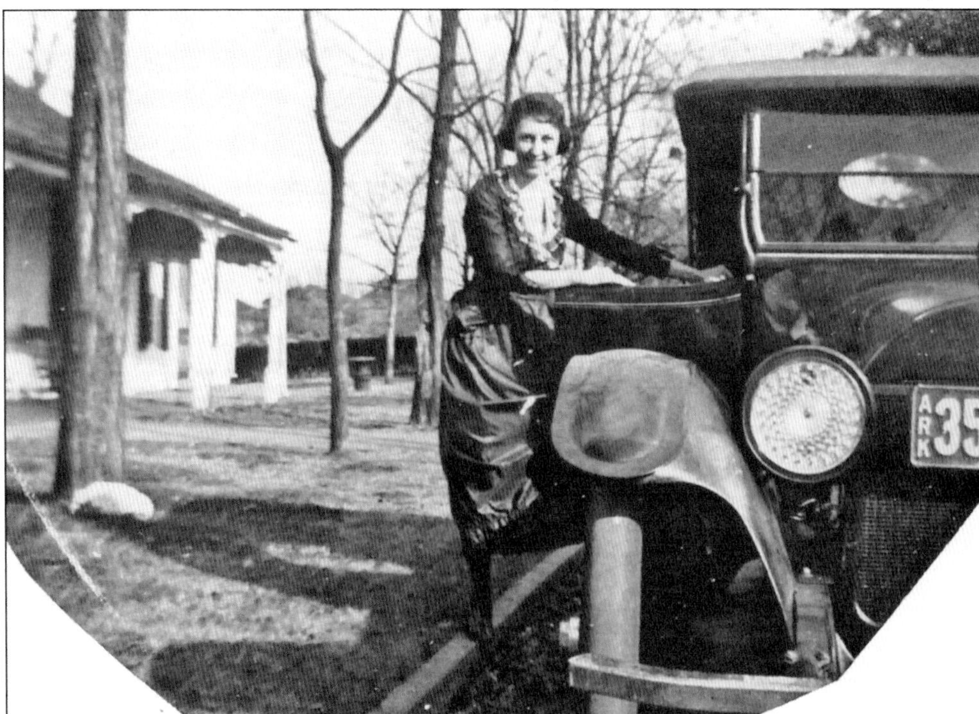

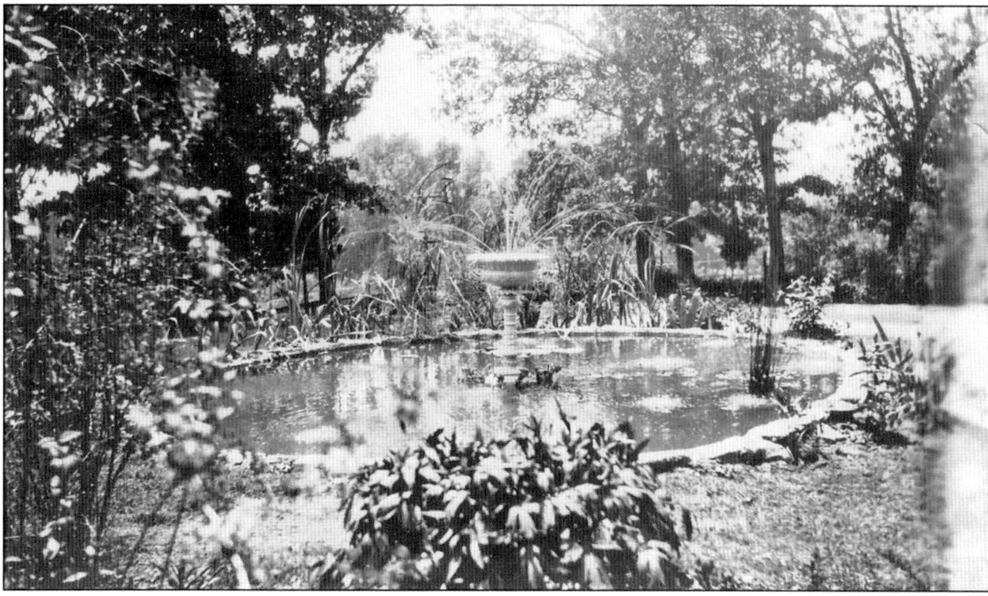

These 1920s photographs include the goldfish pond near the driveway at the Drennen-Scott House and the main garden in bloom. (Both, courtesy of the Historic Arkansas Museum.)

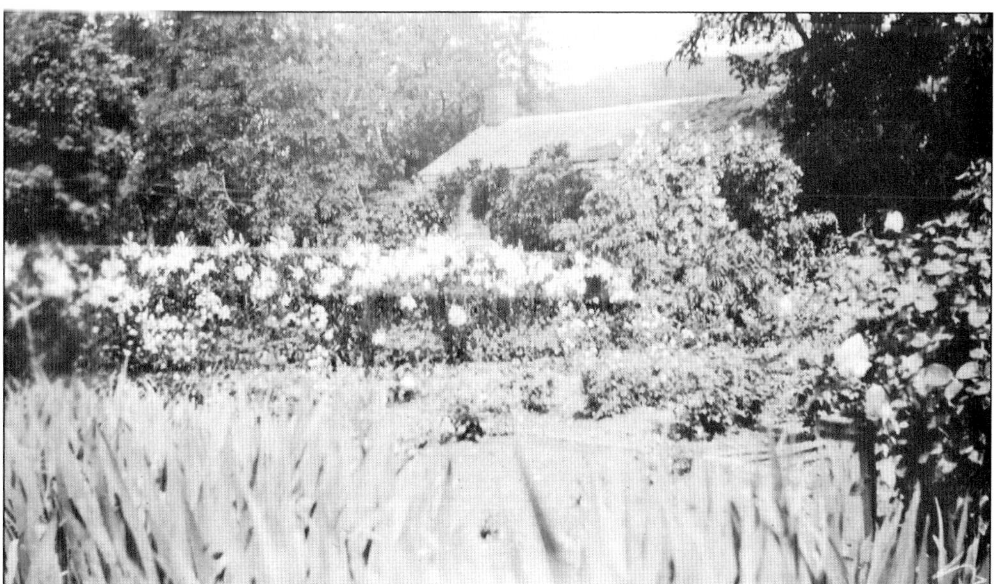

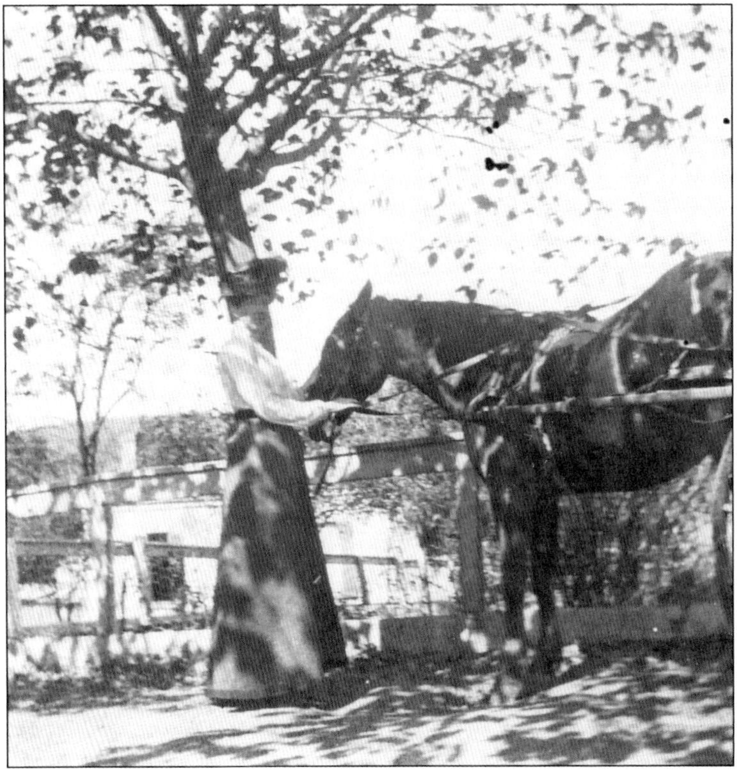

An unidentified woman attends to a horse and buggy in front of the Drennen-Scott House around 1890. (Courtesy of the Historic Arkansas Museum.)

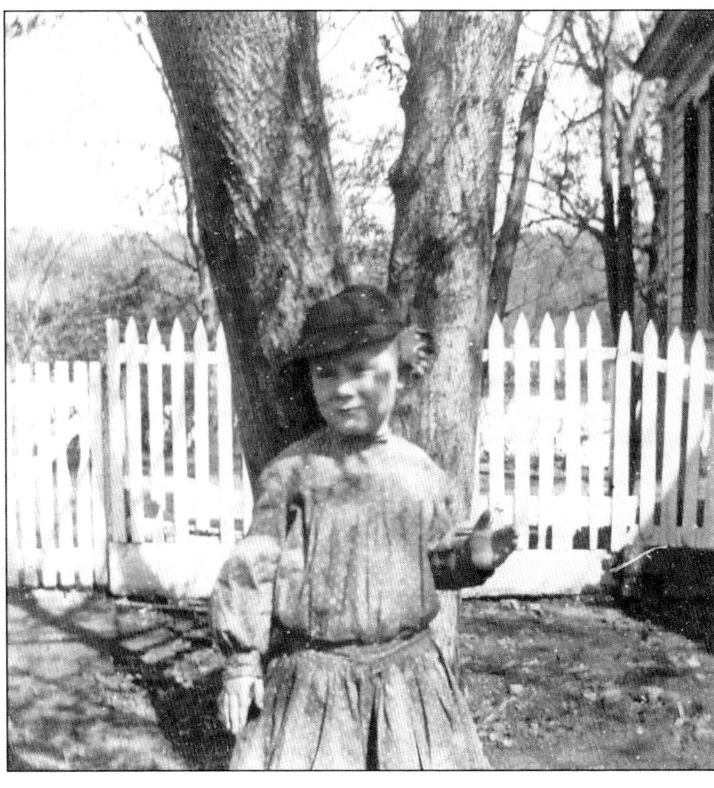

An unidentified girl poses sometime in the 1920s with the white picket fences of the Drennen-Scott House in the background. (Courtesy of the Historic Arkansas Museum.)

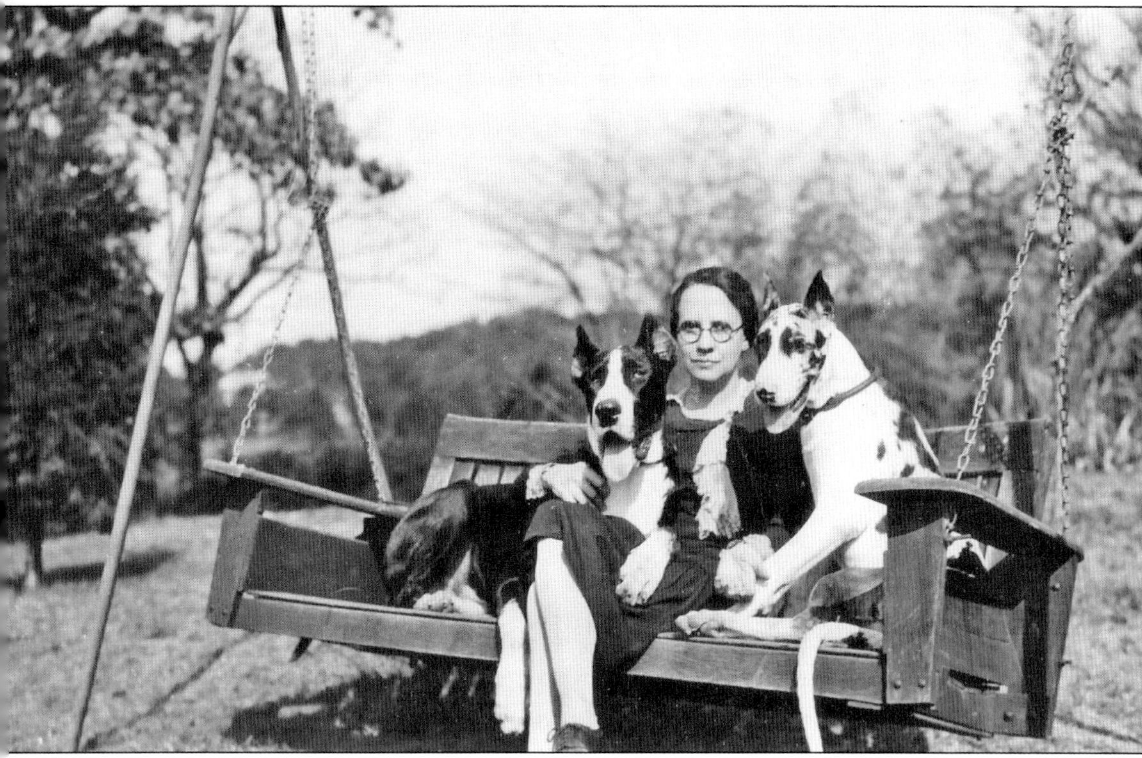

Caroline Mary Scott sits on a swing with two of her dogs at the Drennen-Scott House around 1920. (Courtesy of the Historic Arkansas Museum.)

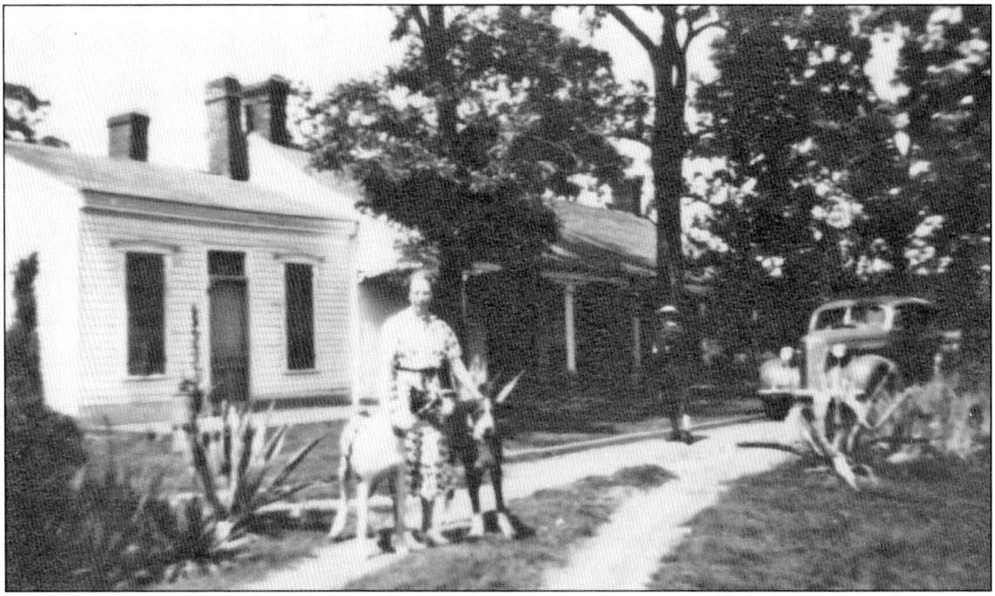

Sometime in the 1930s, Caroline Mary Scott and her dogs stand on the driveway of the Drennen-Scott House. (Courtesy of the Historic Arkansas Museum.)

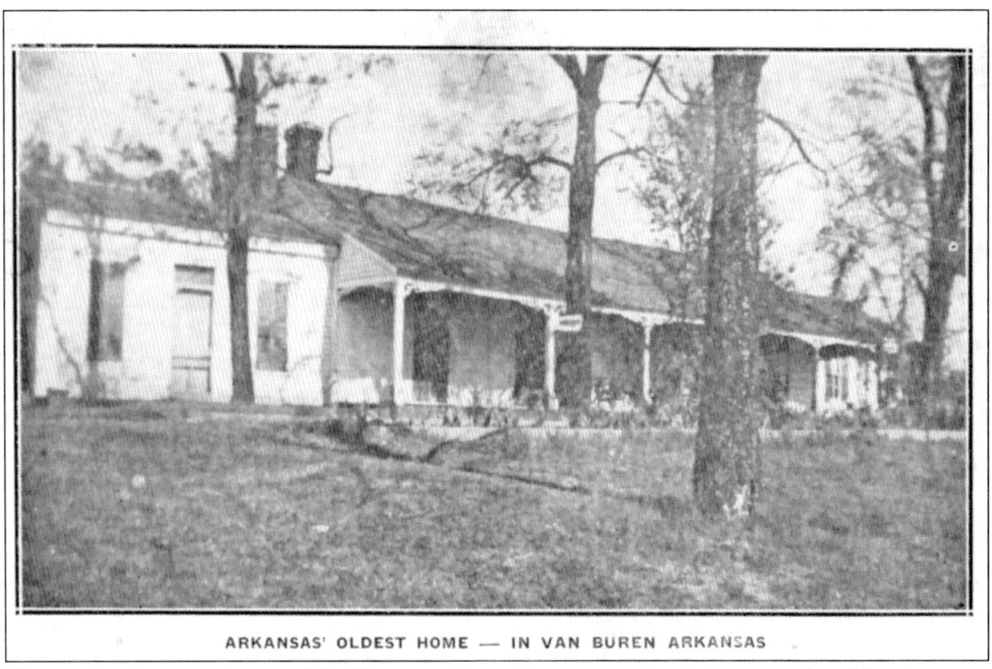

This undated postcard view of the Drennen-Scott House mistakenly lists it as the oldest home in Arkansas. While it is indeed old, and has been occupied continuously by the same family for five generations, there are older homes in the state. (Courtesy of the Historic Arkansas Museum.)

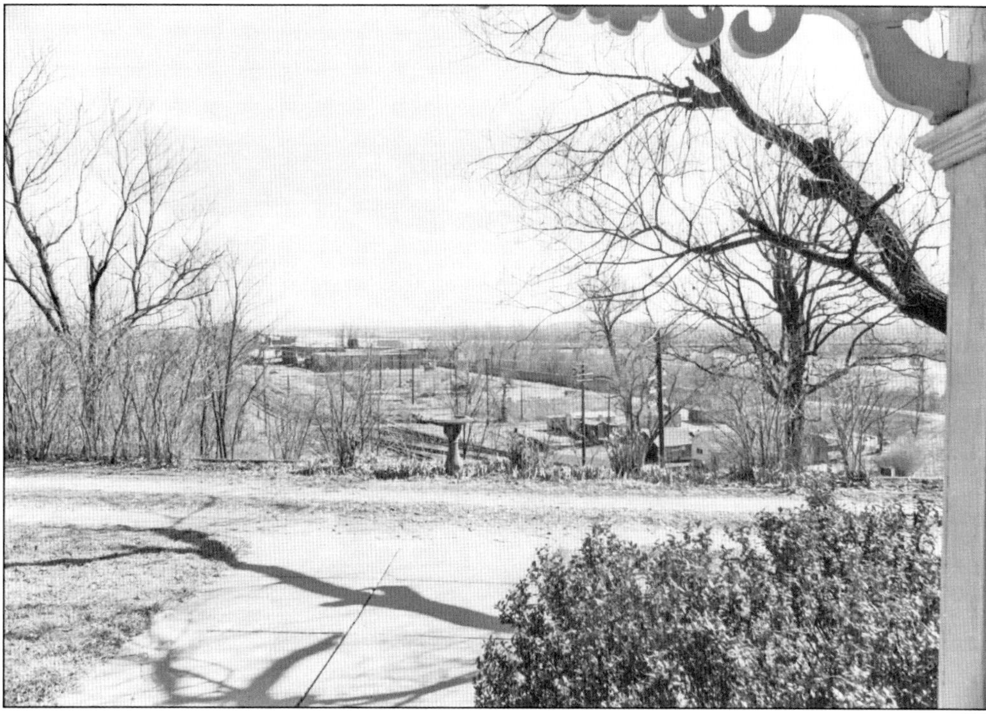

Likely dating between 1945 and 1955, this view of the Van Buren waterfront was taken from the front yard of the Drennen-Scott House. The bare trees reveal a winter landscape, and it is possible that ice is on the river in the distance. The Free Pedestrian Bridge, opened in 1912 and damaged and rebuilt after the Flood of 1943, is also visible. (Courtesy of the Historic Arkansas Museum.)

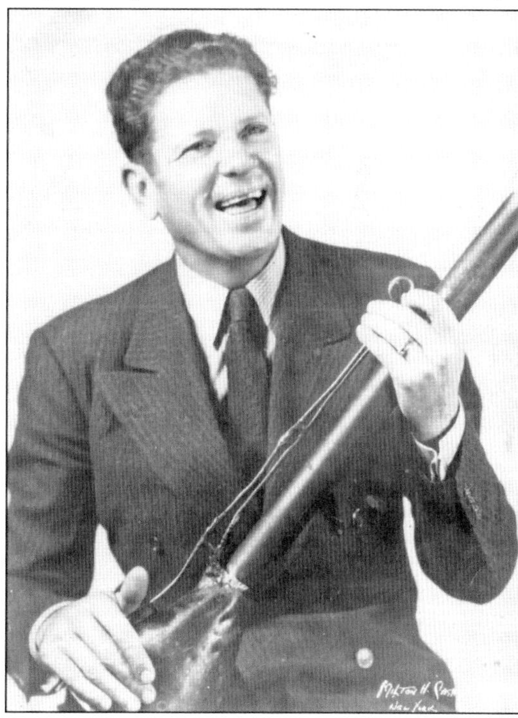

Although he was born in Greenwood, Arkansas, Robin Burn grew up in Van Buren and is fondly remembered as a favorite son. Fashioning a musical instrument from pipes found at the hardware store and calling it the bazooka, Burn would also get credit for naming the shoulder-fired anti-tank weapon of World War II. In the 1930s, he called himself Bob Burns and was a radio personality featured by Paul Whitman and Rudy Vallee. In 1936, Burns joined Bing Crosby on NBC's *Kraft Music Hall* radio show. He also made several movies with Crosby, Martha Ray, and Susan Hayward. Burns died in 1956, but not before trading his entertainment career for a prosperous run as a real estate developer in California. (Courtesy of the UAFS Cobb Collection.)

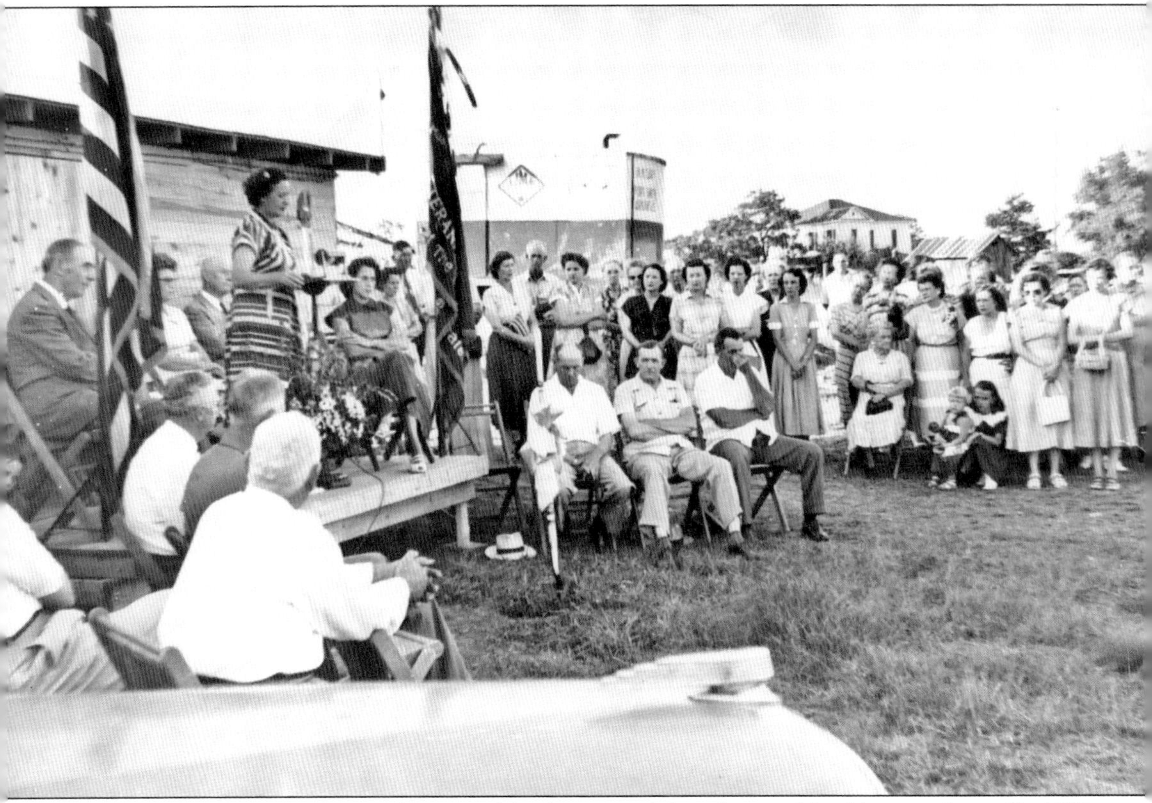

Crawford County Memorial Hospital broke ground for a hospital building on June 28, 1950. Sponsors for its construction included the Business and Professional Women's Club and the Veterans of Foreign Wars. Today, the hospital operates under the name Summit Medical Center. (Courtesy of the UAFS Cobb Collection.)

Two

Origins Unknown

The photographs in this chapter are something of a mystery. They were first captured on glass as early as 1903 and were reproduced and redeveloped digitally in 2014.

Dr. Ray Wallace, an award-winning photographer and former provost and senior vice chancellor of the University of Arkansas–Fort Smith (UAFS), discovered and purchased a tattered box of 80 glass-plate negatives in a Fort Smith antique store in 2013. At first glance, Wallace identified most of these fragile glass plates to be in fair condition, although on further examination noted that some had suffered deterioration from exposure to moisture. Wallace later established that these images had initially been rescued from an old wooden garage scheduled for demolition in Van Buren and surmised they might have a local connection.

It is important to remember that photographic emulsions using a dry-plate technique made on glass-plate negatives were popular from the 1870s until the first quarter of the 20th century, when they were then finally surpassed in both ease of development and popularity by gelatin silver negatives exposed on celluloid roll film. However, this dry-plate technique was probably the process used to first expose the glass negatives shown in this chapter since it was the most popular process in use in the region at that time.

To bring these century-old glass photographs to life, Wallace cautiously scanned each glass negative on a dedicated film scanner, producing a new digital negative of the image. Later, Wallace (now chancellor at Indiana University–Southeast) enlisted the help of historical interpretation students from UAFS to research, identify, and interpret the photographs.

The collection includes local landmarks, both posed and candid shots of Van Buren citizens, and a number of family-oriented photographs. In 2014, some of the images were selected for an exhibit at the UAFS-owned Drennen-Scott Historic Site. Clothing styles, magazine dates, and some furnishings were used to determine approximate dates for the collection. While individual names are not known, the glass-plate negatives and the prints seen here give an interesting yet somewhat mysterious look at a Van Buren that has long since changed.

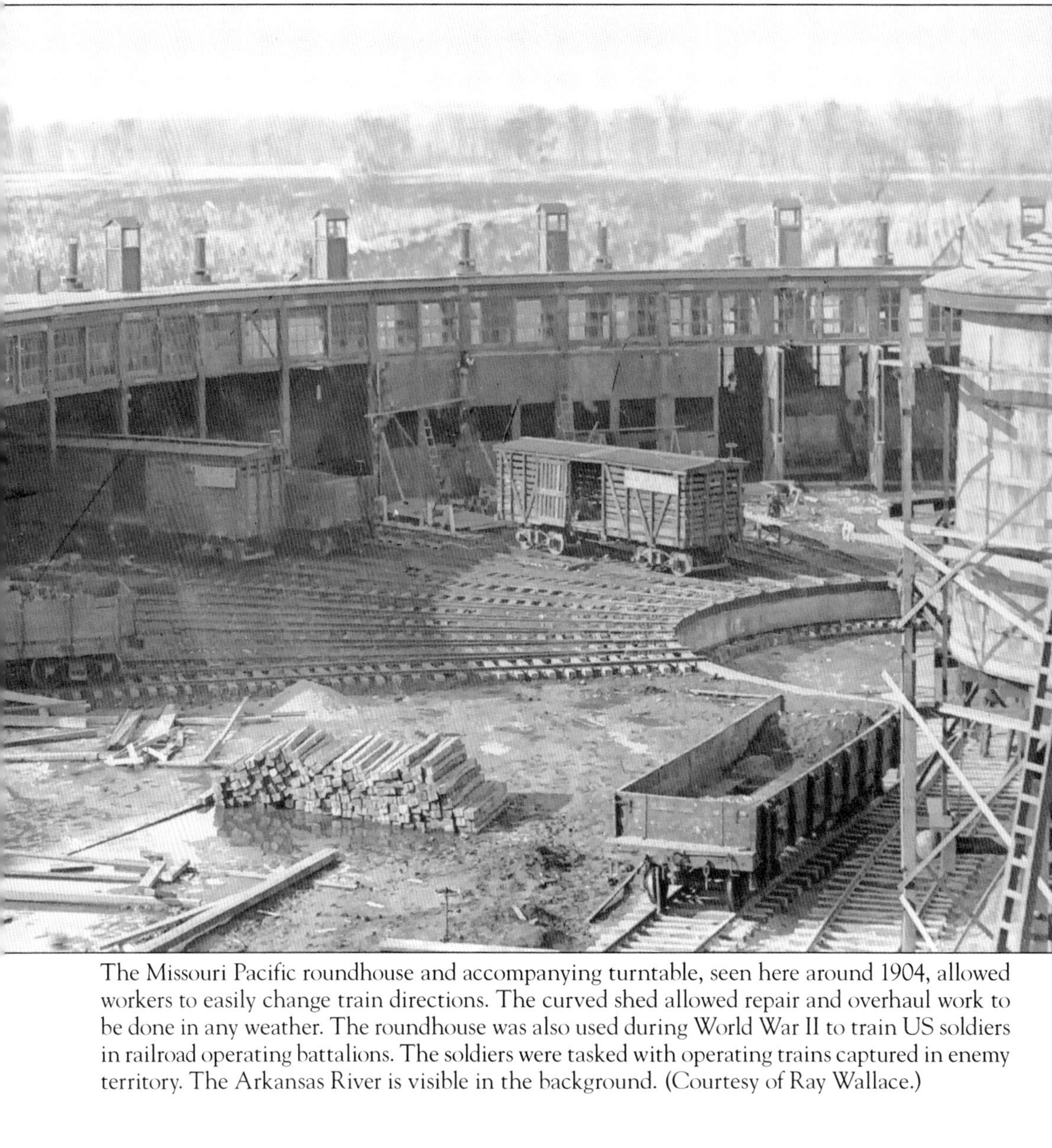

The Missouri Pacific roundhouse and accompanying turntable, seen here around 1904, allowed workers to easily change train directions. The curved shed allowed repair and overhaul work to be done in any weather. The roundhouse was also used during World War II to train US soldiers in railroad operating battalions. The soldiers were tasked with operating trains captured in enemy territory. The Arkansas River is visible in the background. (Courtesy of Ray Wallace.)

The coal elevator of the Missouri Pacific Railroad yard was used to load tender cars. Seen here around 1904, a close examination of the photograph reveals coal in the chutes. The coal-fired boilers produced steam to power the trains before being replaced by diesel engines used widely today. (Courtesy of Ray Wallace.)

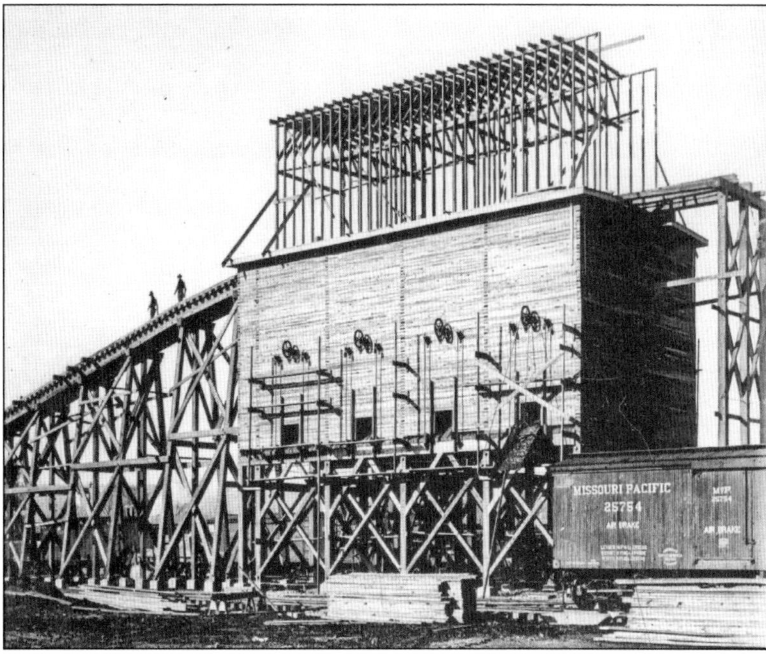

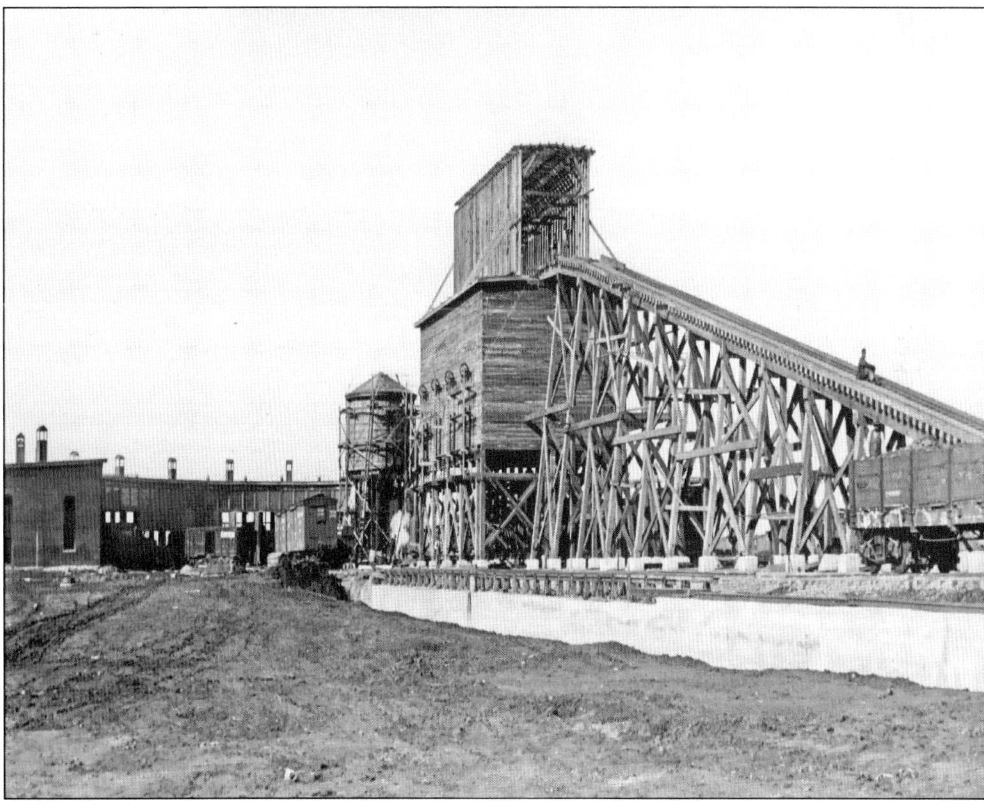

The Missouri and Pacific Railroad yard brought passenger trains and freight service to Van Buren for many years. As the town moved away from the river and steamboat traffic gave way to the railroad, Van Buren became an important rail junction in western Arkansas. (Courtesy of Ray Wallace.)

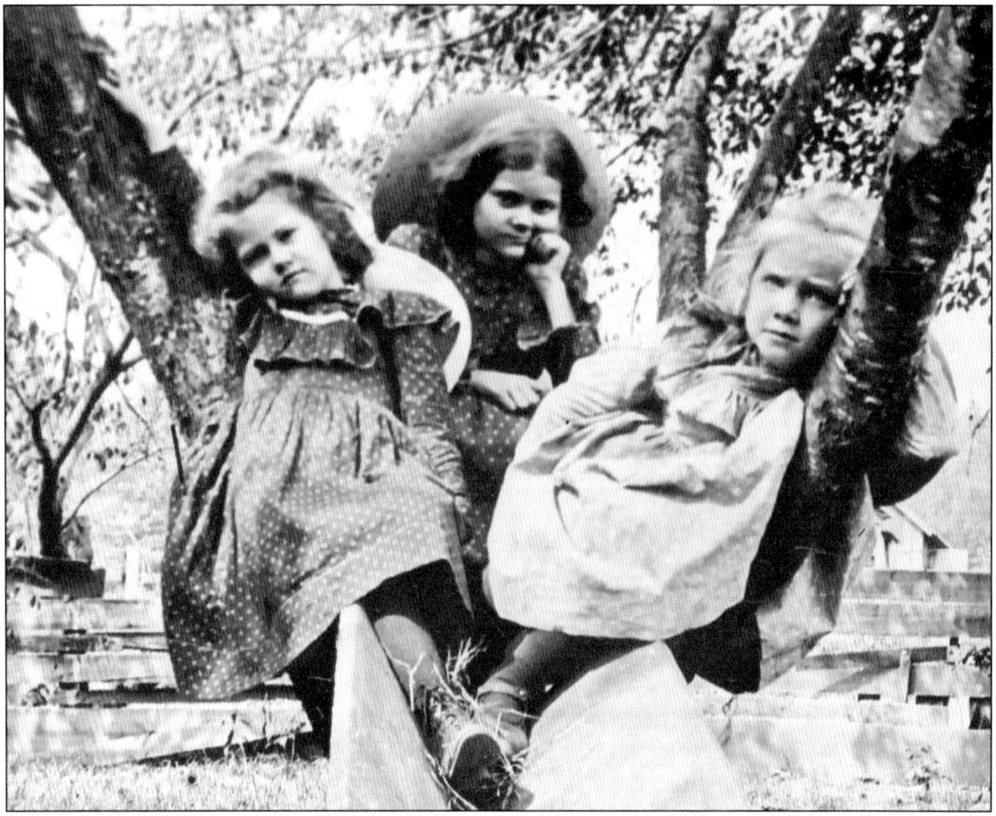

Three girls pose for the photographer. By the early 1900s, camera technology had become available to amateurs, and one of the girls' parents likely took this c. 1904 image. (Courtesy of Ray Wallace.)

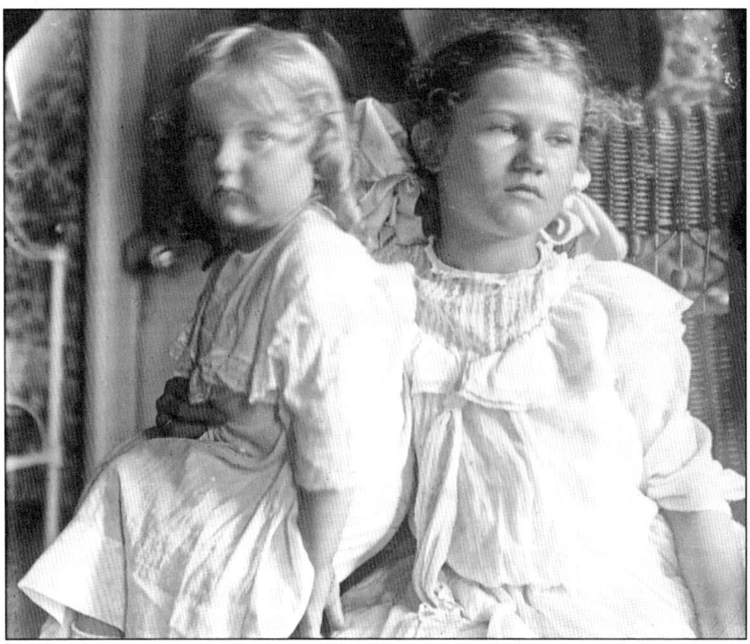

These young girls, possibly sisters, appear to be longing to be something other than the subject of this photograph. Their clothing is typical for children in the early 1900s. (Courtesy of Ray Wallace.)

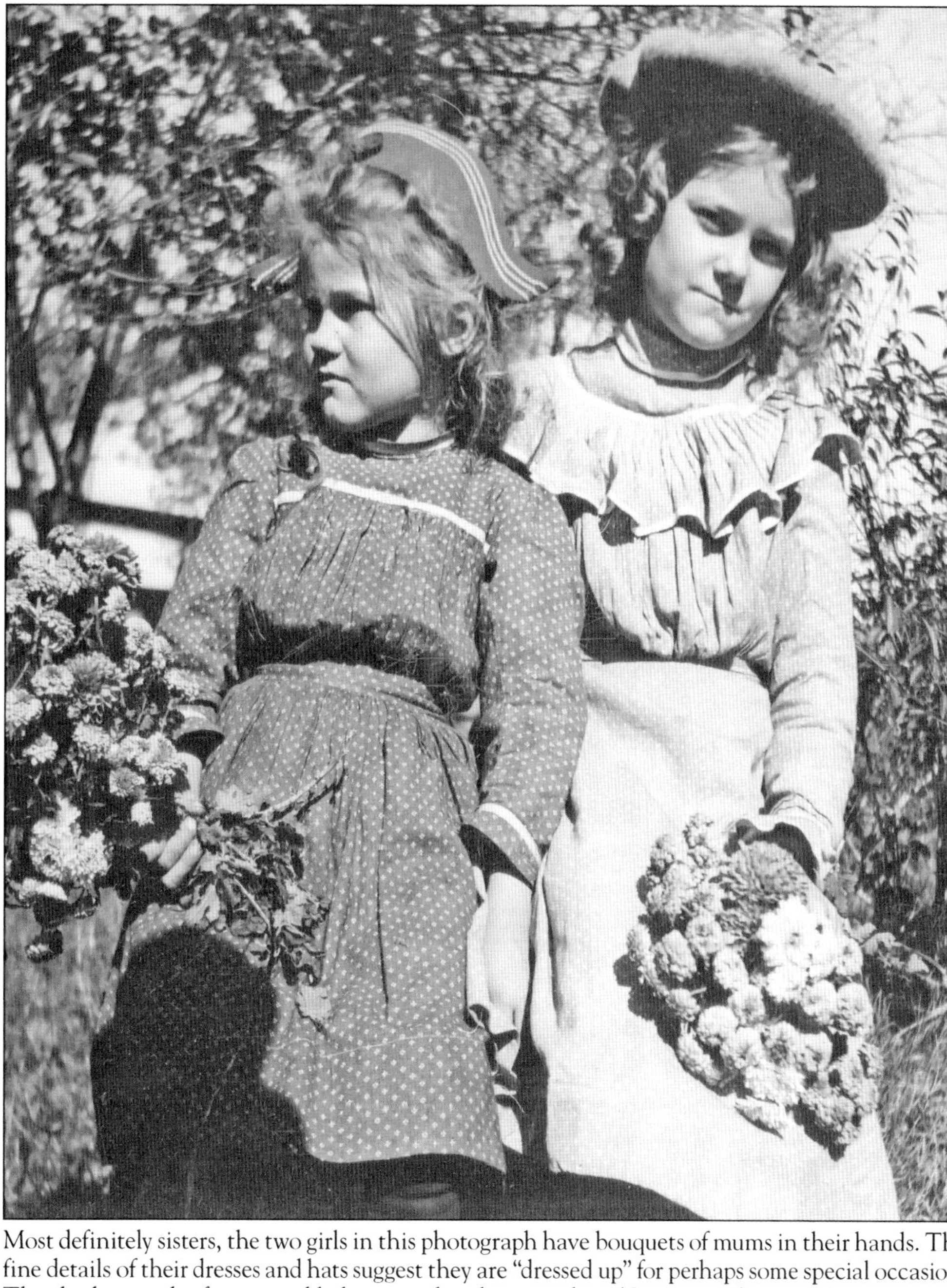

Most definitely sisters, the two girls in this photograph have bouquets of mums in their hands. The fine details of their dresses and hats suggest they are "dressed up" for perhaps some special occasion. The shadow in the foreground belongs to the photographer. (Courtesy of Ray Wallace.)

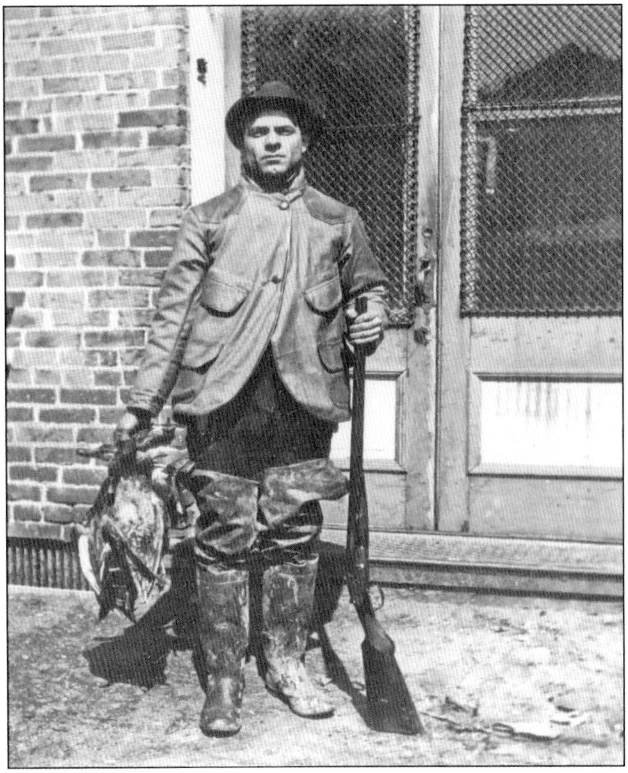

Duck hunting is still popular today along the Arkansas River near Van Buren. This hunter had his photograph taken somewhere on Main Street. His coat protects him from the cold as his tall boots, or waders, allow him to hunt from shallow water. In one hand he holds his double-barrel shotgun and in the other the results of a successful hunt. (Courtesy of Ray Wallace.)

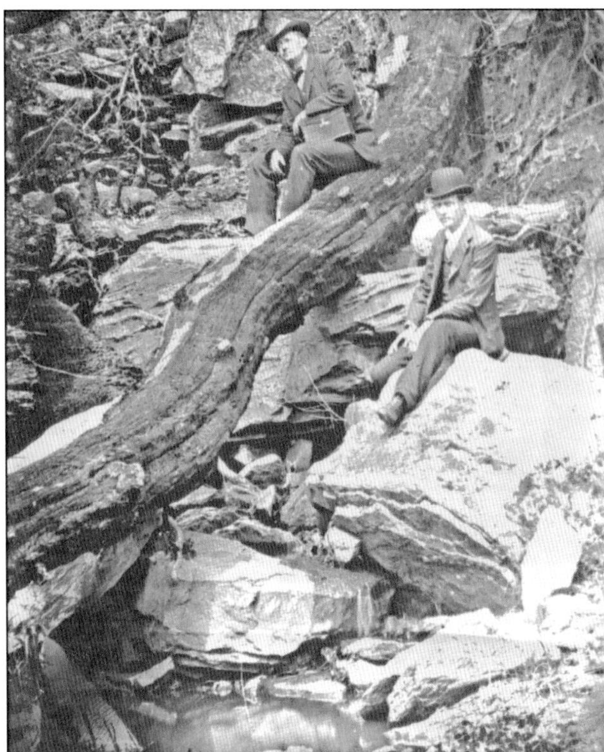

Located where the Ozark Plateau meets the Arkansas River, Van Buren has some interesting terrain, as these two gentlemen can agree. (Courtesy of Ray Wallace.)

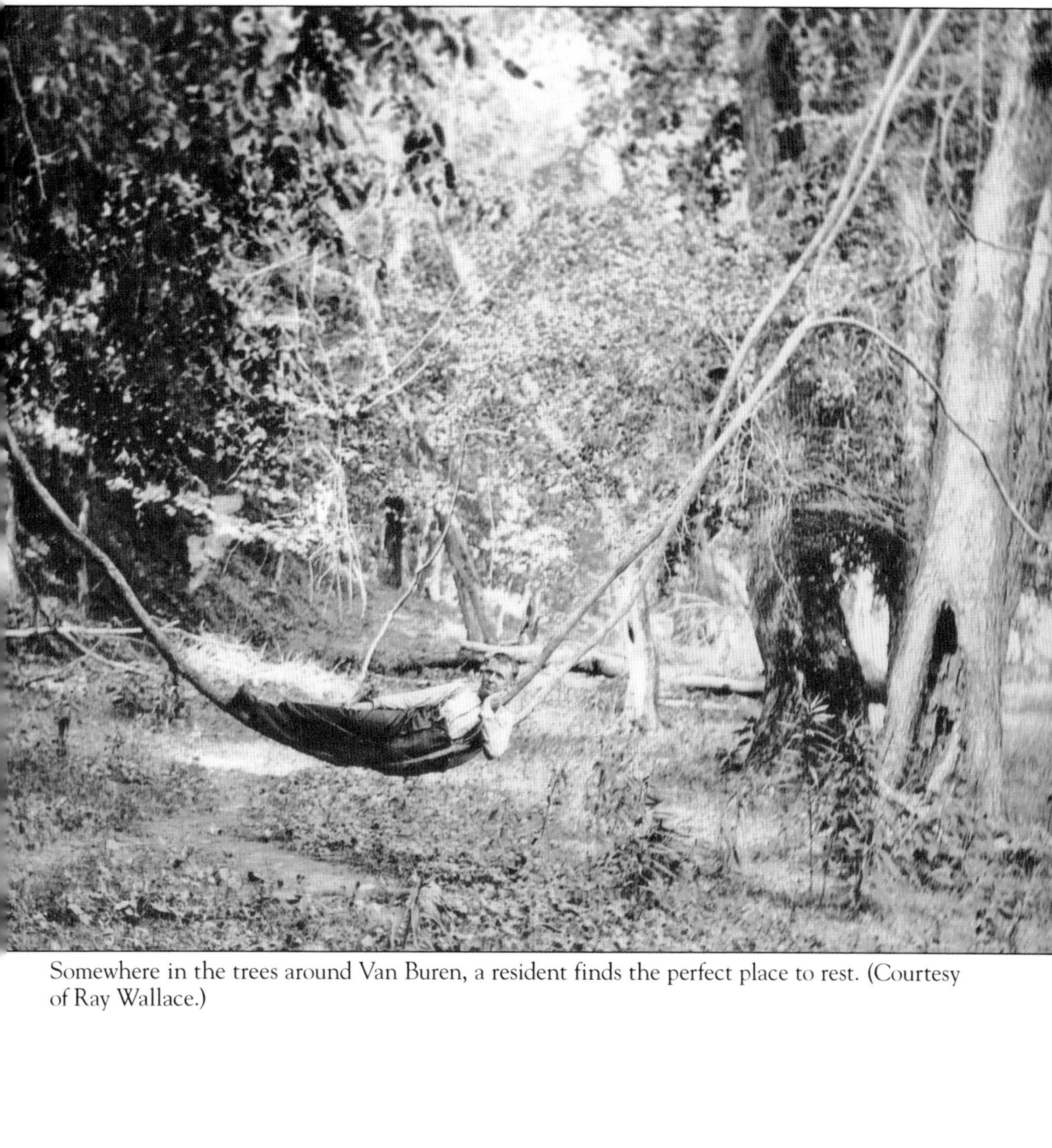

Somewhere in the trees around Van Buren, a resident finds the perfect place to rest. (Courtesy of Ray Wallace.)

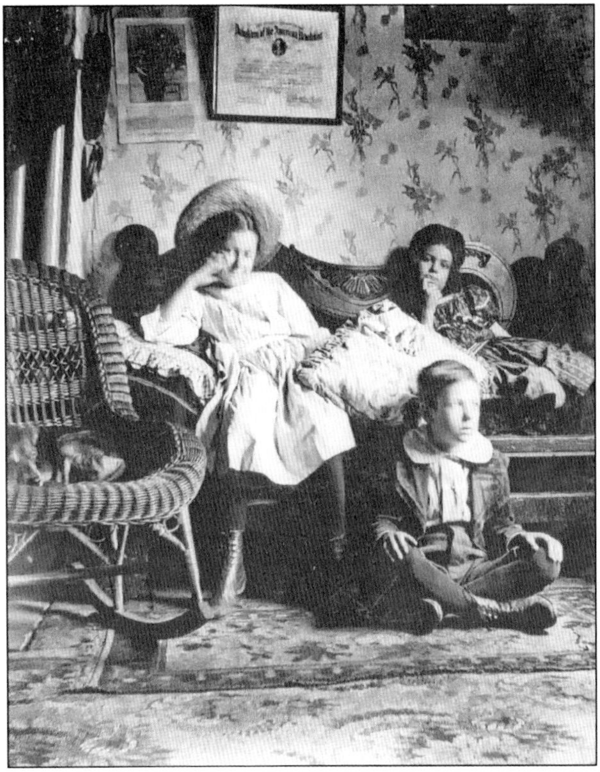

The three children here seem less posed and more candid than in other photographs in this collection. The degree on the wall could mean they are the children of a Van Buren medical doctor. (Courtesy of Ray Wallace.)

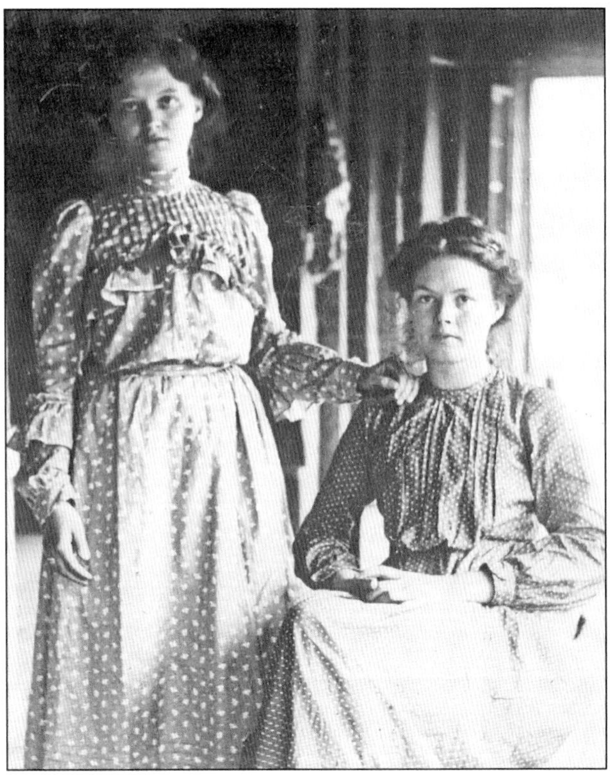

Posing on what appears to be the porch, these likely sisters are frozen in time with somber and dignified expressions. (Courtesy of Ray Wallace.)

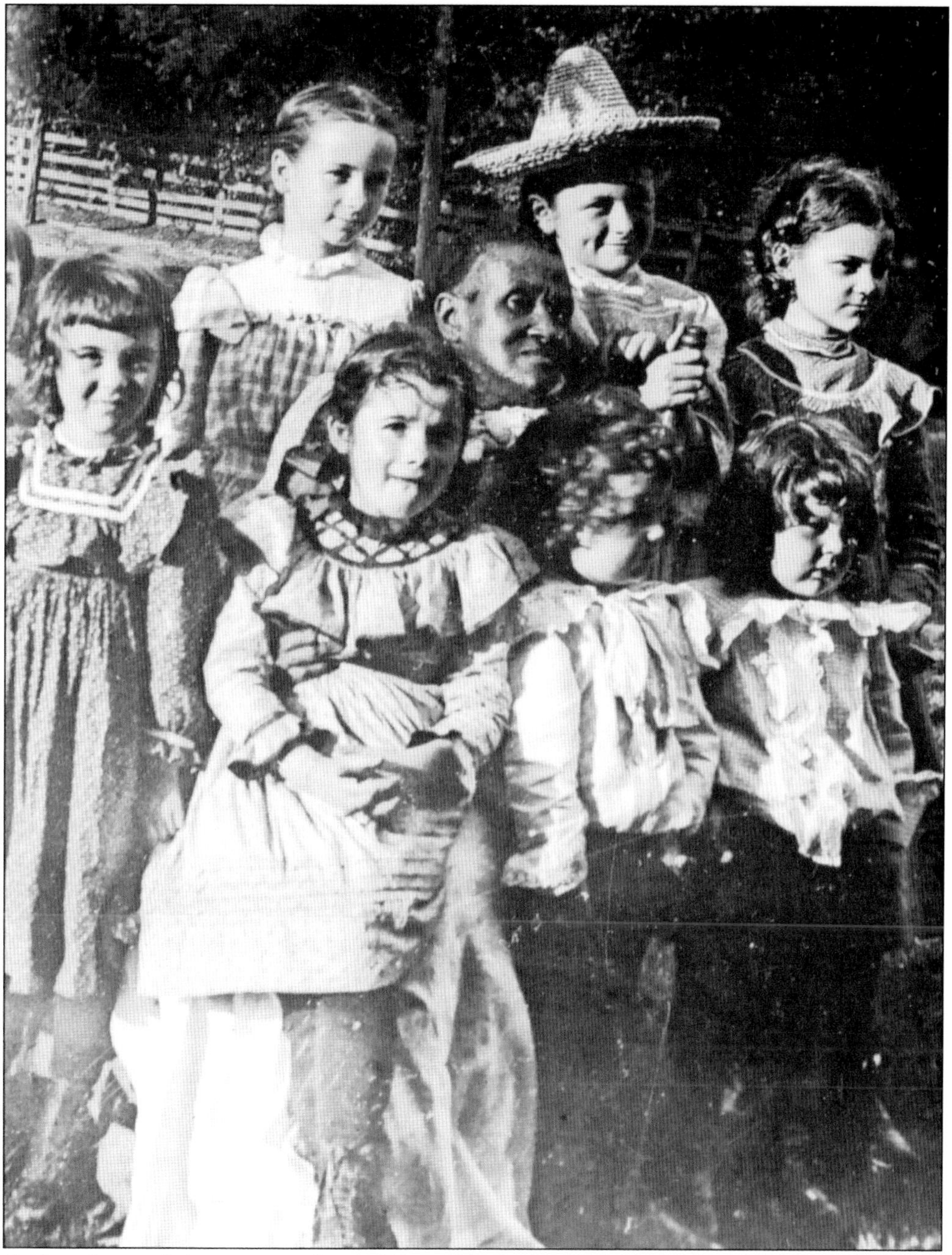

Gathered around their nanny, the children in this image express joy, comfort, and affection for the woman who cared for them. (Courtesy of Ray Wallace.)

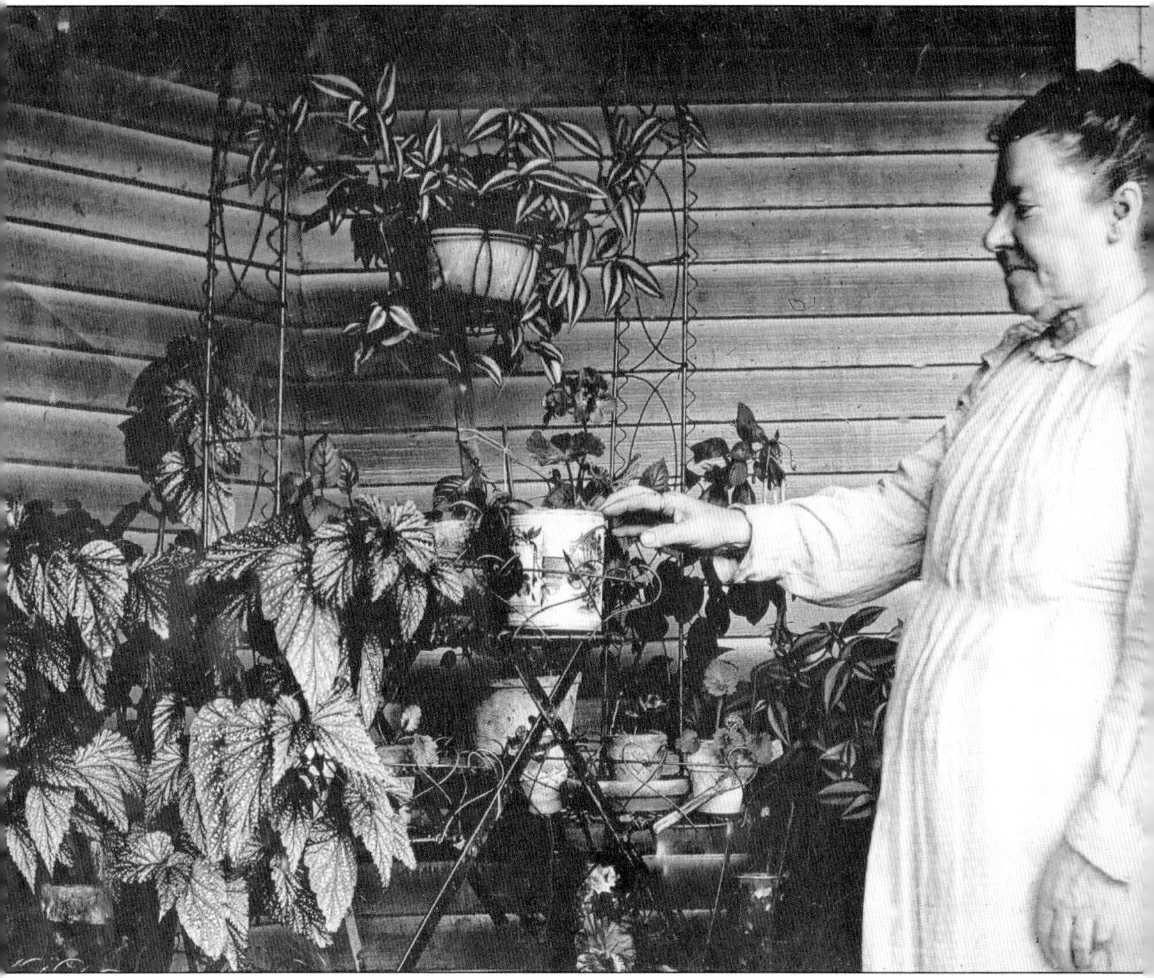

This candid, everyday shot was most likely less about the woman and more about the plants. Watering her elephant's ears with a repurposed coffee can, the woman's healthy plants confirm her green thumb. (Courtesy of Ray Wallace.)

Whether this photograph contains three sisters or a mother and two daughters, it is clear they are closely related. (Courtesy of Ray Wallace.)

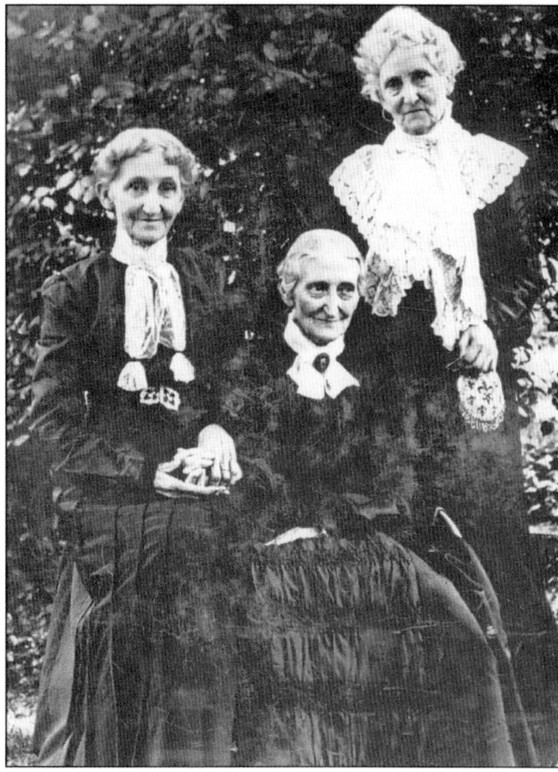

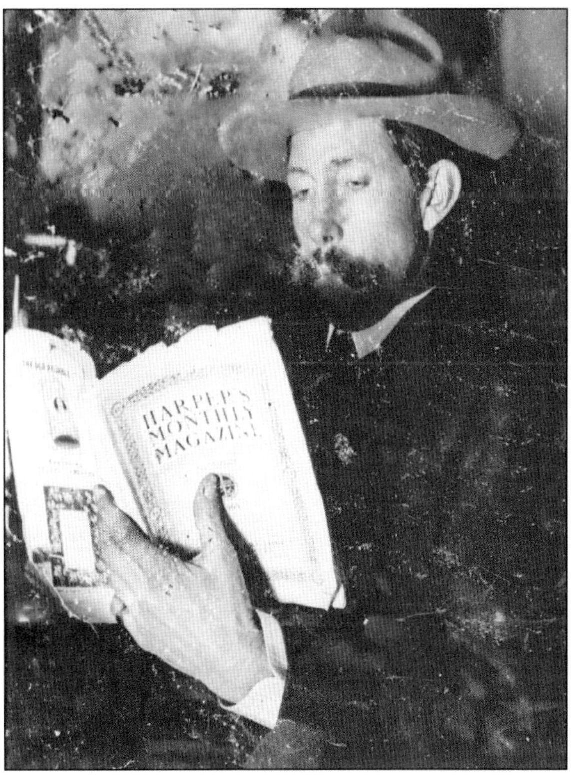

This man is reading the March 1903 copy of *Harper's Monthly Magazine*. *Harper's* was first published in New York in 1850. Part two of the previous month's article about the Dutch founding New York has this man's full attention. (Courtesy of Ray Wallace.)

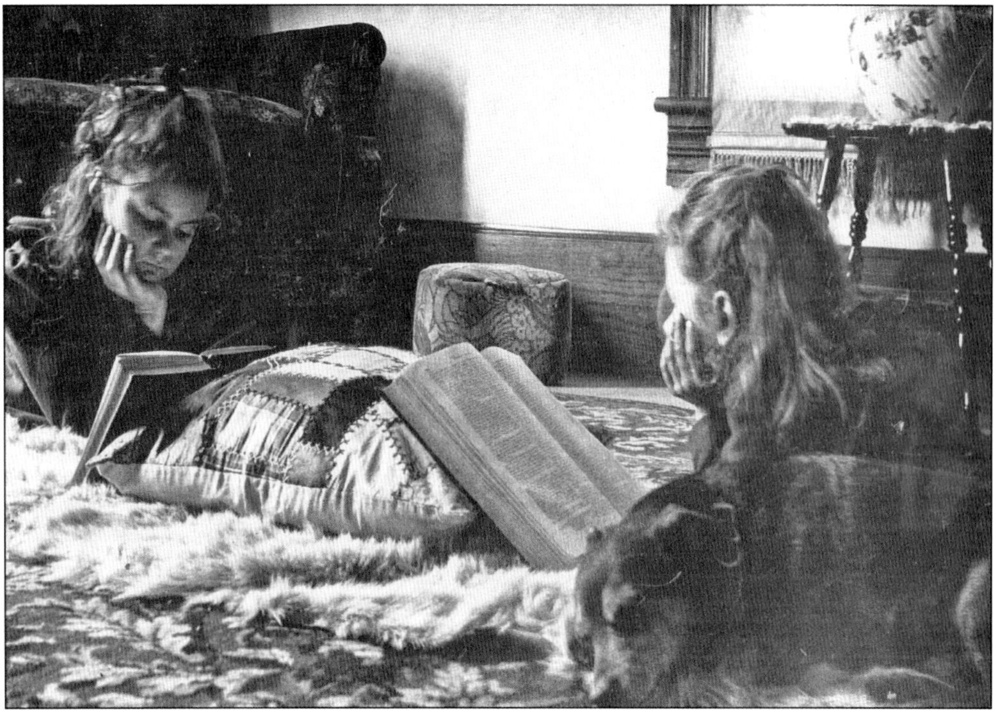

Pillows, plush carpet, and a good book are keeping these young ladies occupied; the family dog rests nearby. (Courtesy of Ray Wallace.)

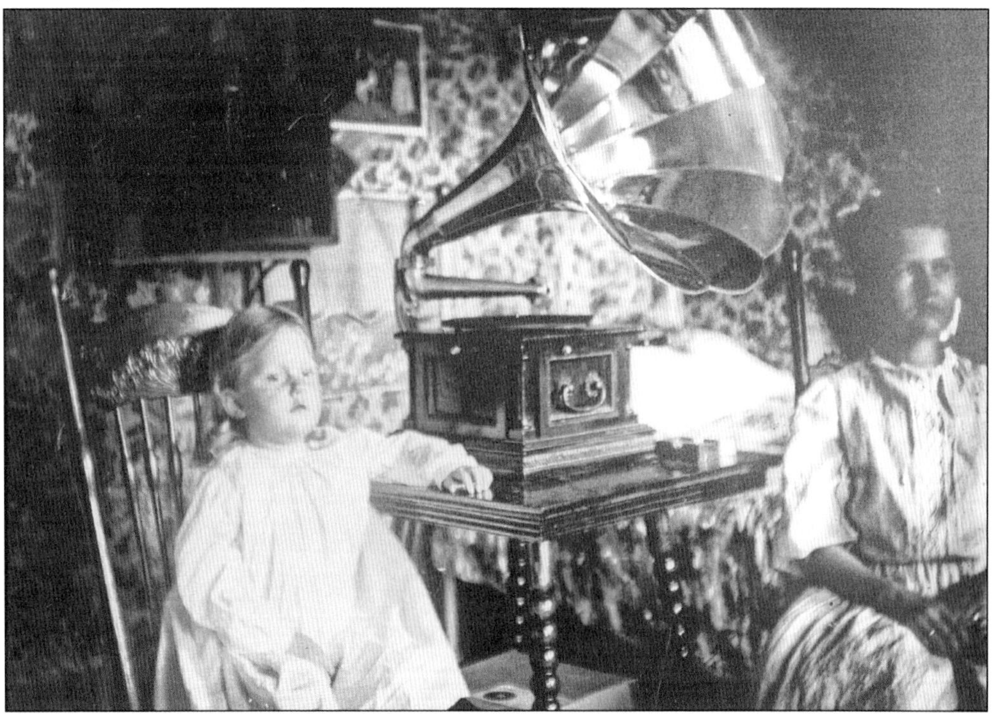

These two girls are sitting next to a post-1902 Victrola phonograph. Many households could not afford the "high tech" record player. (Courtesy of Ray Wallace.)

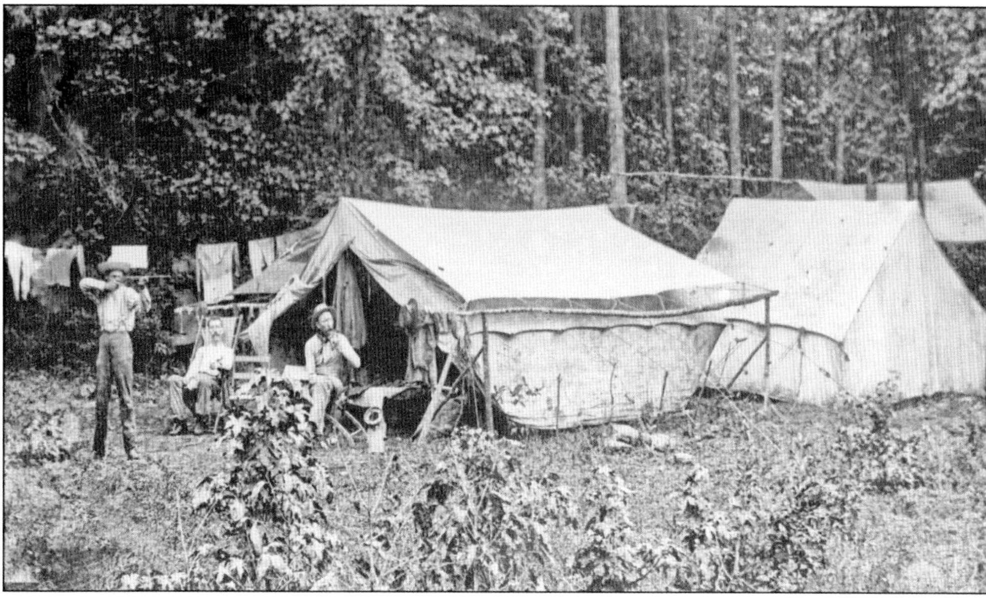

Hunting and camping have been popular pastimes for Van Buren citizens from the early days to the present. These men have all the comforts of home in camp. (Courtesy of Ray Wallace.)

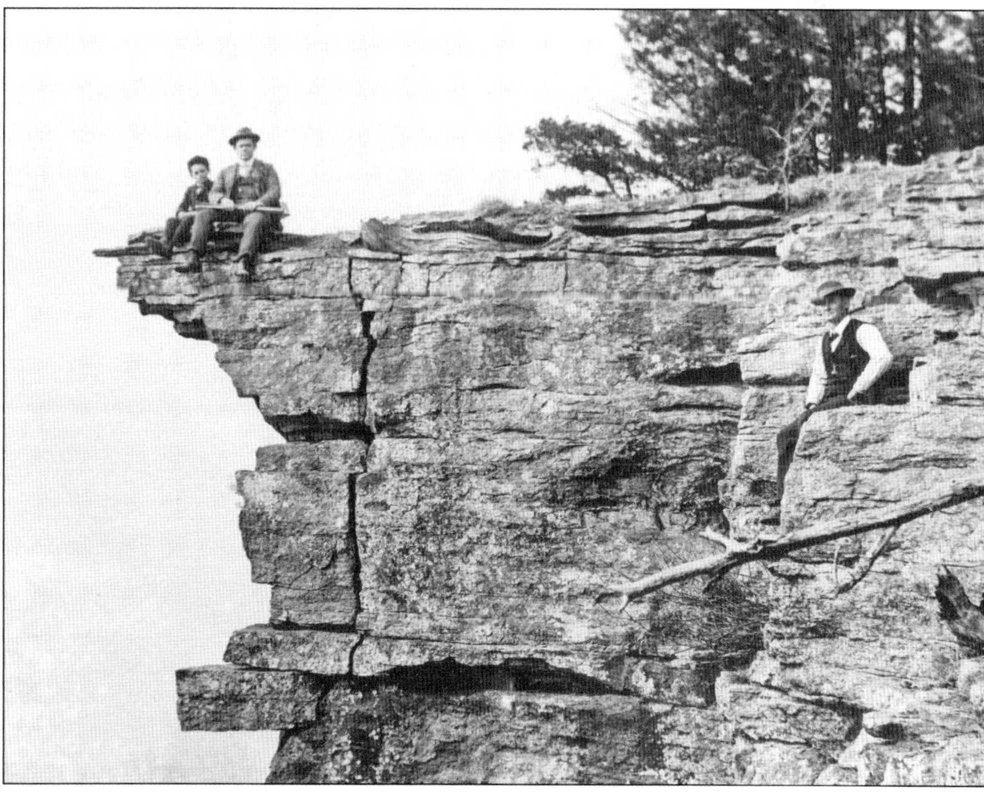

Mount Vista, previously known as Lee Creek Bluff, is located to the west along the river from downtown Van Buren. These men and a boy are enjoying the incredible view of Fort Smith and the river valley. (Courtesy of Ray Wallace.)

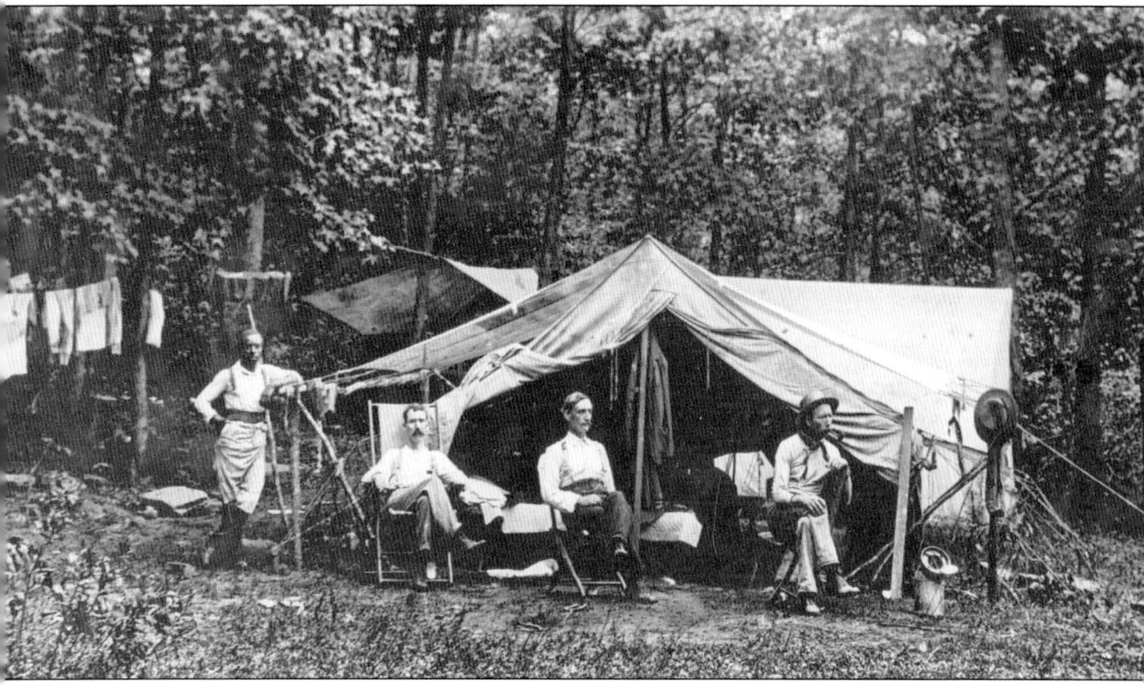

Most likely photographed in Crawford County near Van Buren, this may be a hunting camp or men simply enjoying nature and a break from everyday life. (Courtesy of Ray Wallace.)

Three

Coming Together

Van Buren is beloved for the places in the community where residents can come together. Whether it be on the streets of the city's scenic downtown, at the county courthouse, in a house or worship, or at a final resting place, citizens have a deep sense of pride and responsibility for the places where they commune.

From the time it was selected as county seat in 1842, Van Buren's relationship with the Crawford County Courthouse involved both legal authority and economic development. John Drennen courted Crawford County to relocate the county courthouse to Van Buren. Knowing the necessity of county clerks, records, and the court to a growing community, Drennen sweetened the deal by selling the square block on Main Street where the courthouse now sits for the sum of $1. Still conducting county business today, the Crawford County Courthouse has been active for 173 years.

Van Buren's Main Street has always been the heart of the community, and even today, with the city developing to the north of Interstate 40, the historic charm of downtown and historic buildings on Main Street continue to draw both visitors and locals. Countless parades, festivals, and holiday events have centered on Main Street, as well as a number of defining historical moments. With all the history occurring there, it is perhaps the understated scenes of everyday life that endear the old street to those who spend time there. Once the center of commerce for the city, banks and specialty shops have replaced dealerships, jewelry stores, and other merchants, but a good haircut, a trip to the post office, or a quick bite to eat have always been possible.

With a wide mix of protestant churches and Catholic services as well, a degree of religious diversity remains a part of life in Van Buren and can be traced back to the city's founding. According to Clara B. Eno, a well-known and respected historian of Crawford County, the first church built in Van Buren was Union Church, dating to 1840. It was located near the waterfront, as the early town was much closer to the river. A multitude of religions and respective houses of worship would quickly follow suit.

Finally, Van Buren residents congregate and often come to lie in the common resting place that is Fairview Cemetery.

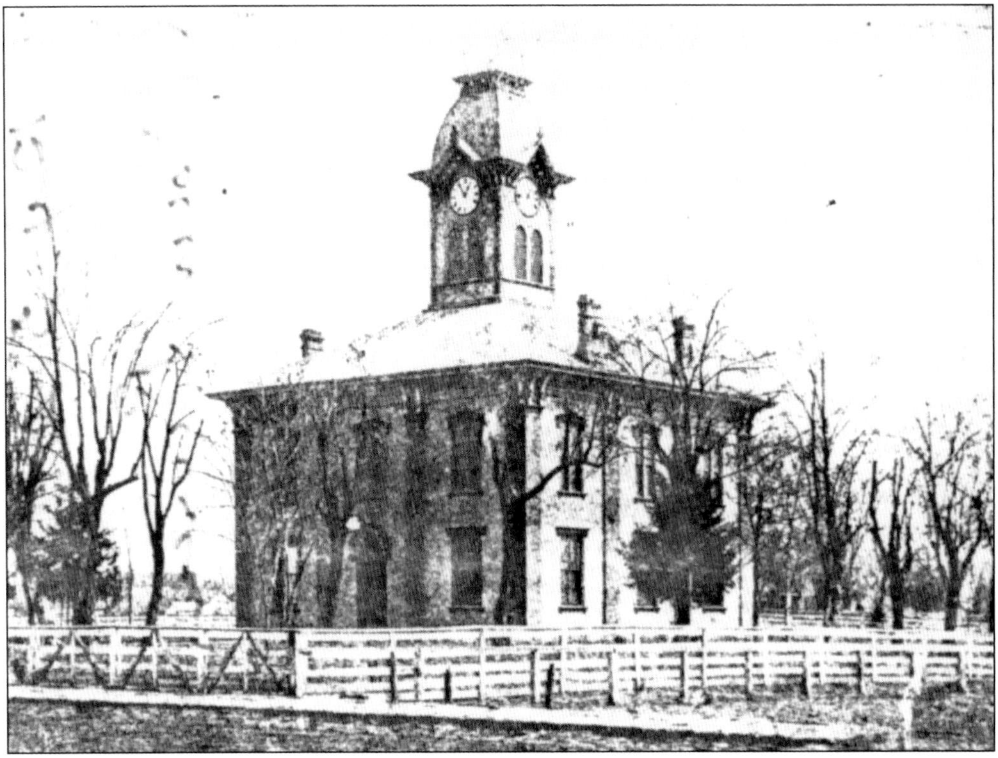

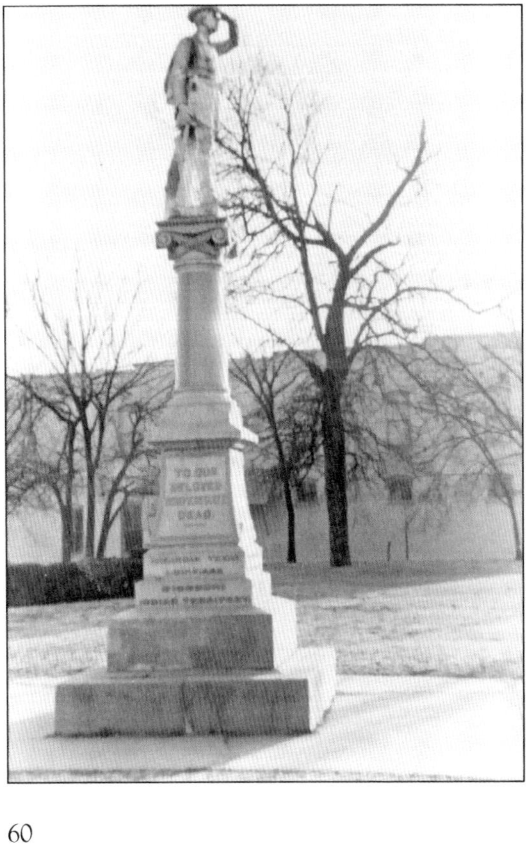

Seen here in 1878, the Crawford County Courthouse features the newly added Seth Thomas clock visible in the tower. Fences around the courthouse served as corrals for artillery battery horses during the Civil War. (Courtesy of the UAFS Cobb Collection.)

Dedicated to the Confederate soldiers who fought the Battle of Wilson's Creek (or Oak Hills) in southwest Missouri in 1861 and the Battles of Pea Ridge and Prairie Grove in Arkansas in 1862, the monument seen here was originally dedicated over the Confederate section of Fairview Cemetery in 1899. Confederates from Van Buren and Crawford County fought alongside other Arkansans and soldiers from Texas, Missouri, Louisiana, and Indian Territory. (Courtesy of the UAFS Cobb Collection.)

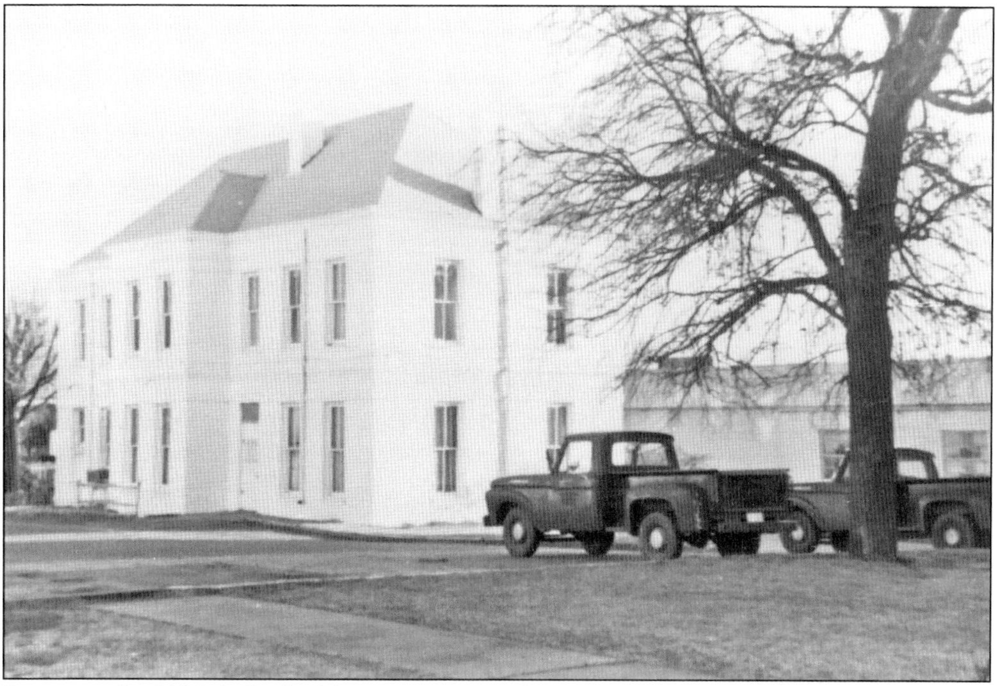

Known as the Old Jail, this building, seen in 1968, has served not only as a place for prisoners but also court offices and storage. The structure sits on the courthouse grounds on the south side of the property. (Courtesy of the UAFS Cobb Collection.)

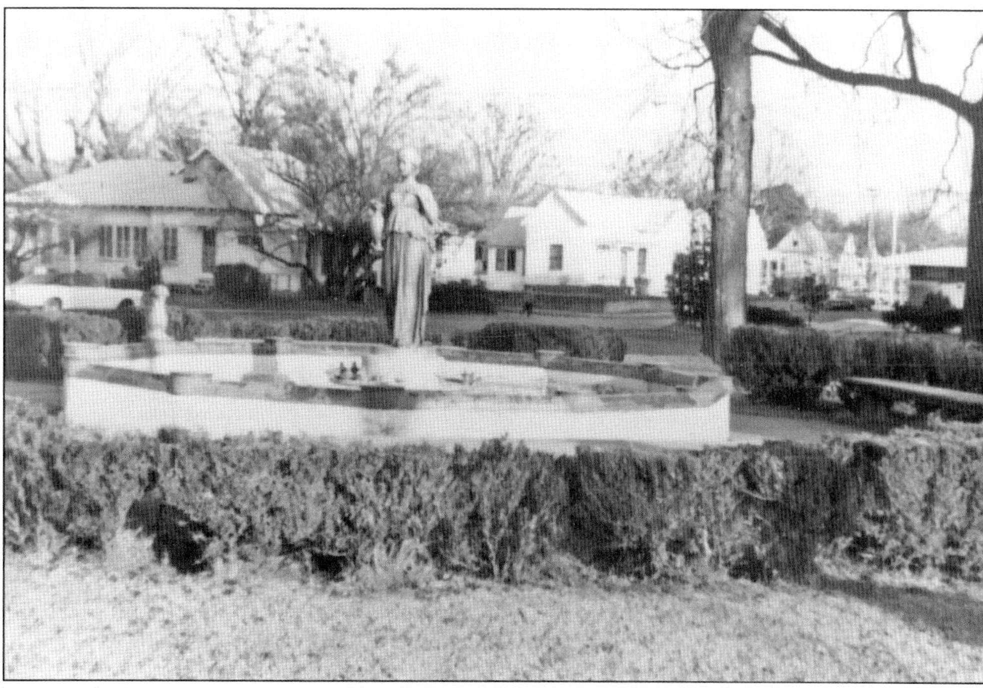

Hebe at the Fountain was sculpted by Giuseppe Moretti and cast by the J.L. Mott ironworks in 1908. The bronze statue deteriorated over time and was replaced by a replica in 2002. Hebe was the Greek goddess of youth. (Courtesy of the UAFS Cobb Collection.)

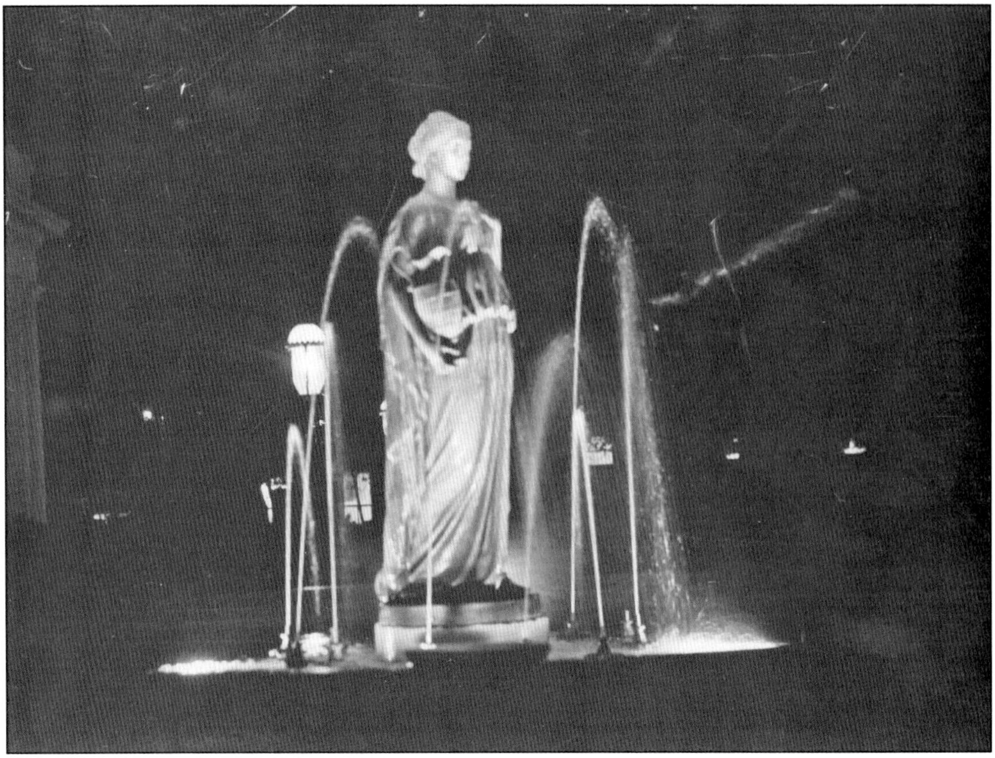

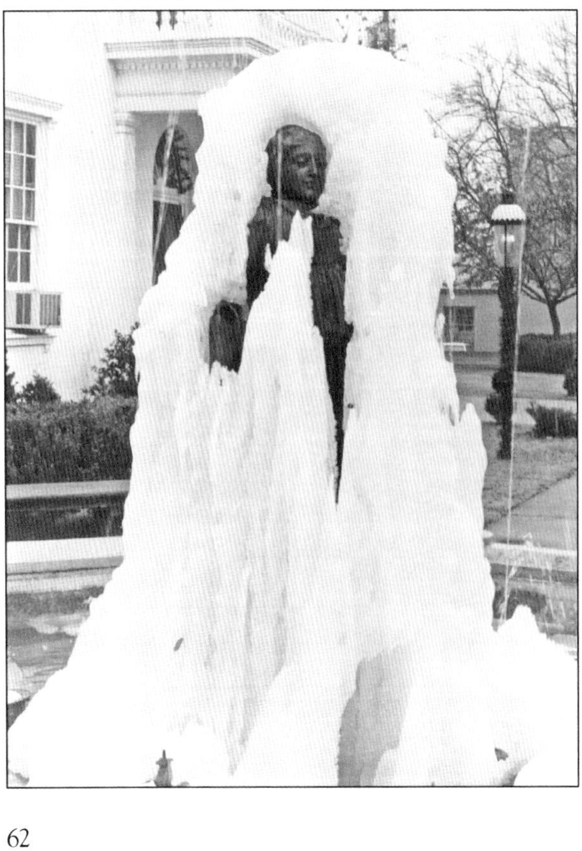

The original *Hebe at the Fountain* is seen above on the courthouse grounds at night in 1973, and at left encased in ice in December 1974. (Both, courtesy of the UAFS Cobb Collection.)

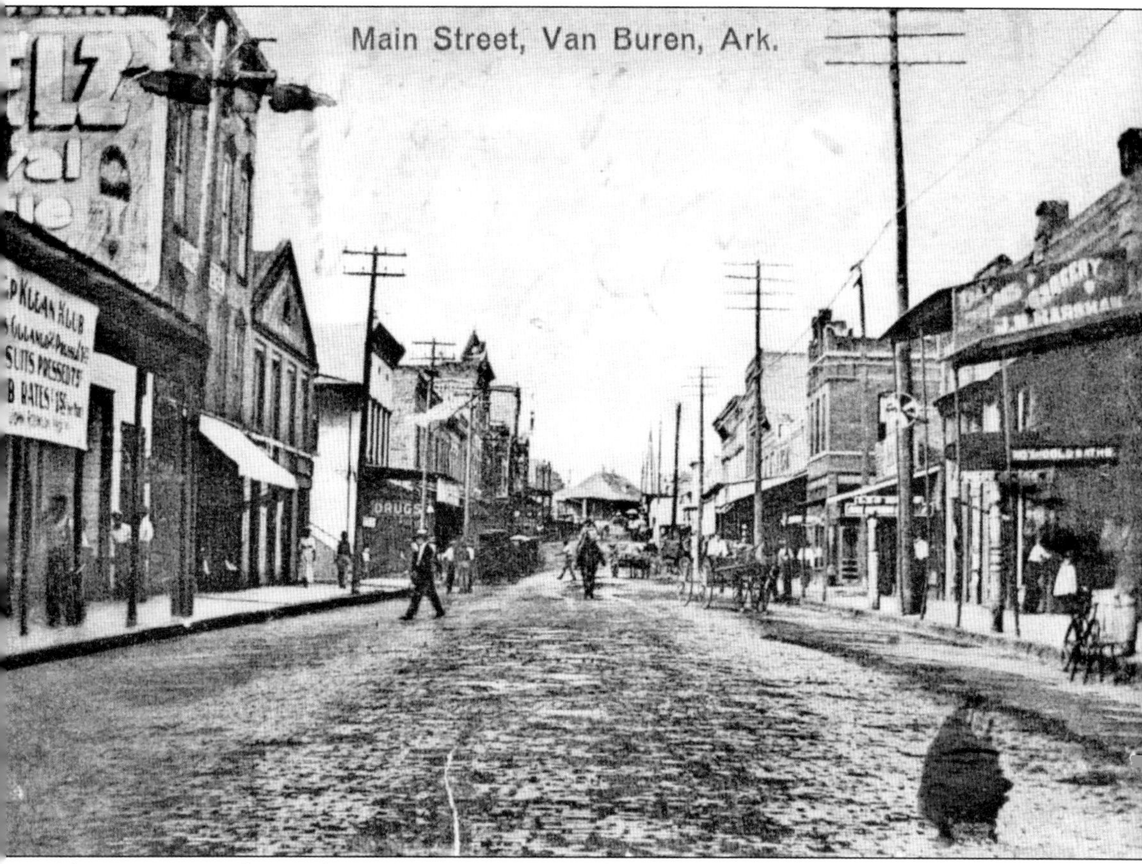

This 1918 postcard view of Main Street in Van Buren has a wealth of details. Seen from the south end of the street near the courthouse, the cobblestone street is clearly visible. Myer Drugstore is not far up on the left, and the iconic Victorian-styled Citizens Bank building is farther up on that side. In the distance, at the head of the street, is the Frisco Depot. (Courtesy of the UAFS Cobb Collection.)

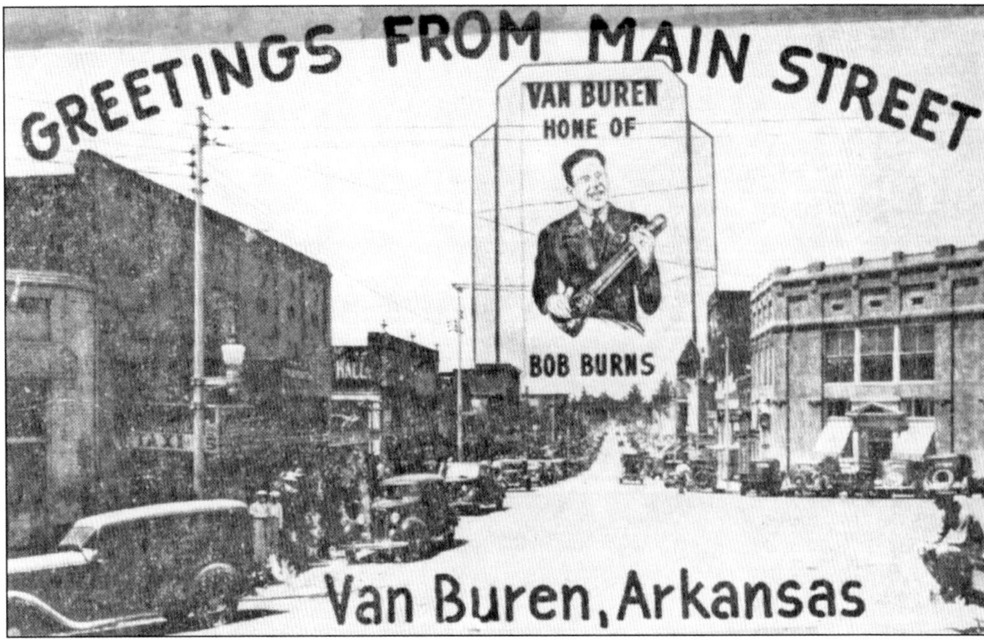

Printed by the *Press Argus* newspaper, this 1930s postcard photograph was taken from the Frisco Depot end of the street looking down towards the river and courthouse. Always searching for an opportunity to promote a "native son," the newspaper hails radio and movie star Bob Burns. (Courtesy of the UAFS Cobb Collection.)

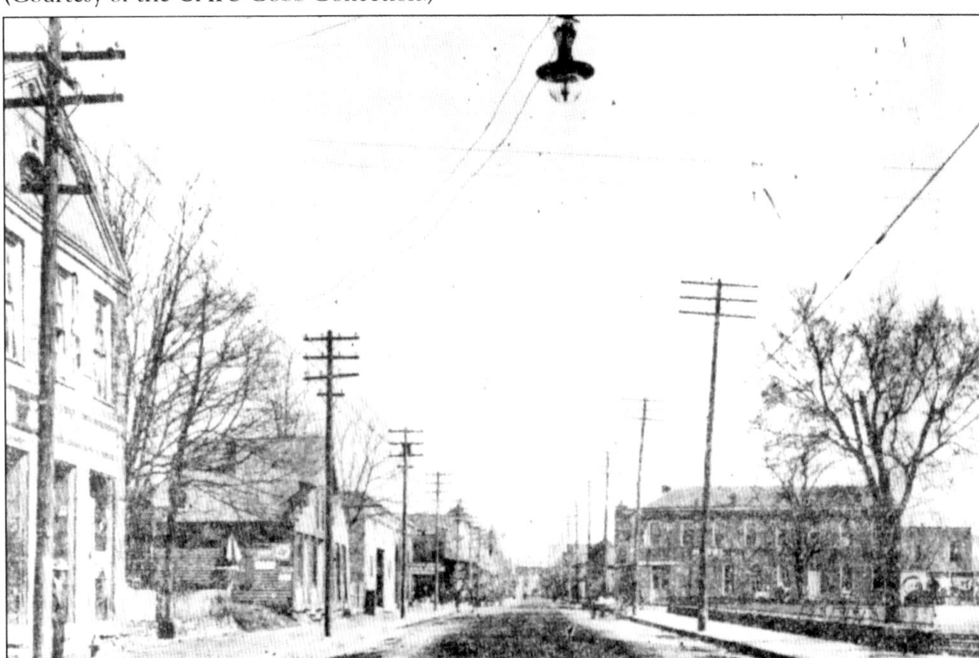

This photograph dates to the spring of 1912, around the time of the dedication of the Free Bridge between Van Buren and Fort Smith. The fenced-in area in the right foreground is the Crawford County Courthouse lawn. In the distance is the Frisco Depot. (Courtesy of the UAFS Cobb Collection.)

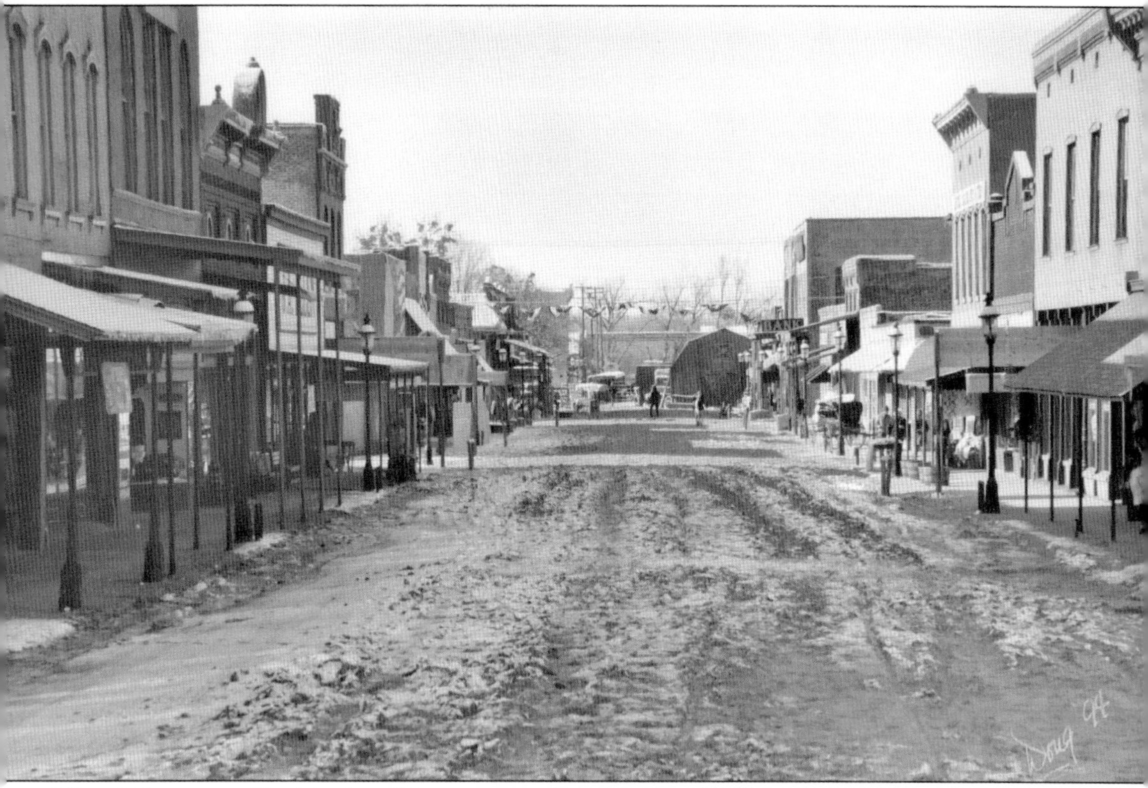

The 1995 western film *Frank and Jesse*, starring Rob Lowe and Bill Paxton, along with country music star Randy Travis, was filmed in Van Buren. Main Street was transformed to appear as a 19th-century town visited by the James gang. Cooperation of the city even included covering the pavement of Main Street with dirt; cleanup after the filming was remembered by many in Van Buren as a laborious process that took quite a bit of time. While the film was not a hit, it was not the only time Van Buren was used as a film location. In 1982, the made-for-TV movie *The Blue and the Gray* was filmed partially in Van Buren, as was 1988's *Biloxi Blues*. (Courtesy of the UAFS Cobb Collection.)

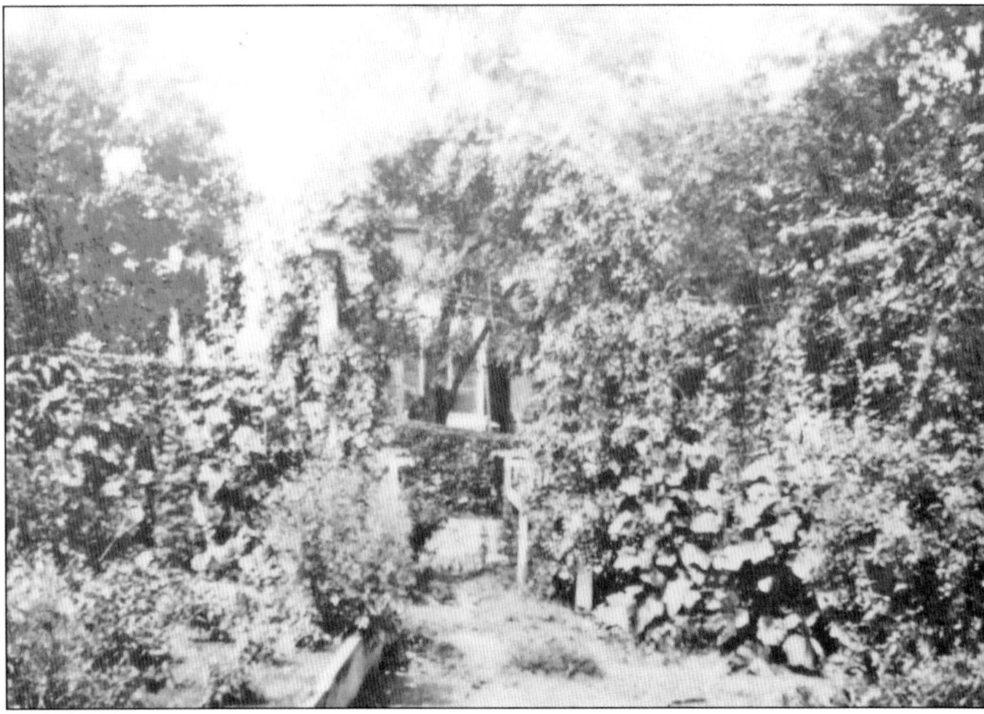

This 1920s view of the Victorian garden at the Drennen-Scott estate shows white roses growing over benched arbors, with the main house visible in the background. Victorian gardens symbolized the wealth and status of the owners. While beauty was the benefit, a vegetable garden with food crops stood nearby out of the camera's view. (Courtesy of the Historic Arkansas Museum.)

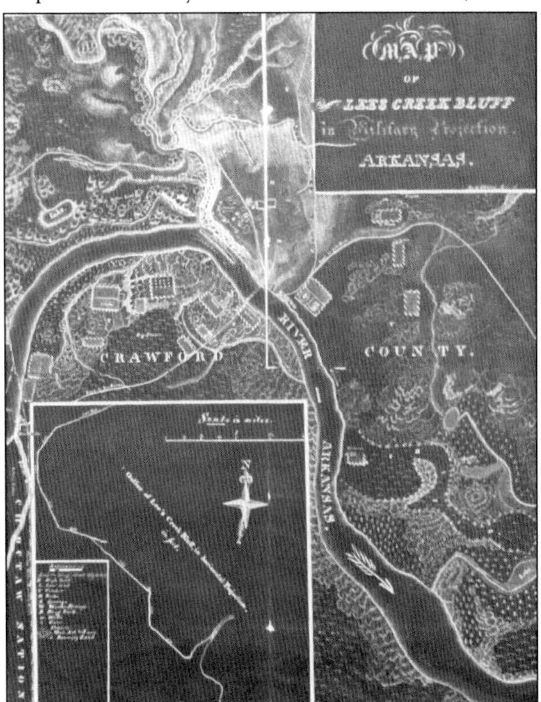

In the late 1830s, the Army, under pressure from Arkansas politicians, decided to build a new outpost in western Arkansas, having vacated the area in 1824. Lee Creek Bluff, the heights above the river and fledgling town of Van Buren, was considered and mapped by Army engineers. The Army eventually built the new fort on the grounds of the previous installation in Fort Smith. Citing difficulty in getting supplies from the waterline up to the bluff and the hard bargaining by Fort Smith businessman John Rogers, Van Buren lost the bid to house the troops. (Author's collection.)

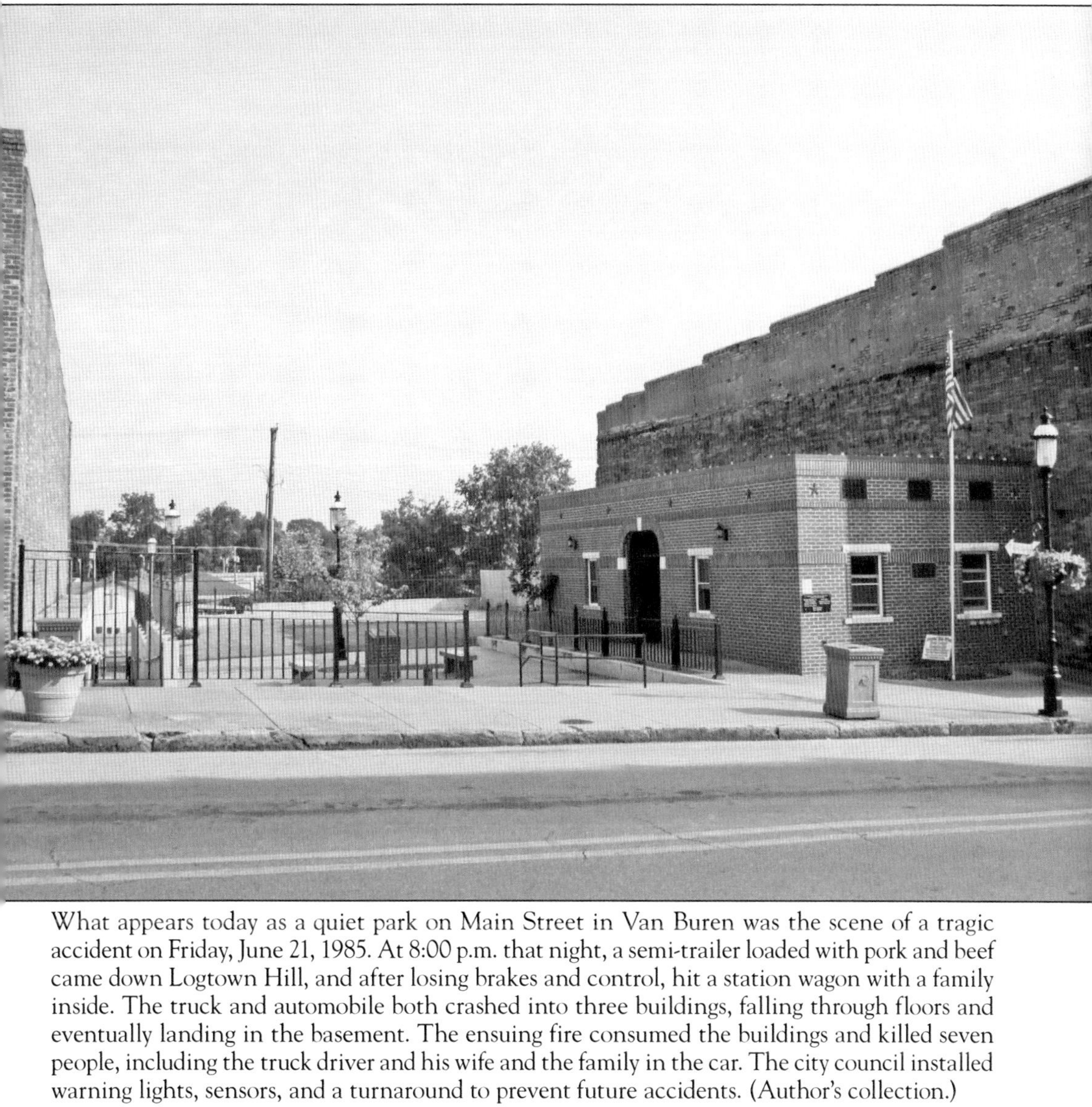

What appears today as a quiet park on Main Street in Van Buren was the scene of a tragic accident on Friday, June 21, 1985. At 8:00 p.m. that night, a semi-trailer loaded with pork and beef came down Logtown Hill, and after losing brakes and control, hit a station wagon with a family inside. The truck and automobile both crashed into three buildings, falling through floors and eventually landing in the basement. The ensuing fire consumed the buildings and killed seven people, including the truck driver and his wife and the family in the car. The city council installed warning lights, sensors, and a turnaround to prevent future accidents. (Author's collection.)

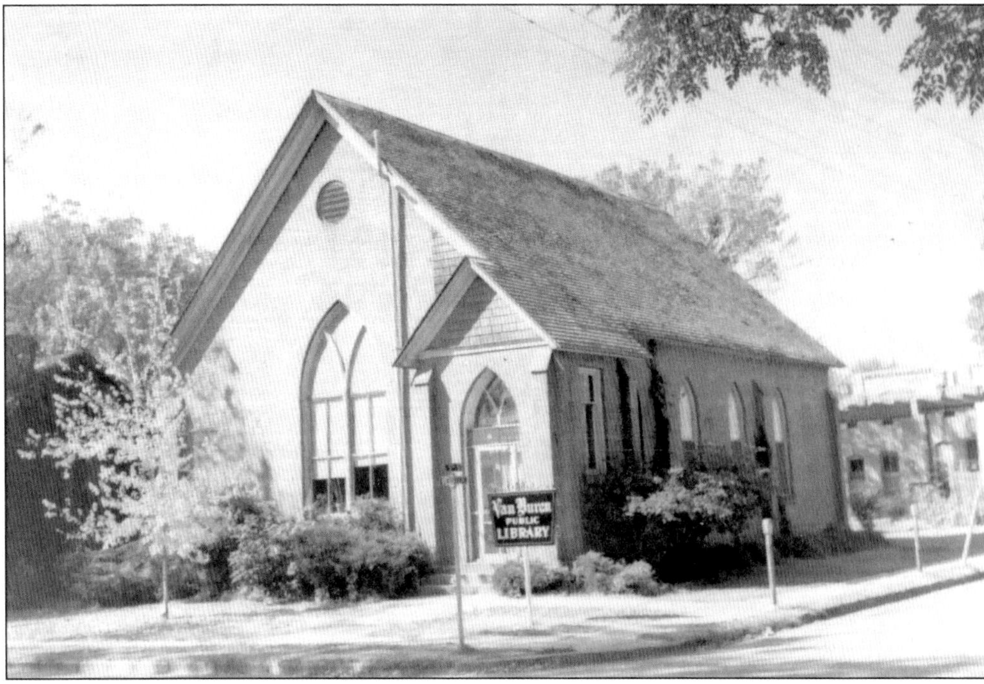

Built in 1848, the old Presbyterian church combined with a Cumberland Presbyterian group in 1906 and built a new building for the combined First Presbyterian congregation. (Courtesy of the UAFS Cobb Collection.)

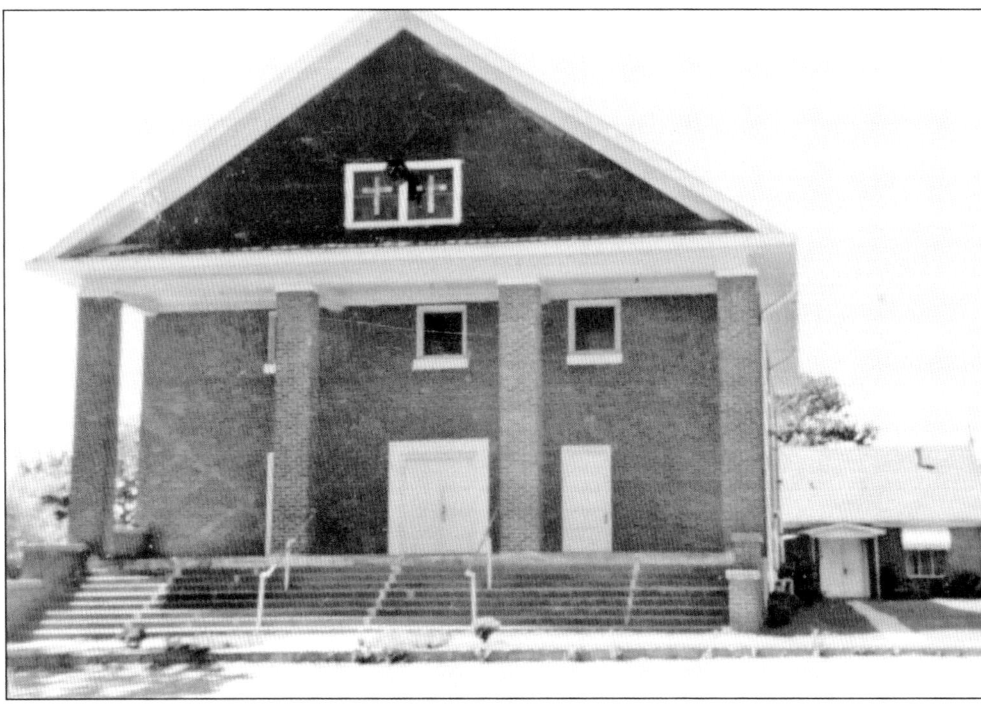

Seen here in 1970, Saint John's Church was located at 619 North Twentieth Street. (Courtesy of the UAFS Cobb Collection.)

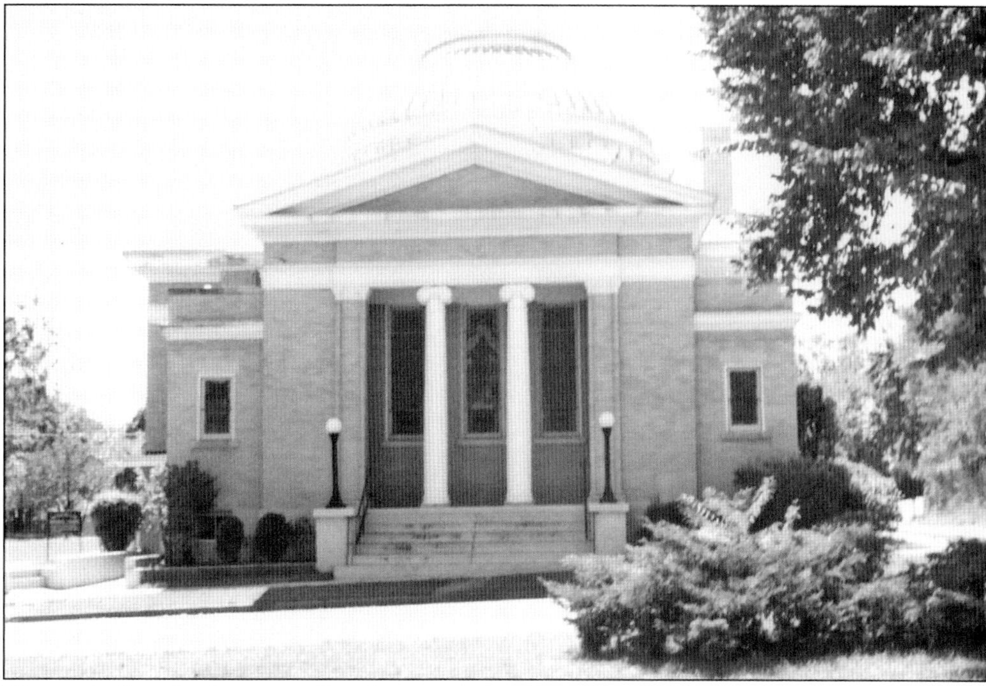

This is the First Presbyterian Church as it appeared in 1970. The congregation resulted from the union of the old Presbyterian and Cumberland Presbyterian churches in 1906. (Courtesy of the UAFS Cobb Collection.)

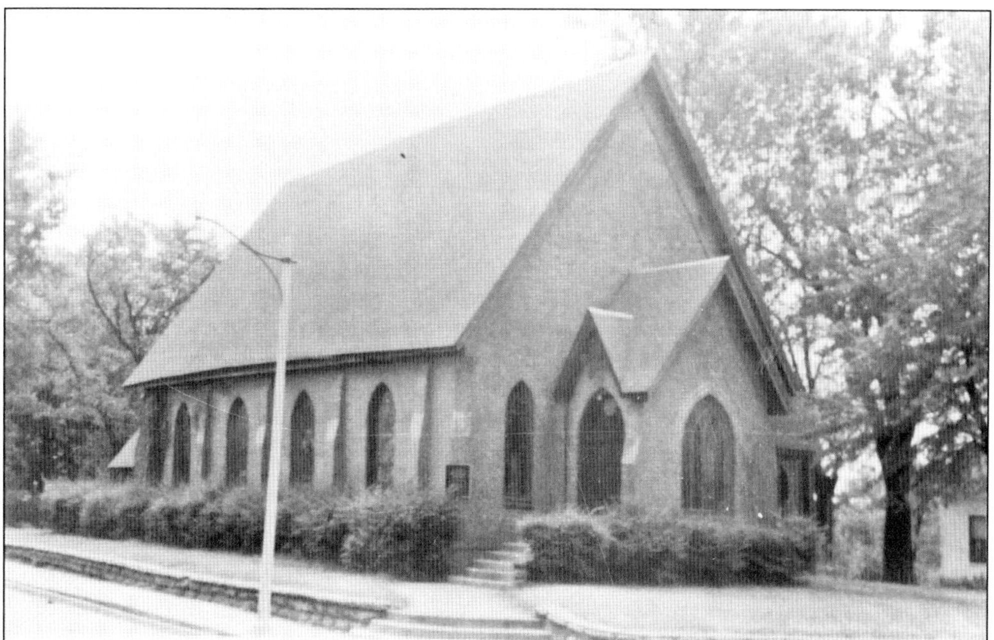

The original Trinity Episcopal Church, seen here in 1952, was constructed at the corner of Webster and Third Streets in 1842. John Drennen gave the lot as a gift. With a congregation still meeting today, Trinity is the oldest continuously attended church in Van Buren. (Courtesy of the UAFS Cobb Collection.)

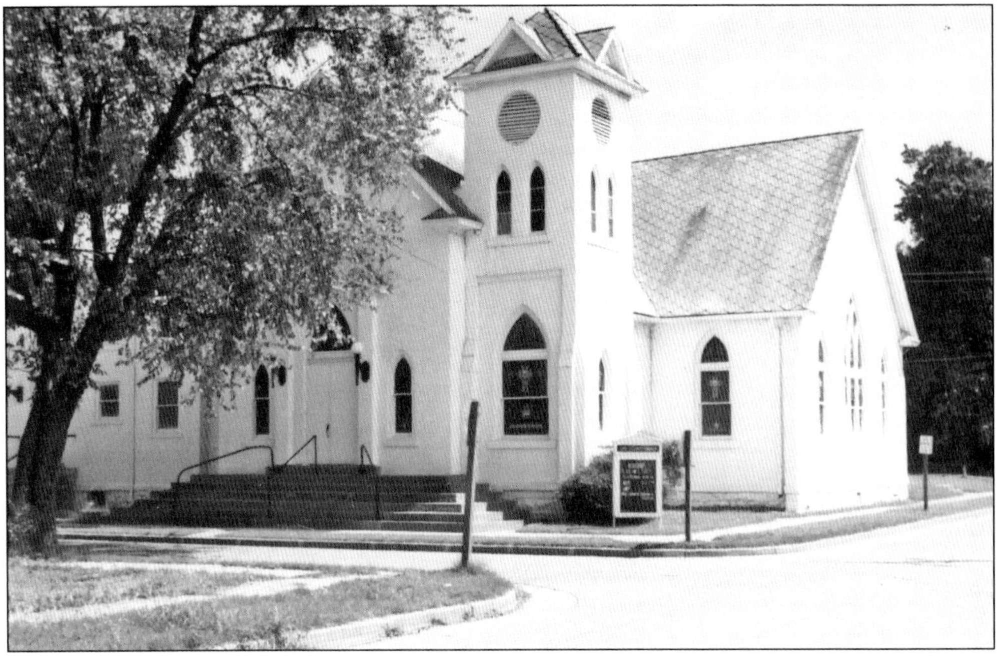

Dating to 1848, the Methodist church seen here in 1970 has a long history in Van Buren. In fact, the main Methodist congregation today attends Heritage Methodist, recalling many years of service to the city. (Courtesy of the UAFS Cobb Collection.)

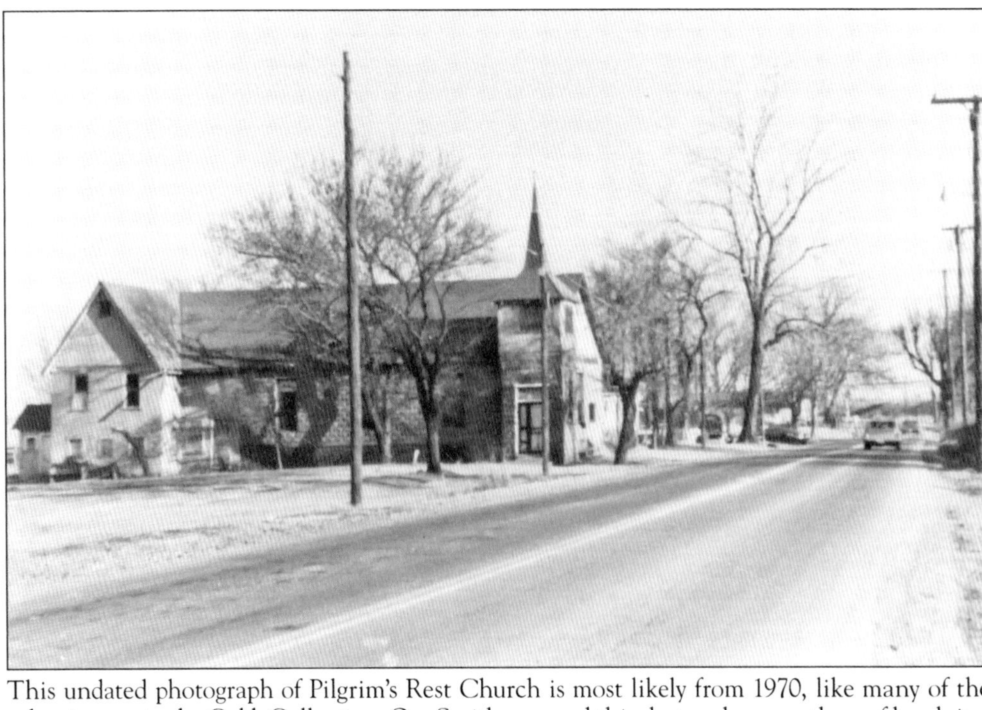

This undated photograph of Pilgrim's Rest Church is most likely from 1970, like many of the other images in the Cobb Collection. Ora Smith snapped this shot and many others of local sites of interest. (Courtesy of the UAFS Cobb Collection.)

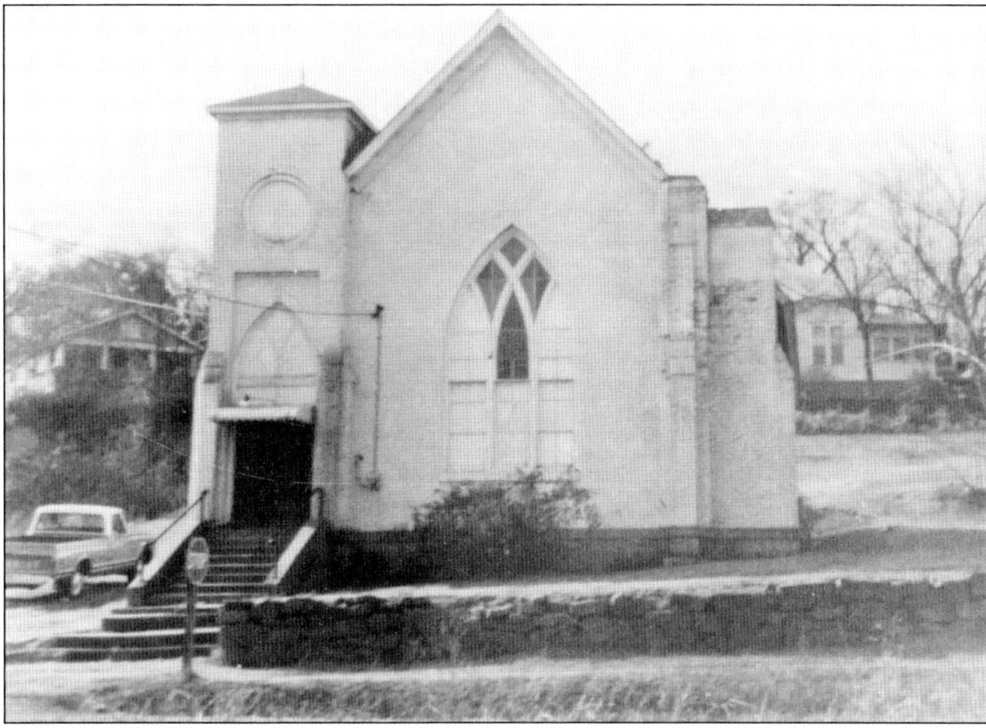

This 1970 view of Mount Olive United Methodist Church documents an African American congregation back to 1889. Built by former slaves, the Gothic Revival–styled church is listed in the National Register of Historic Places. (Courtesy of the UAFS Cobb Collection.)

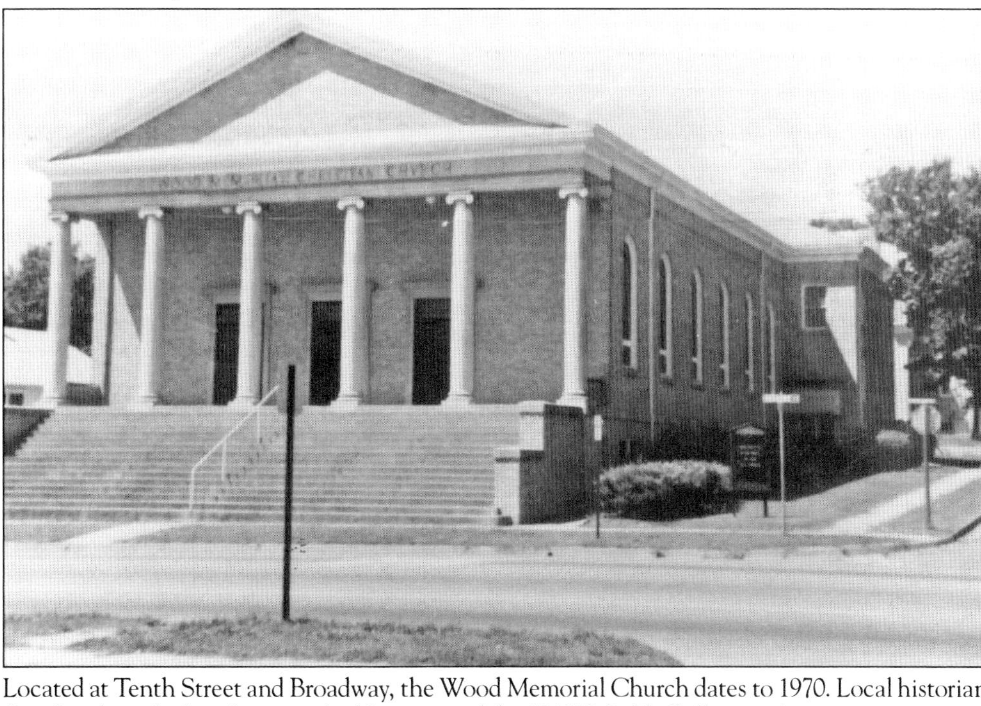

Located at Tenth Street and Broadway, the Wood Memorial Church dates to 1970. Local historian Ora Smith took this photograph. (Courtesy of the UAFS Cobb Collection.)

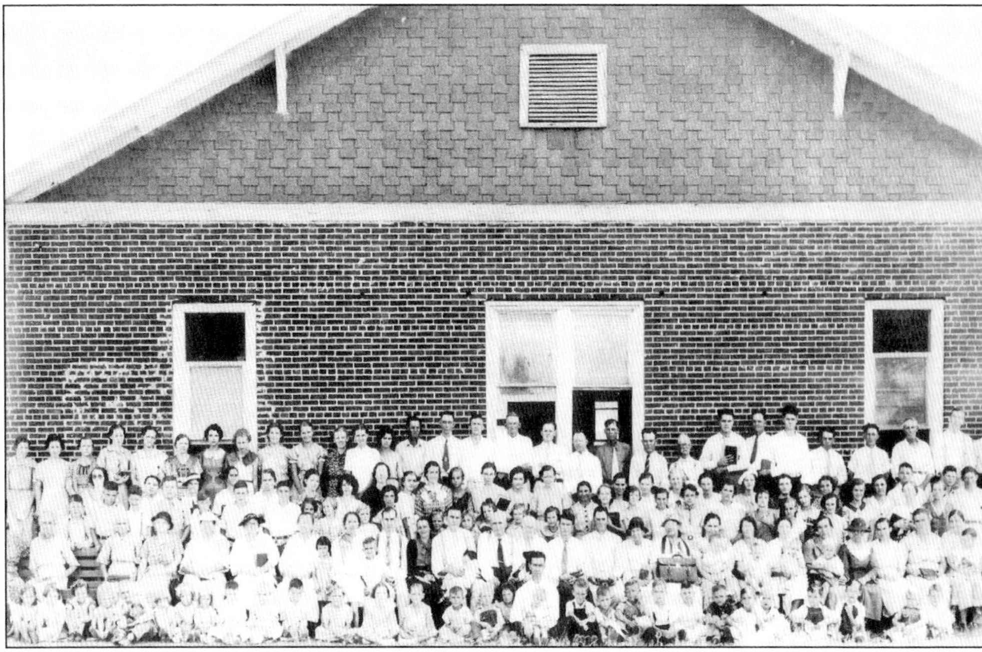

The congregation of First Assembly of God Church is pictured in front of their building, many with Bibles in hand. This photograph was taken in 1936. (Courtesy of Georgia Polk.)

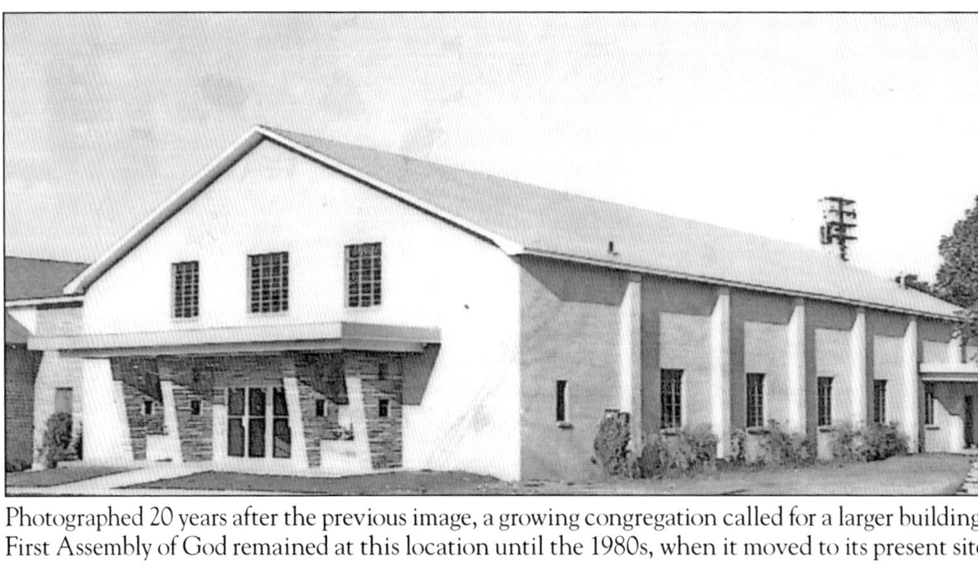

Photographed 20 years after the previous image, a growing congregation called for a larger building. First Assembly of God remained at this location until the 1980s, when it moved to its present site on Fayetteville Road. (Courtesy of Georgia Polk.)

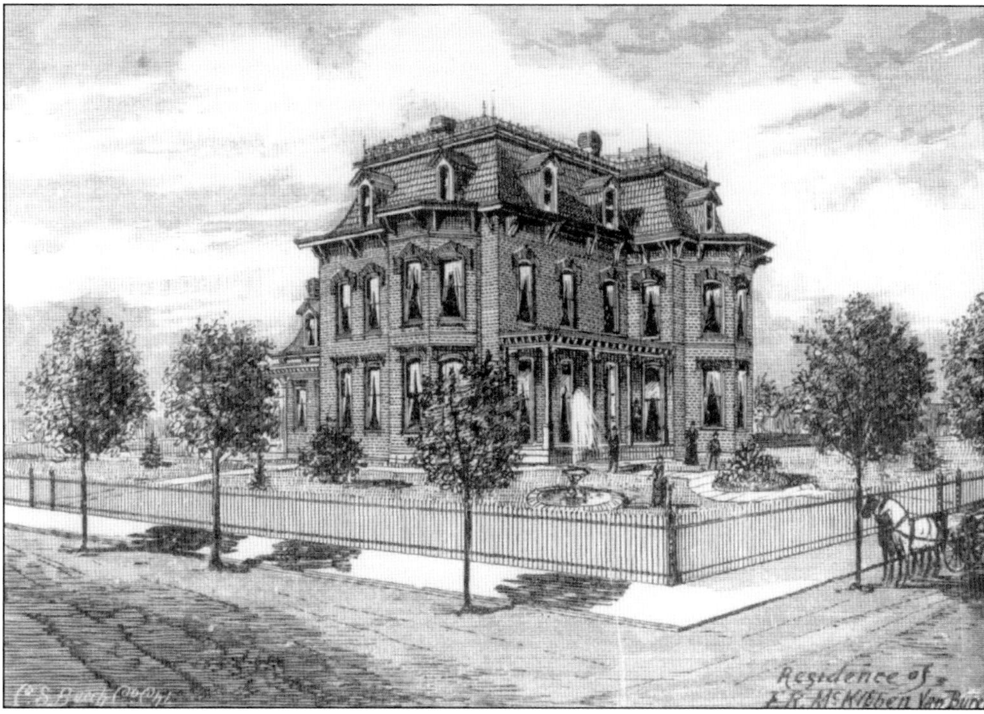

The home of Frank R. McKibben is seen above in an undated sketch and below in a 1964 photograph. McKibben was originally from Ohio and served with the 1st Ohio Cavalry during the Civil War. After the war, he relocated to western Arkansas and in 1871, opened a general store in Van Buren. McKibben eventually partnered with bother-in-law Henry Pape but sold his interest in the business in 1893. After a brief stay in the Creek Nation, he returned to Van Buren and worked as agent for the Union Central Life Insurance Company. (Above, courtesy of the Arkansas History Commission; below, courtesy of the UAFS Cobb Collection.)

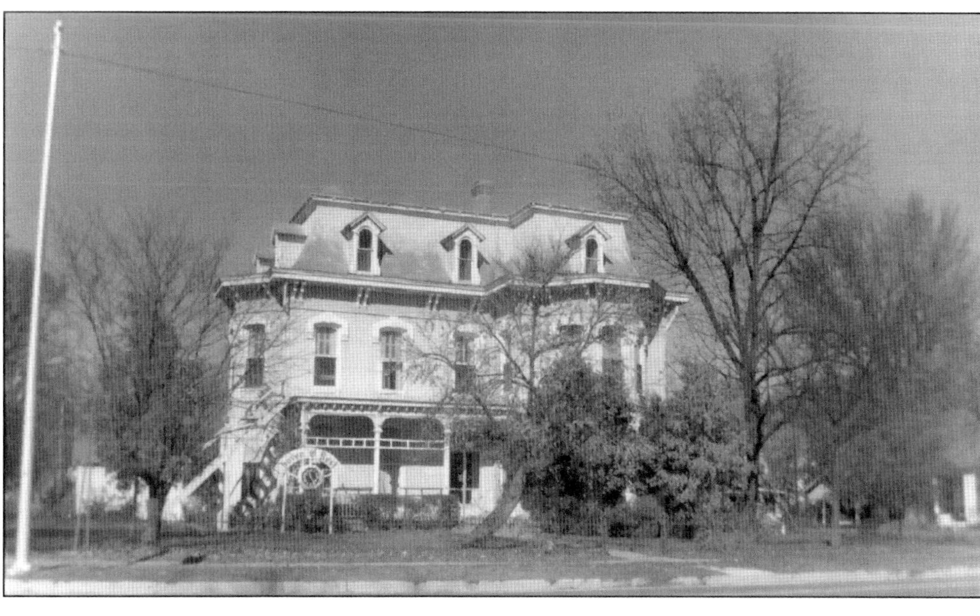

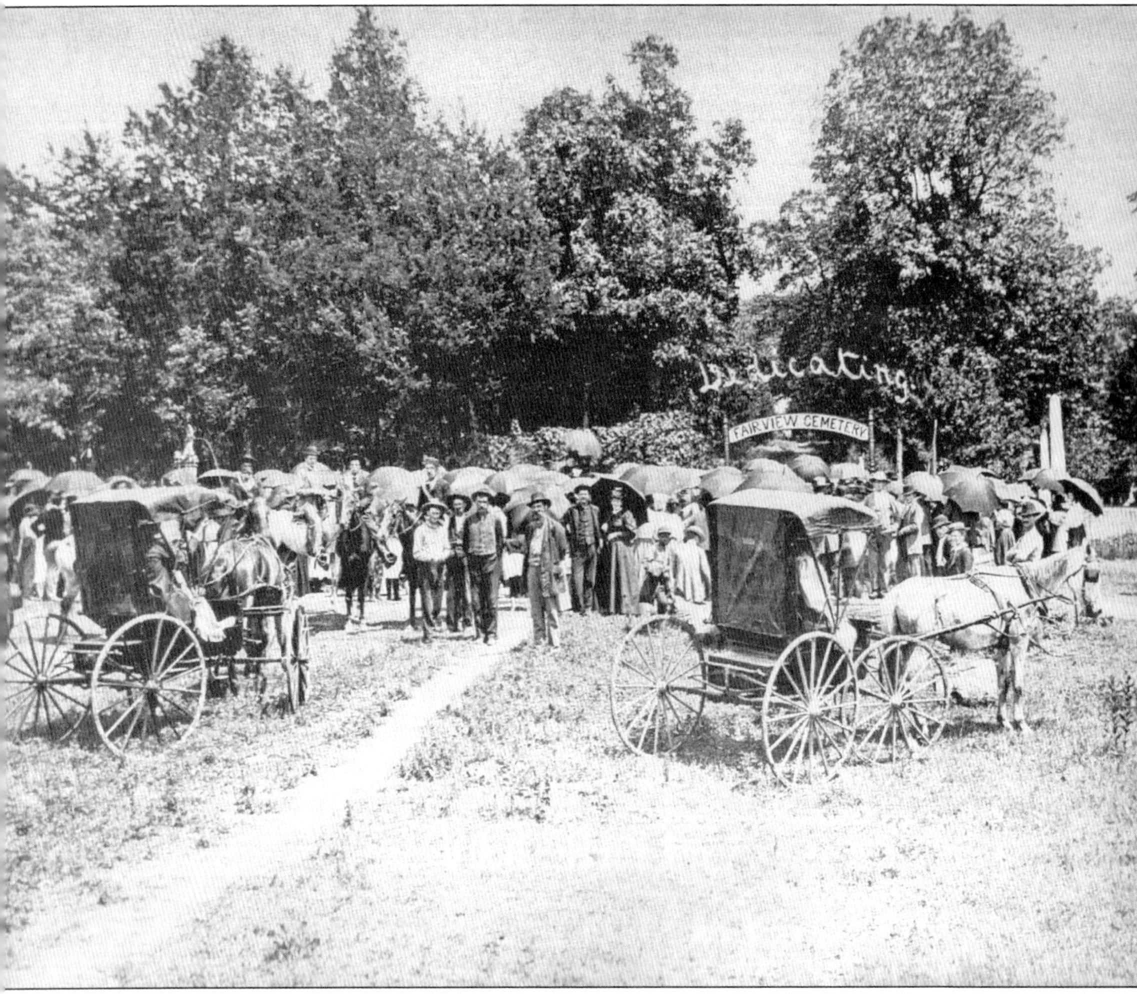

Van Buren's citizens are seen dedicating the gates and fences of Fairview Cemetery in 1896. (Courtesy of the Butler Center for Arkansas Studies.)

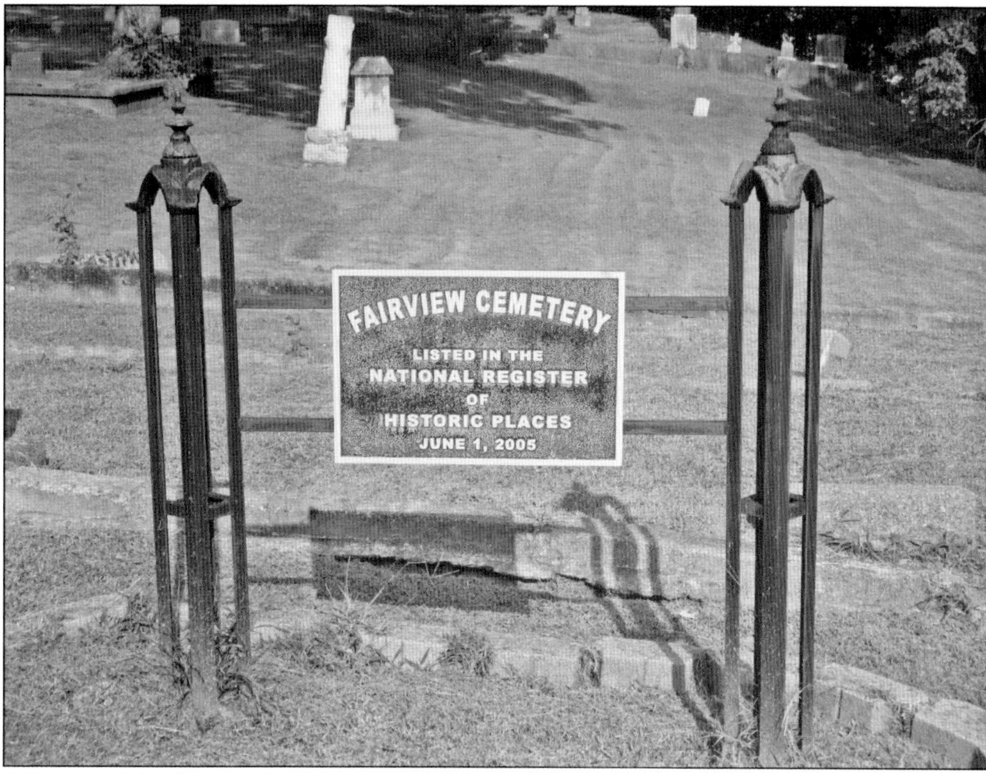

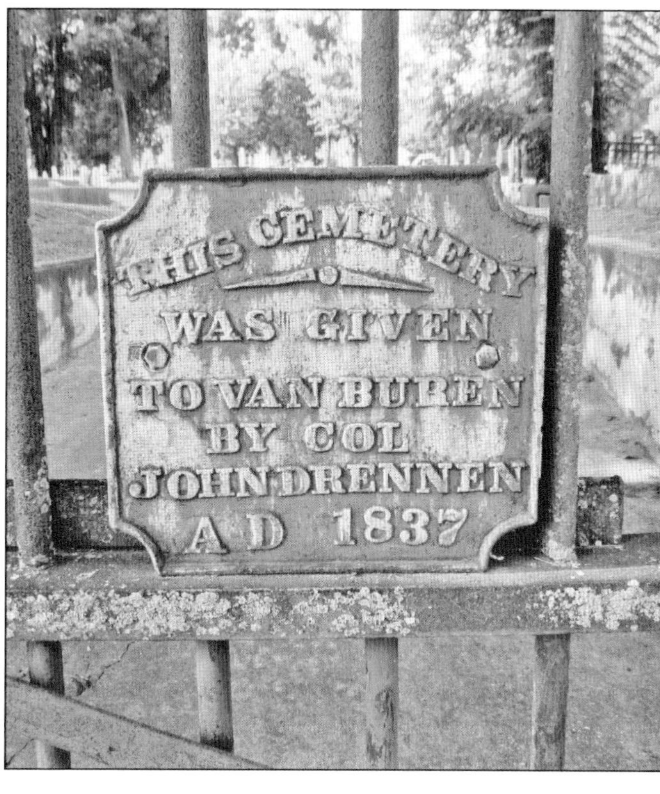

A historical focal point of the community, Fairview Cemetery in Van Buren is listed in the National Register of Historic Places and is the final resting place for soldiers, community leaders, business owners, professionals, and members of the working class. The cemetery is a true cross-section of the town and the diversity present from its beginnings. (Author's collection.)

John Drennen, cofounder of Van Buren, gave 10 acres of land for the cemetery in 1837. Buried there himself, Drennen rests with many of his contemporaries and others who were affected by his legacy. (Author's collection.)

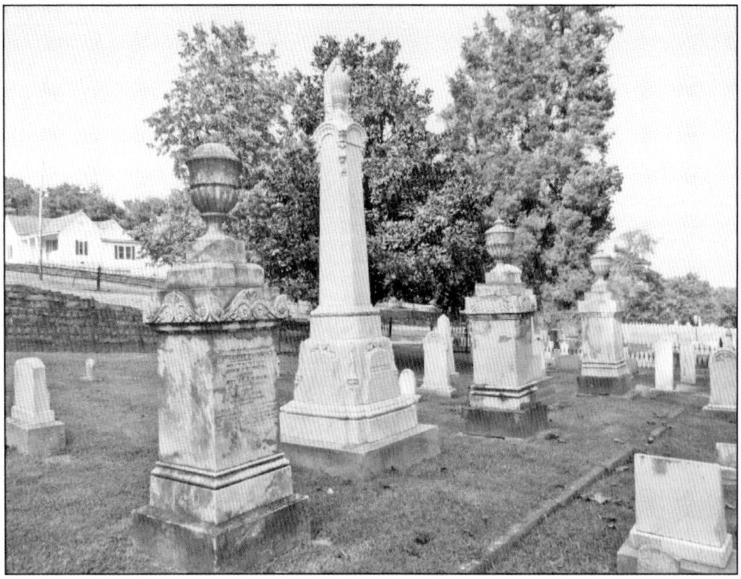

John Drennen's memorial marker is seen here, the obelisk at center, with his second wife, Kate, on the left and first wife, Emily, on the right. Other family members are buried in the iron-fenced plot, along with close friends and business partners such as Phillip Pennywitt, the steamboat captain and associate. (Author's collection.)

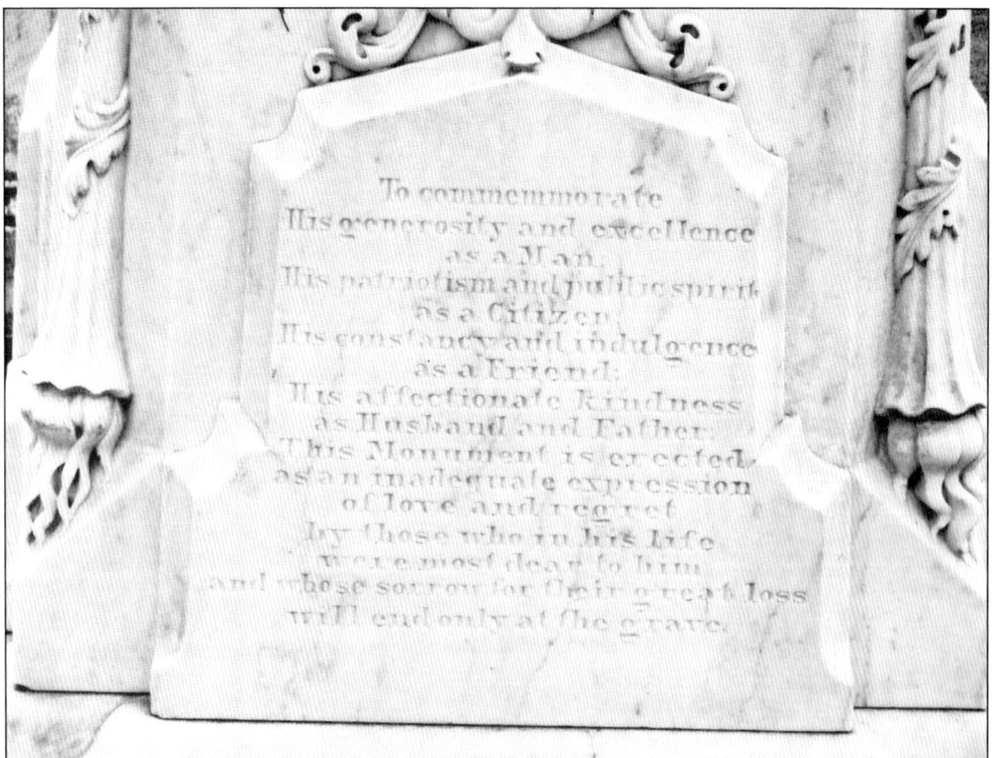

John Drennen's epitaph commends him as a man, citizen, friend, husband, and father. His friend and legal counsel, Albert Pike, wrote the epitaph four years after Drennen's death in 1855. Pike's hand-written epitaph and letter addressed to Caroline Scott, Drennen's daughter, explained the delay and was found among the family possessions when the house was acquired by the University of Arkansas–Fort Smith in 2005. (Author's collection.)

Within the family plot, in what was originally an unmarked grave under a Magnolia tree not far from his owner, Patrick Drennen rests for eternity. Patrick was one of over 90 slaves John Drennen owned. In an inventory of Drennen's property years after his death, Patrick's death date was confirmed along with his original sale price of $2,000. Known as his owner's personal servant, Patrick was trusted and allowed to pursue a relationship with Lydia Talkington, a slave from a neighboring farm. Angela Walton Raji is a fifth-generation descendent of Patrick and Lydia. Patrick's final resting place was recently marked with the cooperation of all the families involved and Randy Smith, director of Fairview Cemetery. (Both, author's collection.)

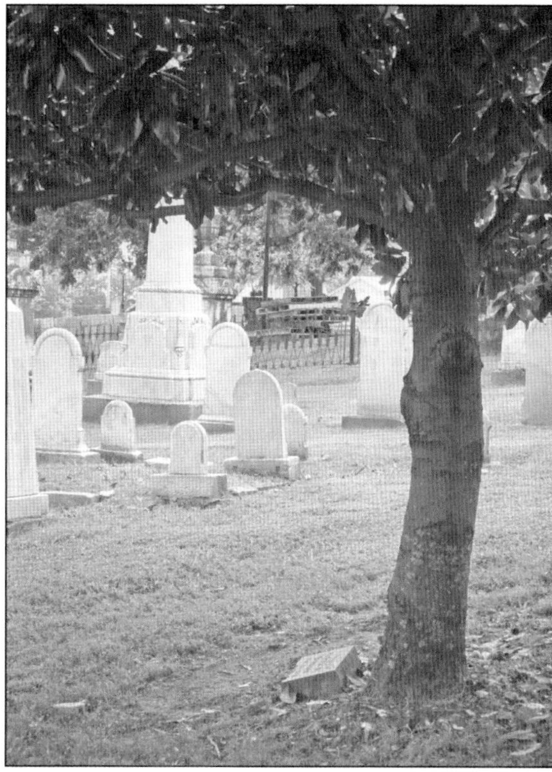

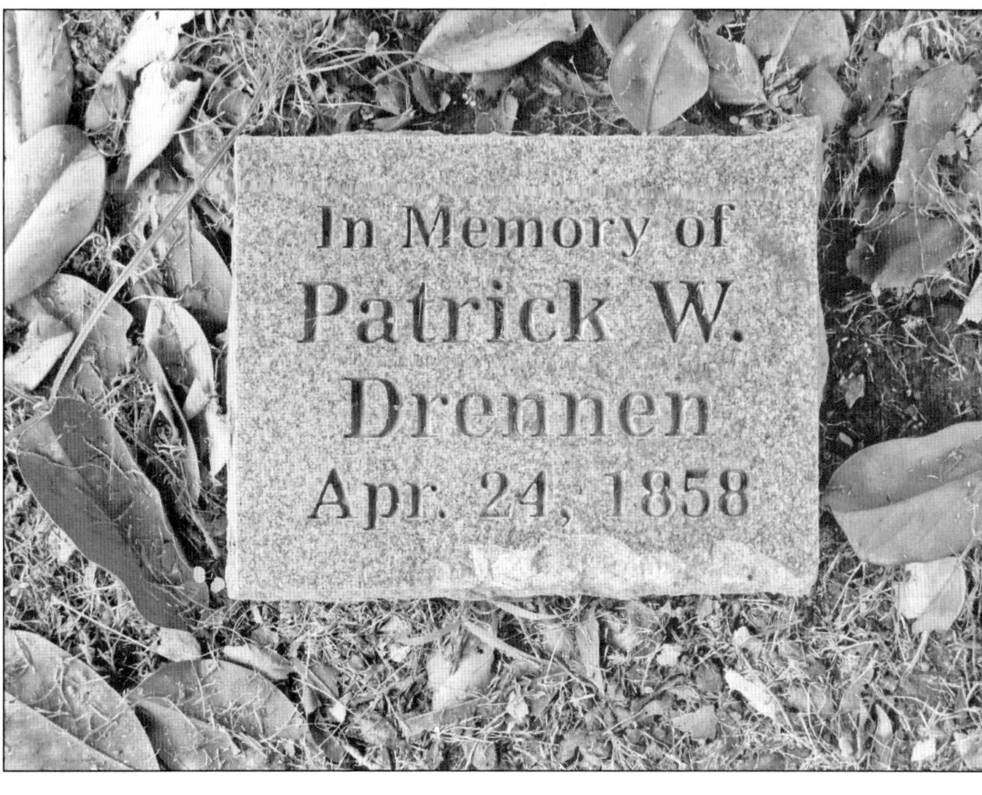

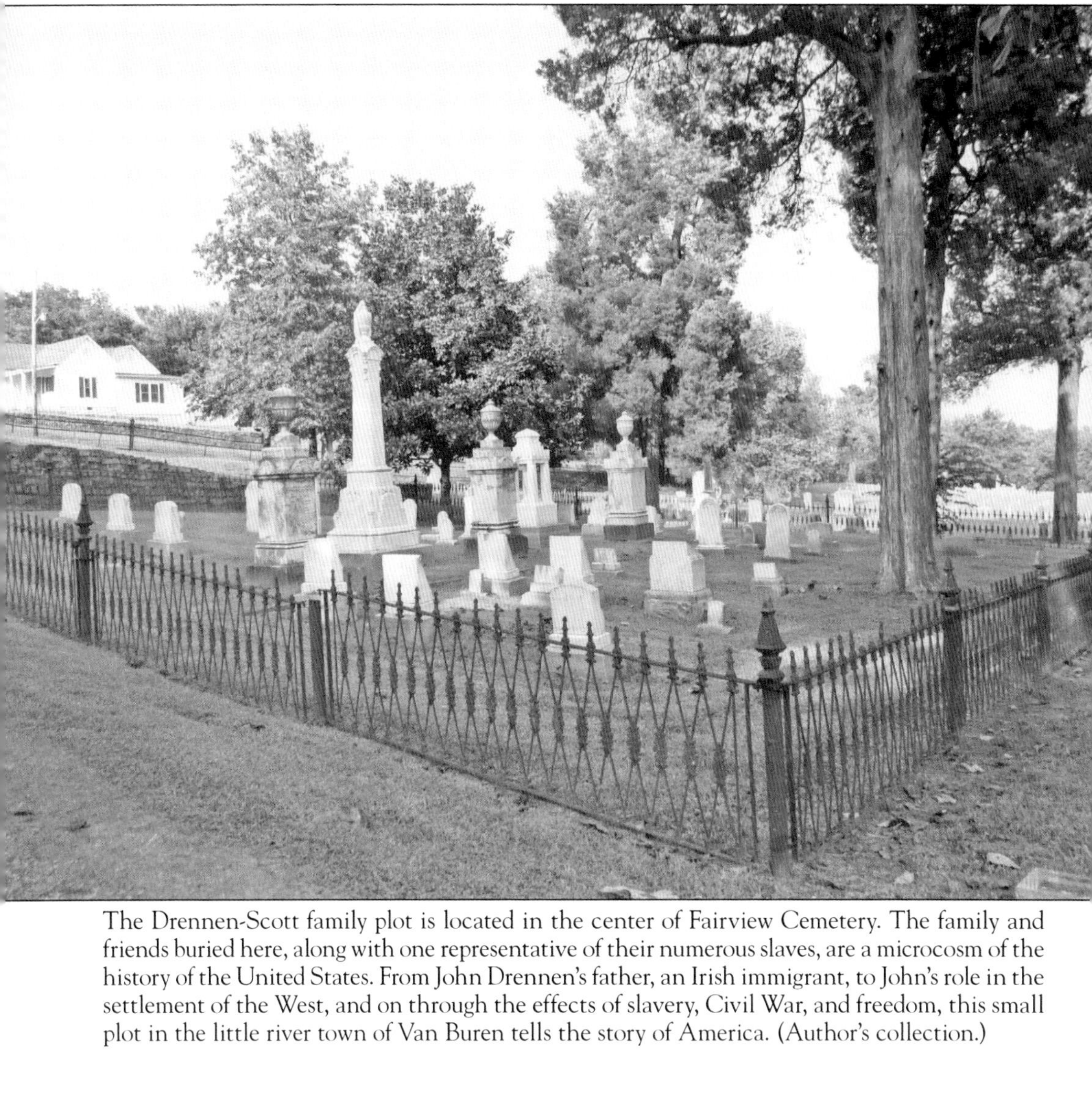

The Drennen-Scott family plot is located in the center of Fairview Cemetery. The family and friends buried here, along with one representative of their numerous slaves, are a microcosm of the history of the United States. From John Drennen's father, an Irish immigrant, to John's role in the settlement of the West, and on through the effects of slavery, Civil War, and freedom, this small plot in the little river town of Van Buren tells the story of America. (Author's collection.)

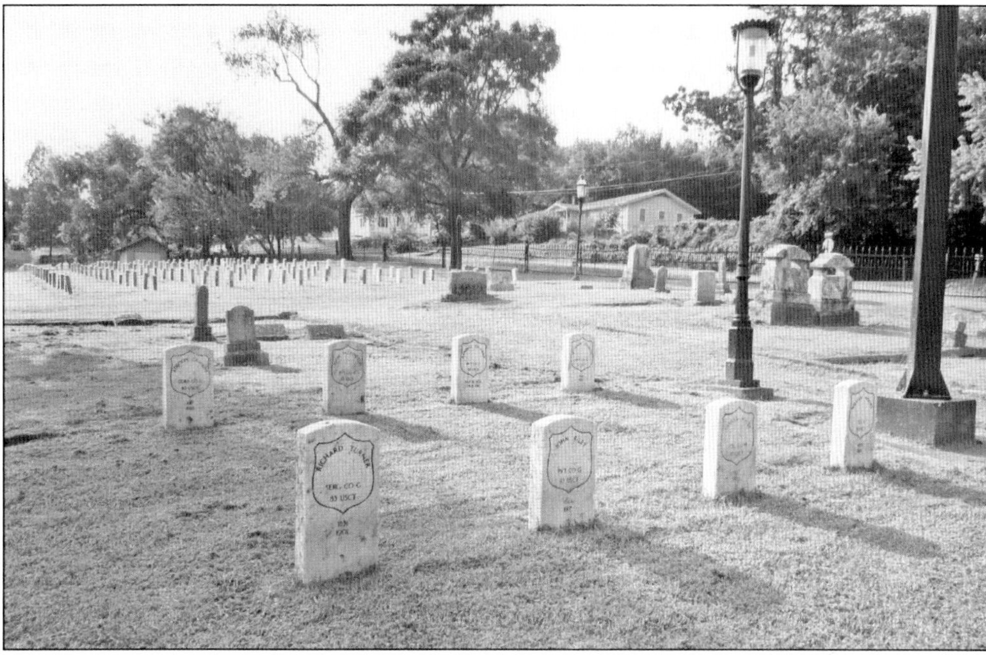

Next to the Confederate section, eight graves mark the resting places of members of the US Colored Troops. Made up of escaped and emancipated slaves as well as free men of color, the regiments of the USCT committed over 100,000 men to fight for the Union during the Civil War. In silent reconciliation, these soldiers rest a few feet from those they fought against. Angela Walton Raji and Tonia Holliman worked to acquire Veterans Administration headstones and honor these men. (Author's collection.)

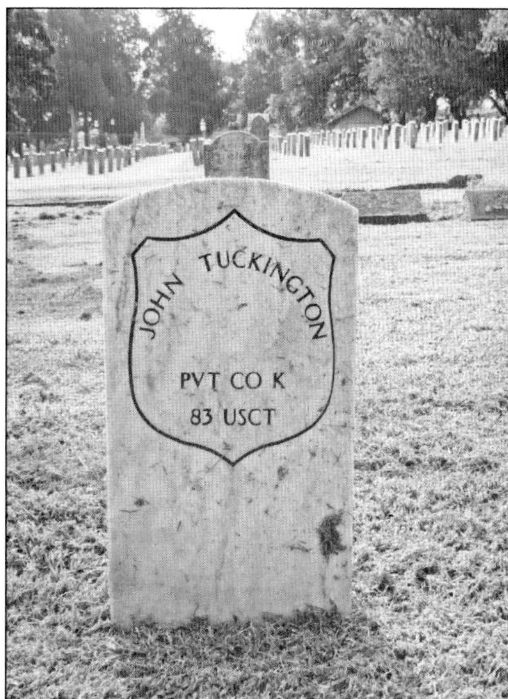

John Tuckington watched as federal troops occupied Van Buren for two weeks in December 1862 during a raid that pushed Confederates across the Arkansas River to Fort Smith. When the blue coats headed back north having accomplished their mission, Tuckington walked away from his slave owner in Crawford County and joined the 83rd US Colored Infantry. Wounded in action in south Arkansas in the spring of 1864, Tuckington later died and was buried in Van Buren. He was the second husband of Lydia Talkington, widow of Patrick Drennen, a slave owned by John Drennen. (Author's collection.)

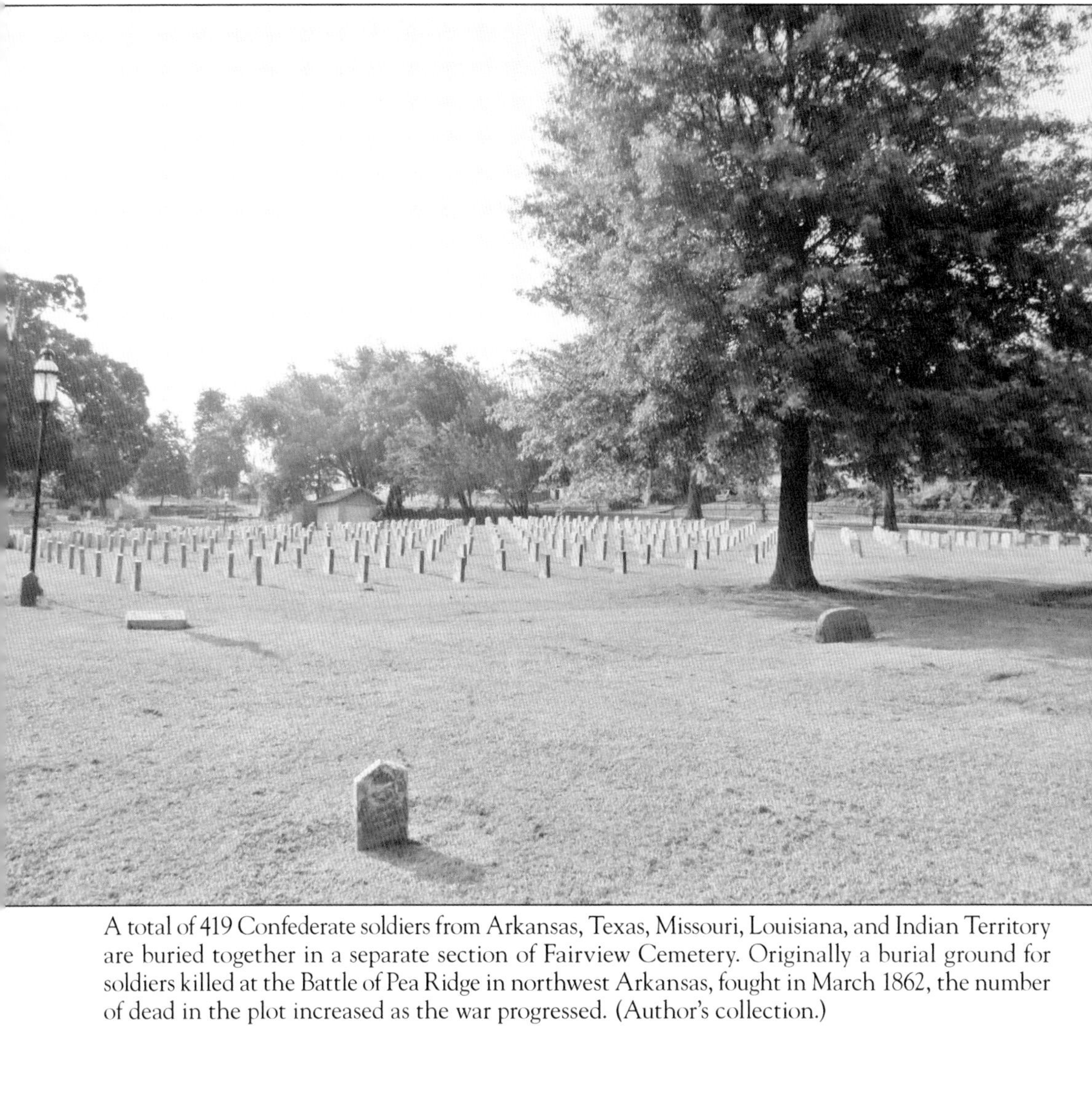

A total of 419 Confederate soldiers from Arkansas, Texas, Missouri, Louisiana, and Indian Territory are buried together in a separate section of Fairview Cemetery. Originally a burial ground for soldiers killed at the Battle of Pea Ridge in northwest Arkansas, fought in March 1862, the number of dead in the plot increased as the war progressed. (Author's collection.)

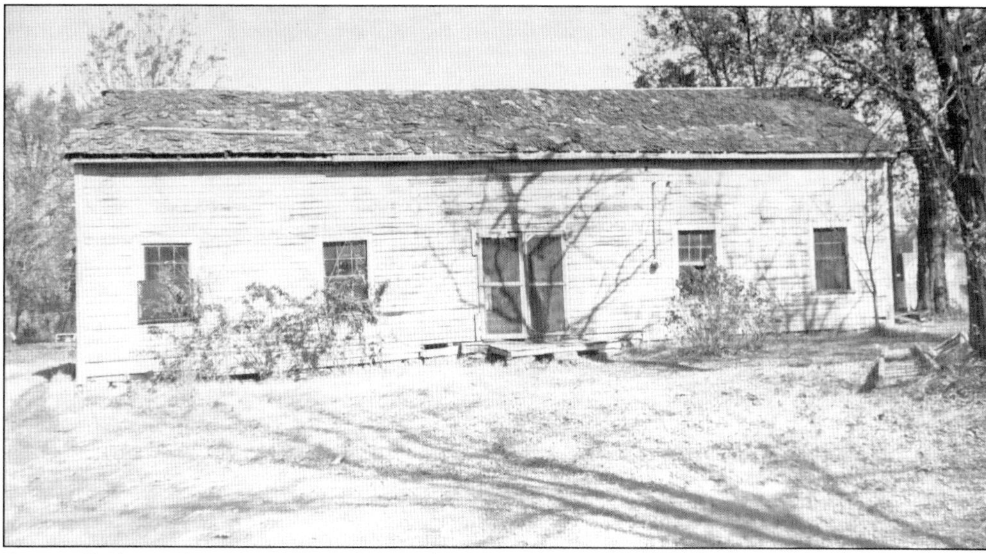

Originally located at 19 Fayetteville Road, the Knox house, built by George Washington Knox, is seen here before its demolition in the 1950s. George Knox was born in Louisville, Kentucky, in 1812 and his father, Hugh, had a large plantation on the south side of the Arkansas River near present-day Barling, Arkansas. George married Eudora Rose and had four daughters. In 1851, Knox was appointed the first US marshal for the newly created Federal Court for the Western District of Arkansas, located in Van Buren. The court eventually moved to Fort Smith in 1871. (Courtesy of the UAFS Cobb Collection.)

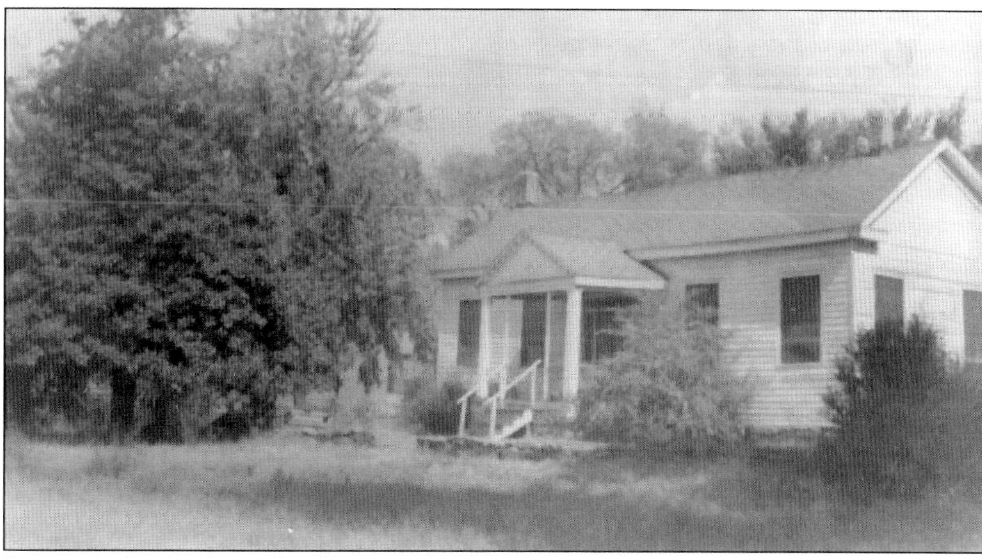

Built around 1838, the Wilhauf house is the second oldest residence still standing in Van Buren. Located just down the hill from the Drennen-Scott property, the building site was sold to Leonard Wilhauf by John Drennen in 1837. Wilhauf (1813–1866) was a German immigrant who settled in Crawford County in the 1830s. He is best remembered for his role in the Mexican War, when he served as color bearer for the Van Buren Avengers, a company of mounted troops who served under Archibald Yell. Wilhauf successfully defended the company banner in all engagements and brought the cherished flag back to Van Buren after the war. After the war, he operated a bakery on Main Street. (Courtesy of the UAFS Cobb Collection.)

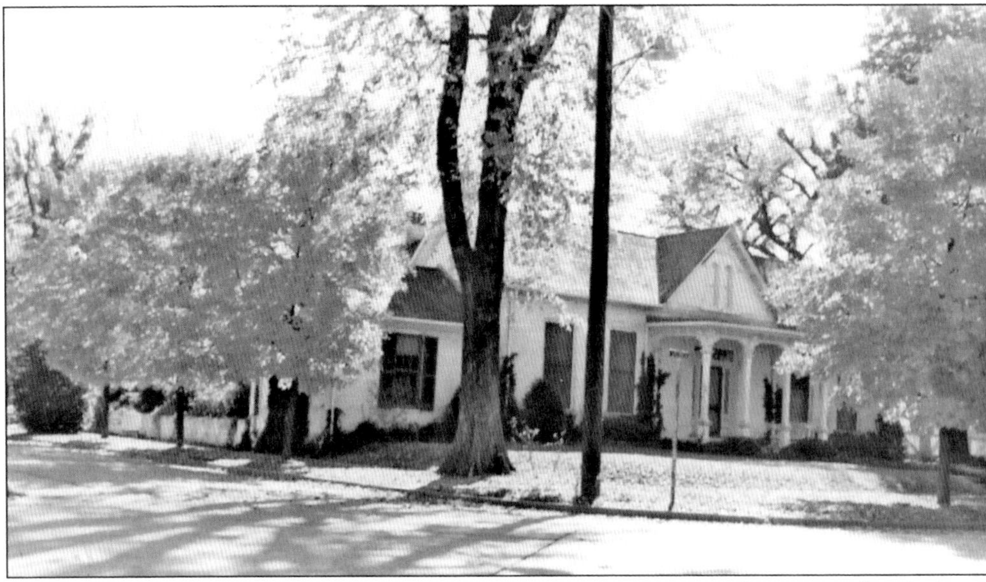

Dr. Charles Fox Brown was born in Virginia in 1820. As a young man, he migrated to St. Louis and then Fayetteville, Arkansas, where he studied medicine. He eventually graduated from the Ohio Medical College in 1848 and set up practice in Van Buren. In 1858, he married Heeland Mary Bostick, and together they had four children. Dr. Brown was the surgeon of the 3rd Battalion Arkansas Infantry during the Civil War. He also served as president of the Crawford County Medical Association. He died in 1889. This photograph was taken in 1955. (Courtesy of the UAFS Cobb Collection.)

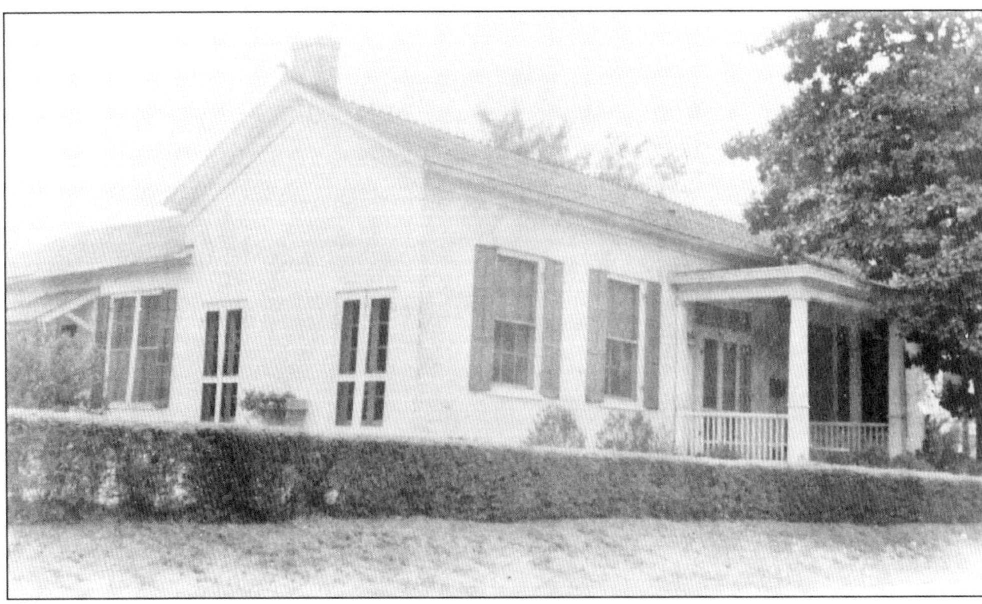

Located at 400 Broadway was the home of Dr. James A. Dibrell, seen here in 1952. Dr. Dibrell was born in Nashville, Tennessee, and graduated from the medical department of the University of Pennsylvania in 1839. Dibrell first practiced medicine in Van Buren in the 1840s and raised seven children spanning two marriages before he died in 1897 at the age of 80. (Courtesy of the UAFS Cobb Collection.)

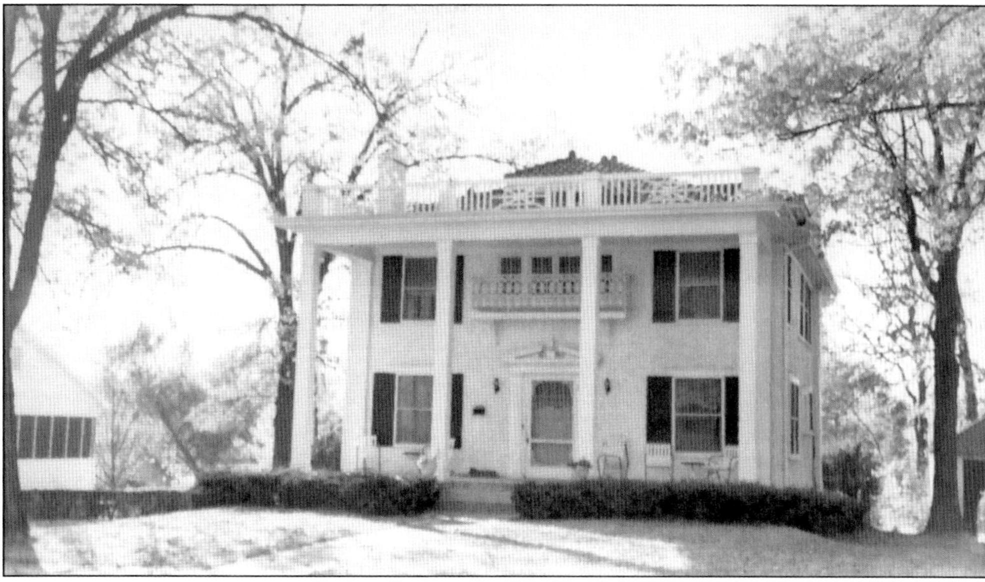

John J. Izard came to Van Buren from Wynn, Arkansas, in the early 1900s. He was a bookkeeper and sales clerk before eventually becoming president of the People's Bank and Trust Company. He married Della Cory of Van Buren. J.J. Izard Elementary School is named for him due to his 46 years of service on the school board and his work to better the community. This photograph dates to 1952. (Courtesy of the UAFS Cobb Collection.)

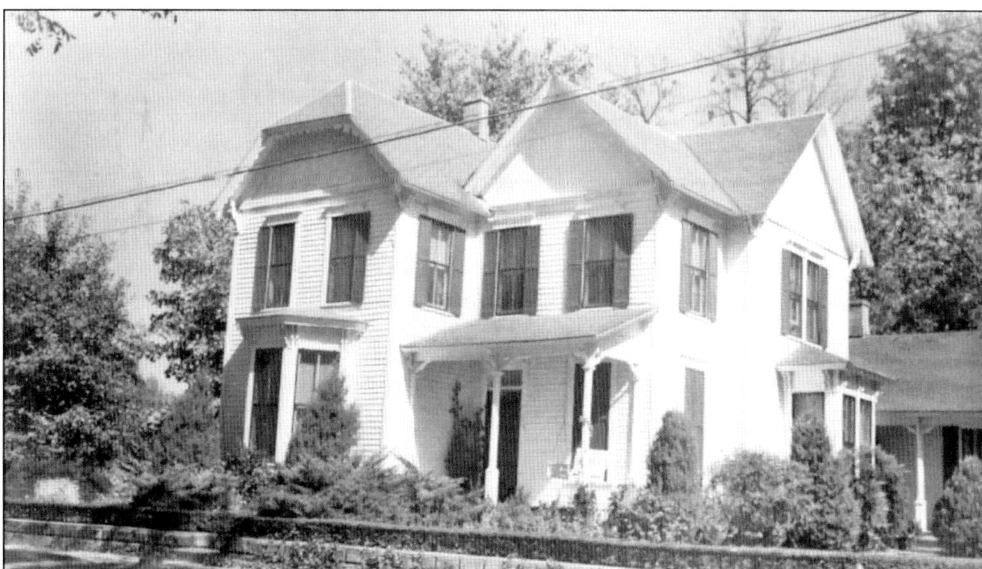

Leonard Southmayd was born in Connecticut in 1822. After working for his father as a store clerk, Leonard relocated to Van Buren in 1845. He worked for Wallace and Ward for a number of years until Wallace retired, later becoming a partner in Ward and Southmayd. He also served three terms as county clerk. He married Susannah Howell, and together they had five children. He died in Van Buren in 1906 and is buried in Fairview Cemetery. This photograph of the Southmayd home was taken in 1952. (Courtesy of the UAFS Cobb Collection.)

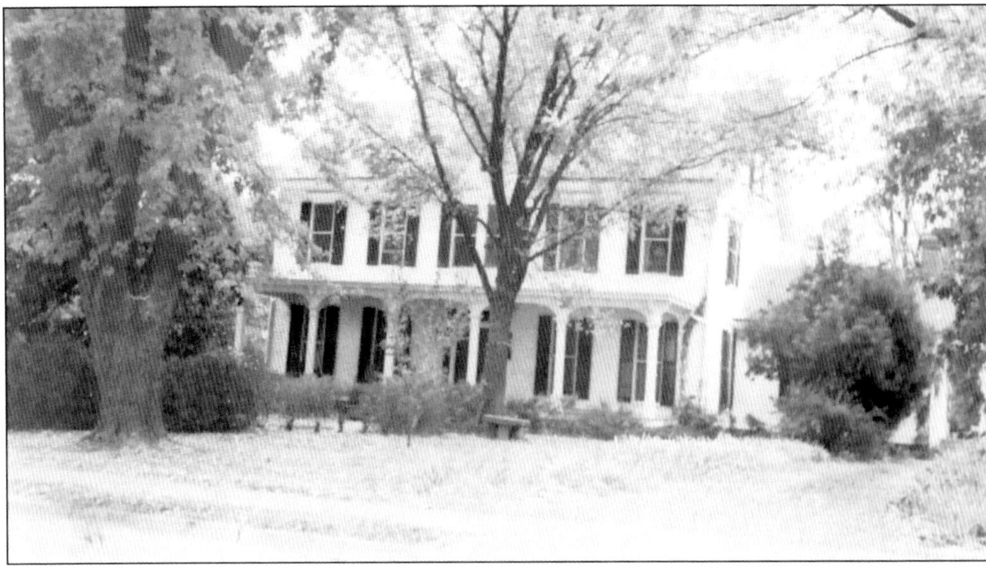

Pictured is the Jesse Turner home on Fourth Street in 1950. Turner was born in North Carolina in 1805 and was a self-educated law student who passed the bar exam by the time he was 20 years old. He came to Van Buren in 1838, where he spent the rest of his days. He married Violet Drennen, a niece of John Drennen, who died before their first anniversary. Turner took a second wife, Rebecca Allen, and together they had one son. He served as a state representative, federal district attorney, presidential elector, West Point examiner, railroad president, and Arkansas Supreme Court judge. He died in 1894 at the age of 89. (Courtesy of the UAFS Cobb Collection.)

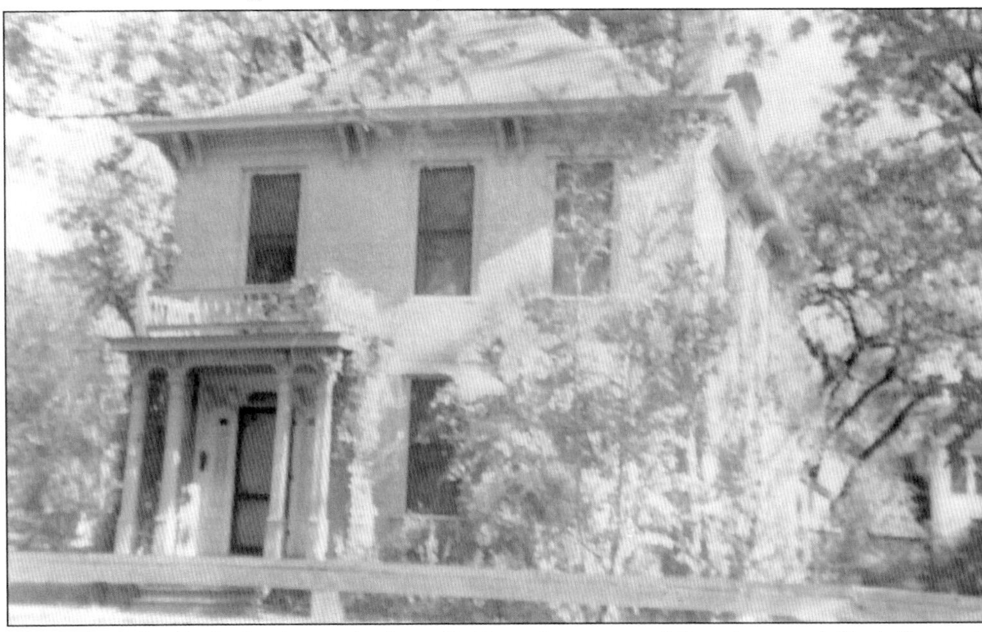

The Judge John B. Ogden home, built in 1846 on the corner of Broadway and Sixth Street, is shown in 1952. The Ogden family occupied the home until the judge's death in 1889. John Ogden came to Van Buren from Tennessee in the 1840s. He was a lawyer and served as commissioner and judge for the Federal Court for the Western District of Arkansas, established in 1851. He is buried in Fairview Cemetery. (Courtesy of the UAFS Cobb Collection.)

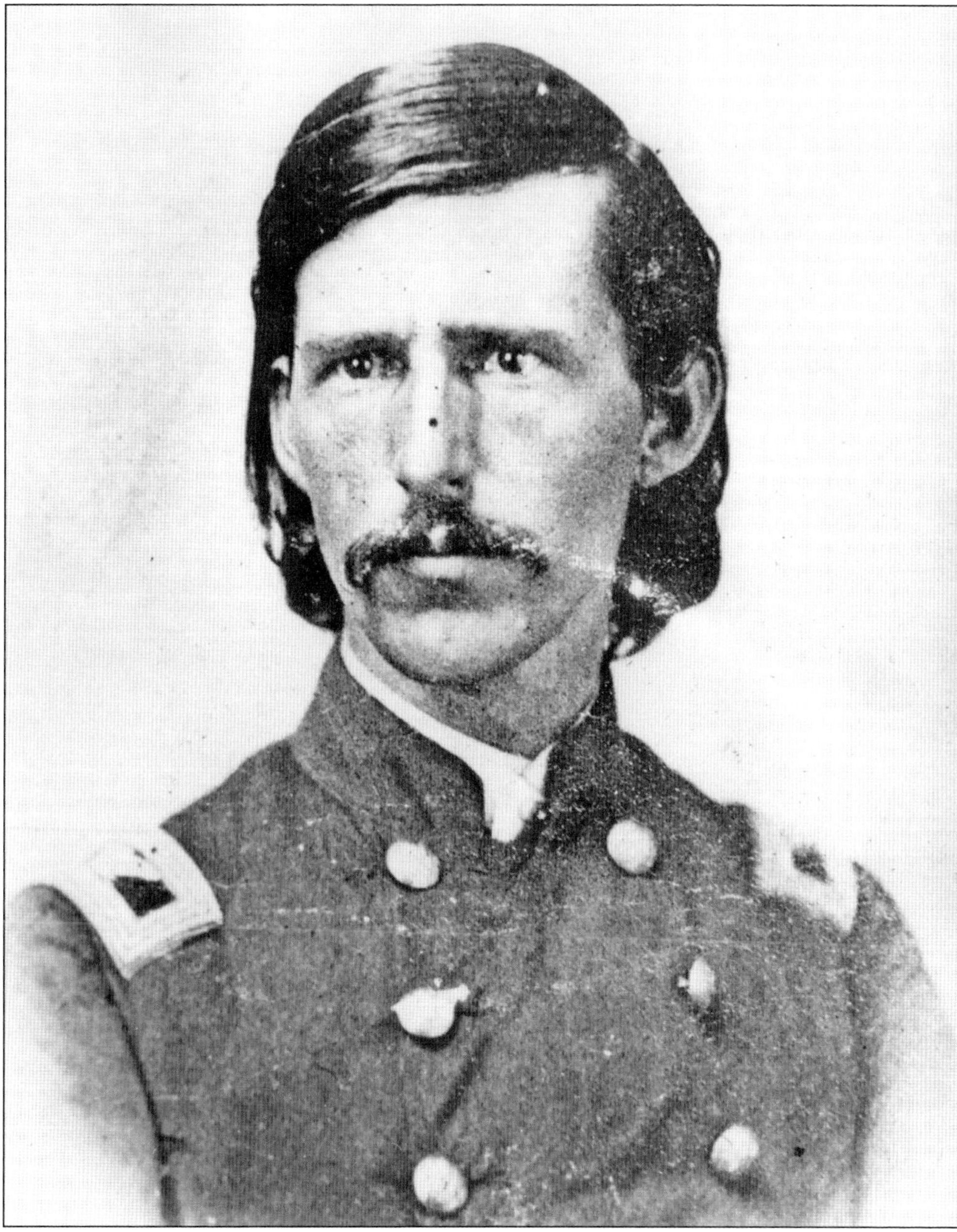

Col. Thomas Bowen of the 13th Kansas Infantry served as garrison commander at Van Buren from 1863 to 1865. Bowen's troops defended the river crossing from possible Confederate attack and carried mail between Van Buren and Fayetteville along the Wire Road. On August 12, 1864, soldiers under Bowen's command were ambushed north of Van Buren en route to Fayetteville. While in Arkansas, Bowen met and married Margaretta Thurston, daughter of Dr. Richard Thurston. (Courtesy of the UALR Center for Arkansas History and Culture.)

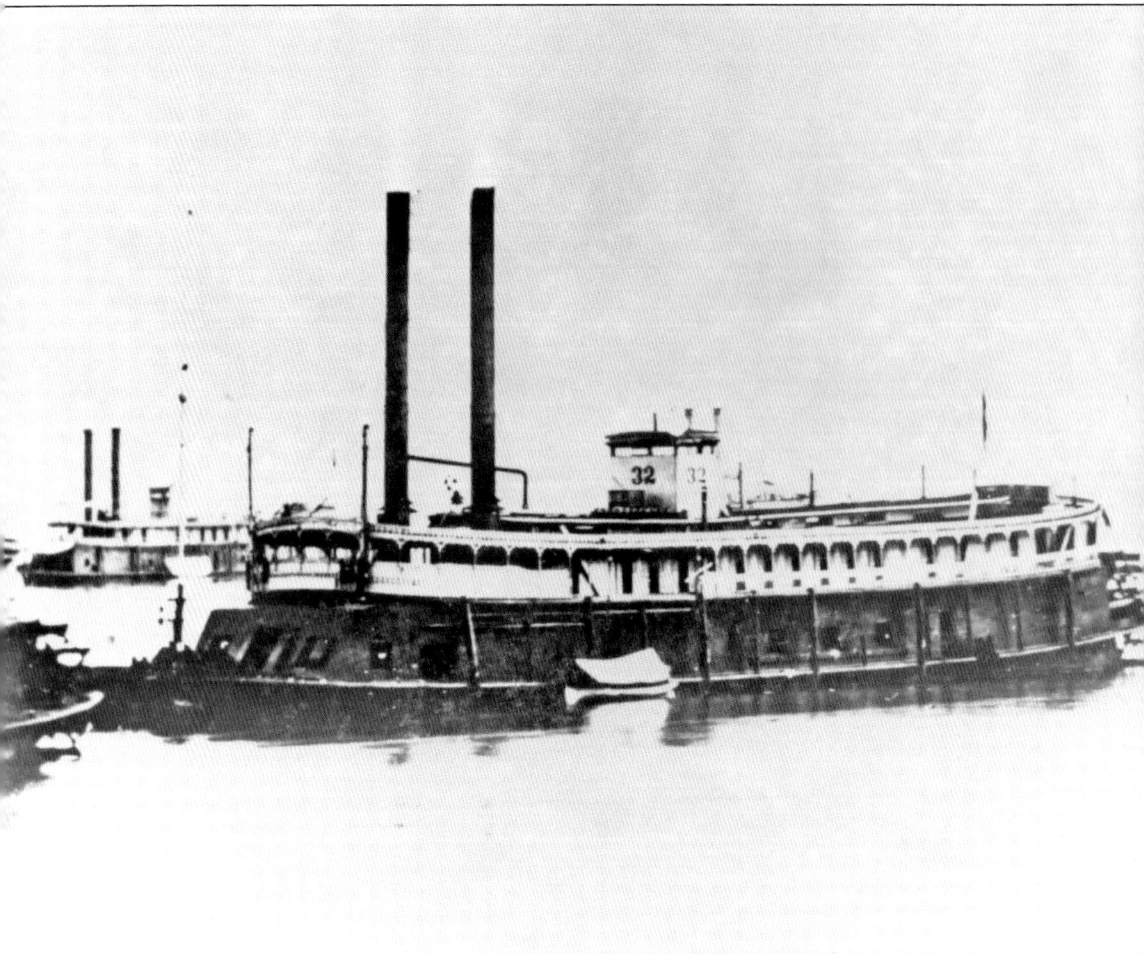

The 169-ton stern-wheel steamboat *Key West* is seen here. Built in 1857 in Elizabeth, Pennsylvania, the boat was appropriated for hauling supplies for Confederate forces in Arkansas during the Civil War. The boat was docked at Van Buren in December 1862 when federal forces raided western Arkansas and skirmished with Confederates across the river at Fort Smith. The *Key West* was captured, and its cargo of corn and cotton was burned along with the ship before the Federals retreated back to northwest Arkansas. (Courtesy of the UALR Center for Arkansas History and Culture.)

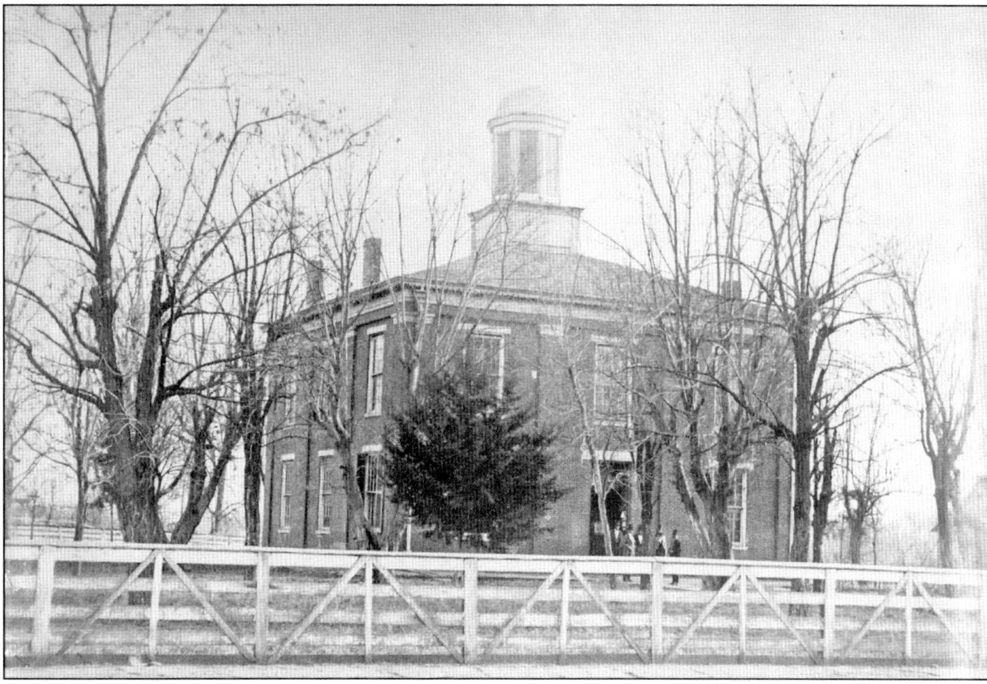

This 1870s view of the Crawford County Courthouse shows its appearance before the fire in 1876 and subsequent remodeling. (Courtesy of the UALR Center for Arkansas History and Culture.)

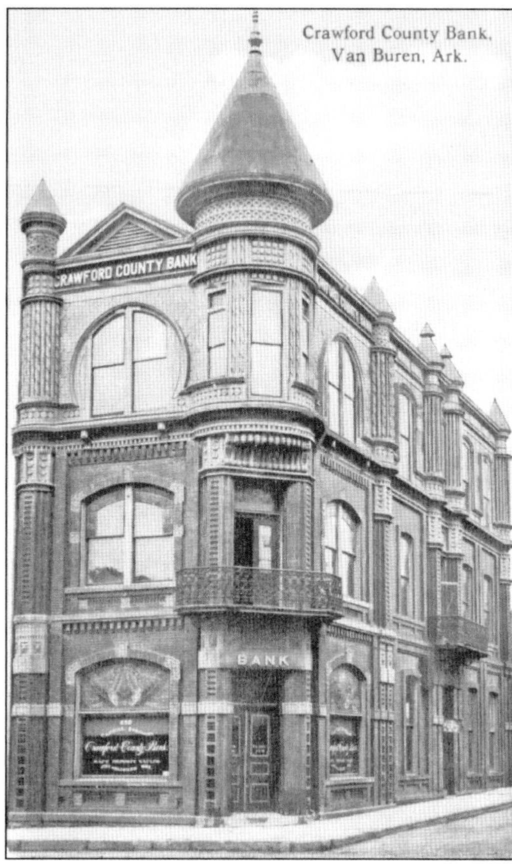

One of many surviving buildings on Main Street today, the Crawford County Bank building was constructed in 1889. Gothic Revival in style with turrets, spires, and stained glass, the building has served as the iconic image for downtown Van Buren for many years. (Courtesy of the UALR Center for Arkansas History and Culture.)

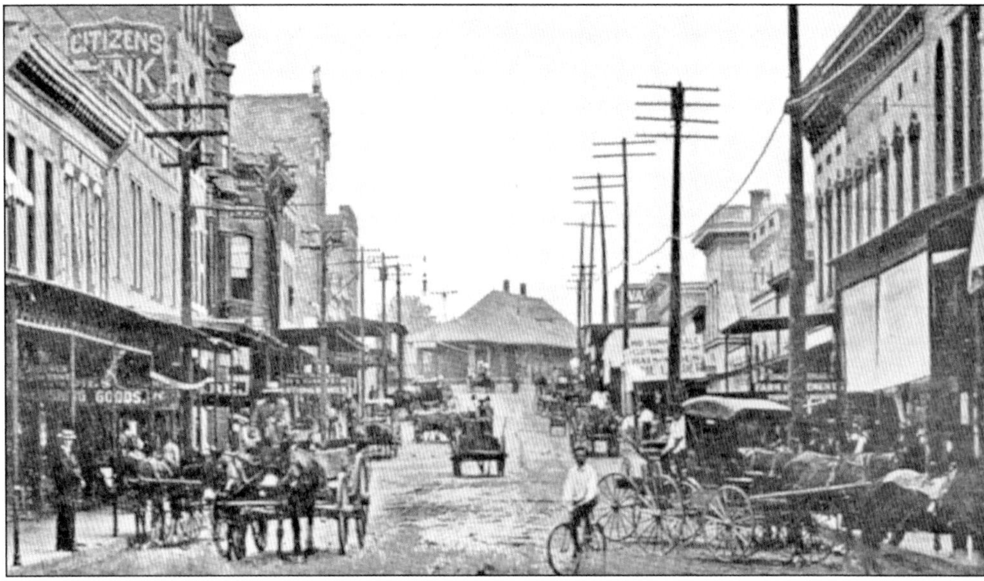

This view along Main Street in Van Buren is looking to the northeast and was taken in the 1880s. (Courtesy of the UALR Center for Arkansas History and Culture.)

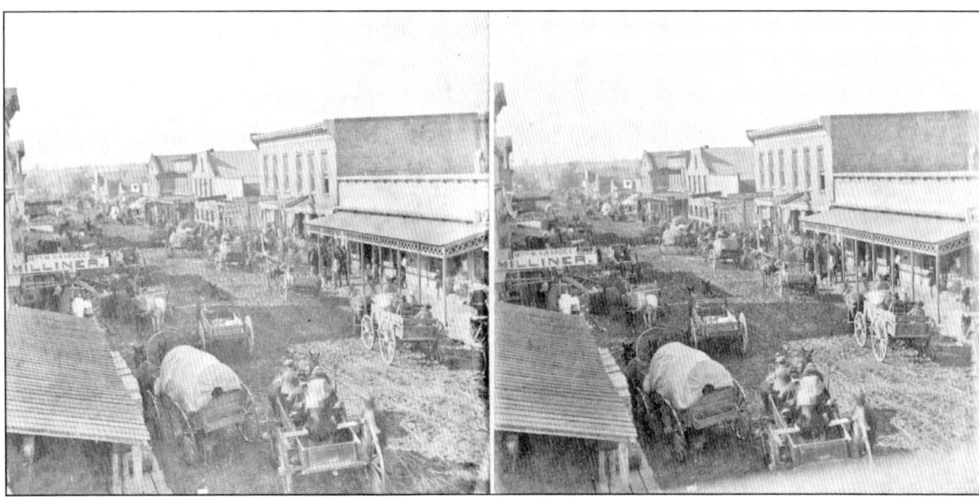

This stereo view along Main Street in Van Buren looks to the southwest and was taken in the 1880s. The dual images produced a three-dimensional effect when seen through a special viewer. (Courtesy of the UALR Center for Arkansas History and Culture.)

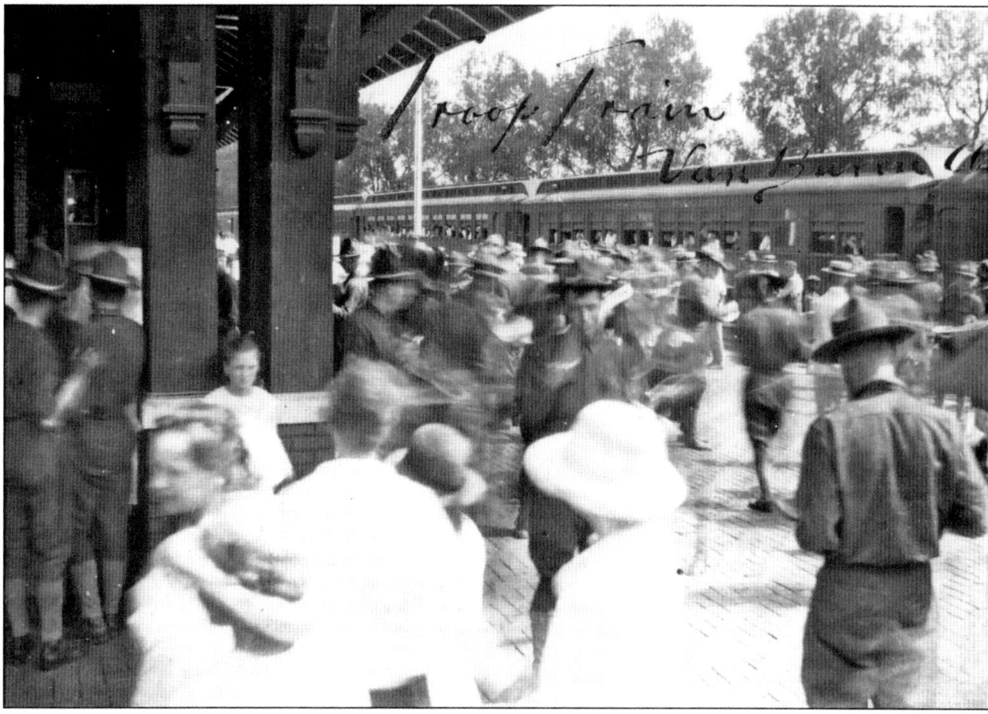

Soldiers heading overseas during World War I are seen passing through Van Buren in this photograph taken between 1914 and 1918. Crawford County and Van Buren had numerous veterans who served in both the Army and Navy. (Courtesy of the UALR Center for Arkansas History and Culture.)

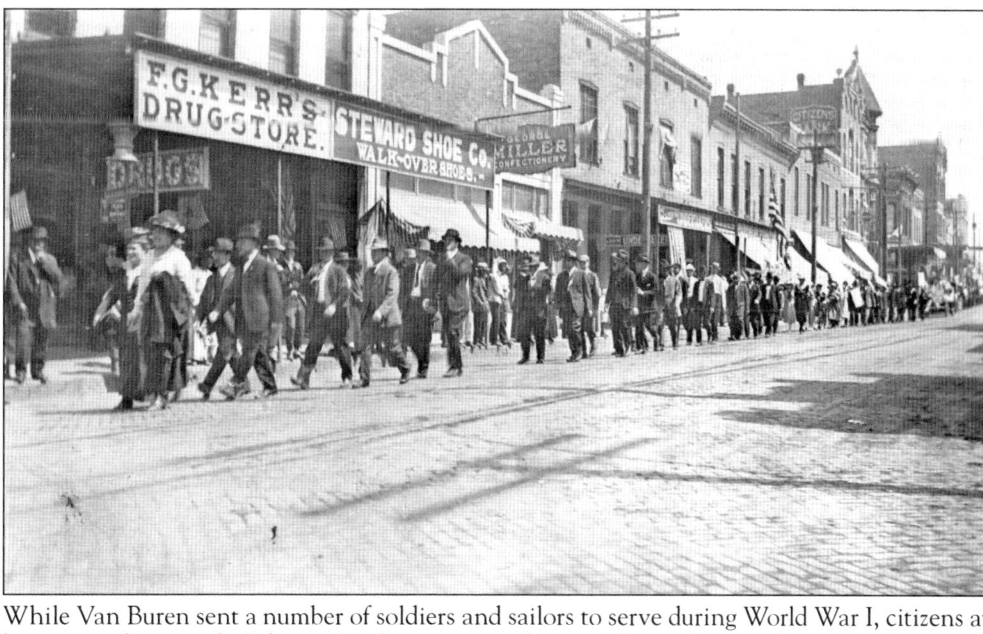

While Van Buren sent a number of soldiers and sailors to serve during World War I, citizens at home raised money for Liberty Bonds to support the war effort. This parade was held on Main Street to draw attention to the cause. (Courtesy of the UALR Center for Arkansas History and Culture.)

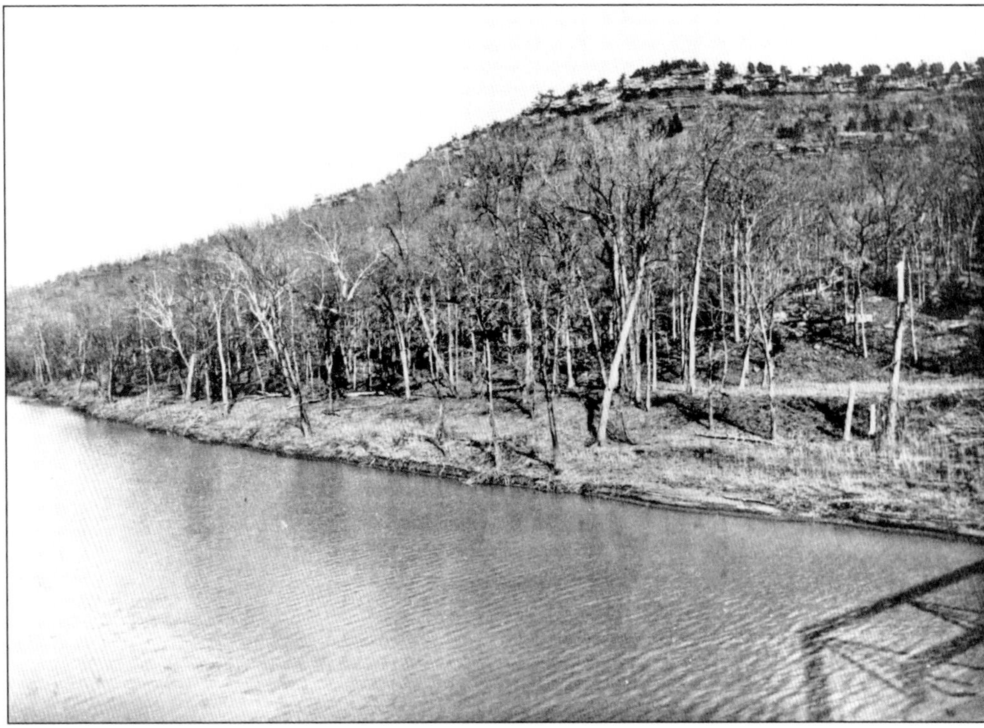

This view of the Lee Creek and Mount Vista bluff area illustrates the geographical fact that Van Buren is located where the Ozark Highland Plateau meets the Arkansas River Valley. (Courtesy of the UALR Center for Arkansas History and Culture.)

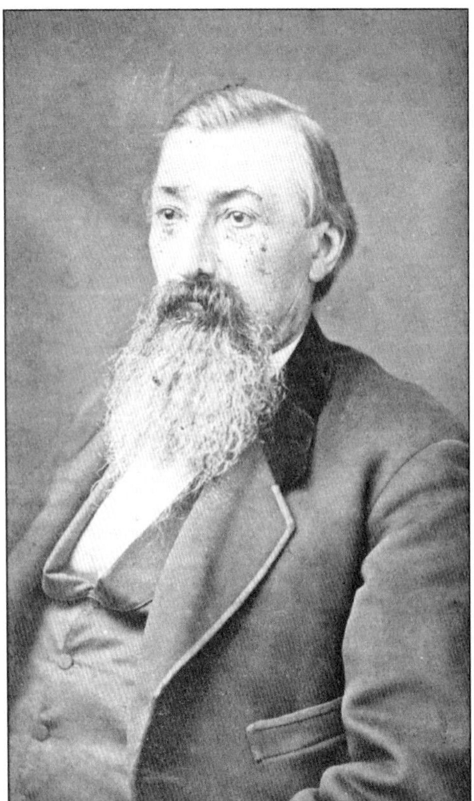

Dr. Henri Pernot was a French immigrant to the United States who established a medical practice in Van Buren before the Civil War. During the conflict he served as a surgeon for the Confederate army while his wife and children lived in Van Buren. He resumed his practice in Van Buren in 1865. (Courtesy of the UALR Center for Arkansas History and Culture.)

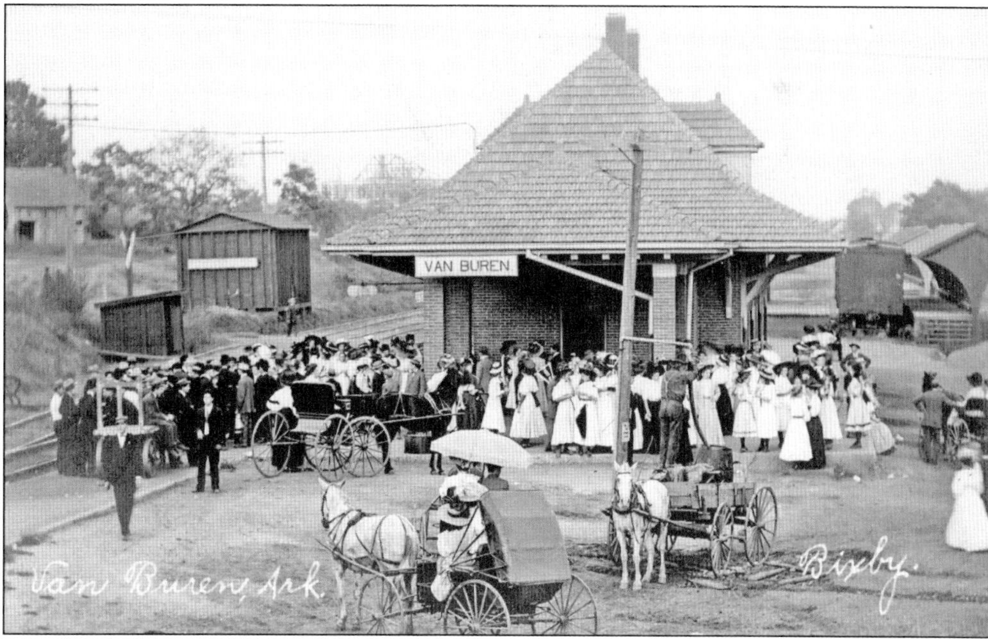

Passengers are seen waiting for the train at the Frisco Depot in this c. 1910 photograph. The depot was often the focal point of activity in Van Buren and serves as its tourist welcome center today. (Courtesy of the UALR Center for Arkansas History and Culture.)

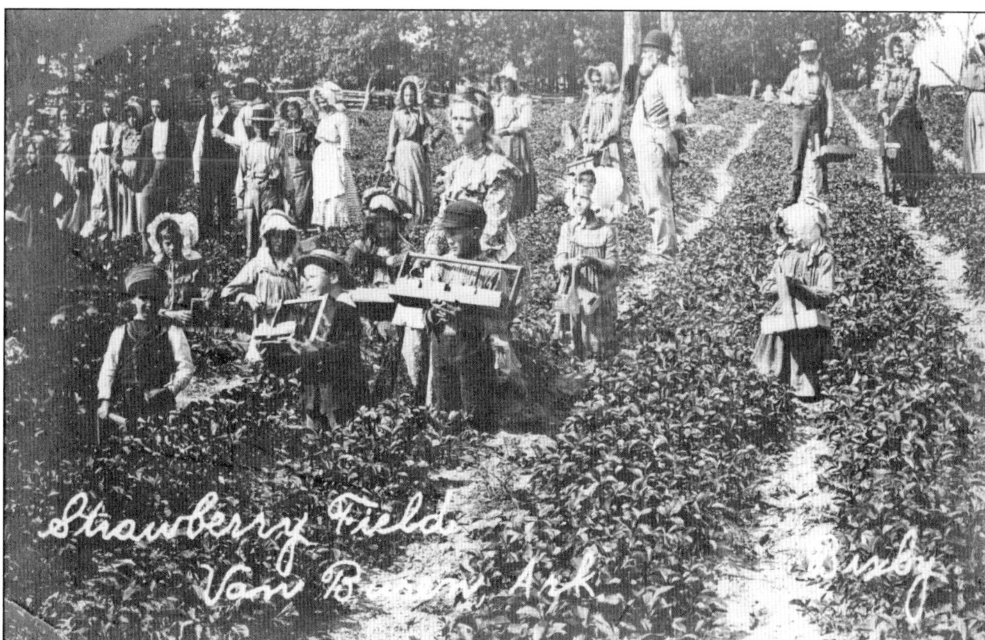

Crawford County was once a national leader in strawberry cultivation. Pickers in fields near Van Buren are seen here in the early 1900s. (Courtesy of the UALR Center for Arkansas History and Culture.)

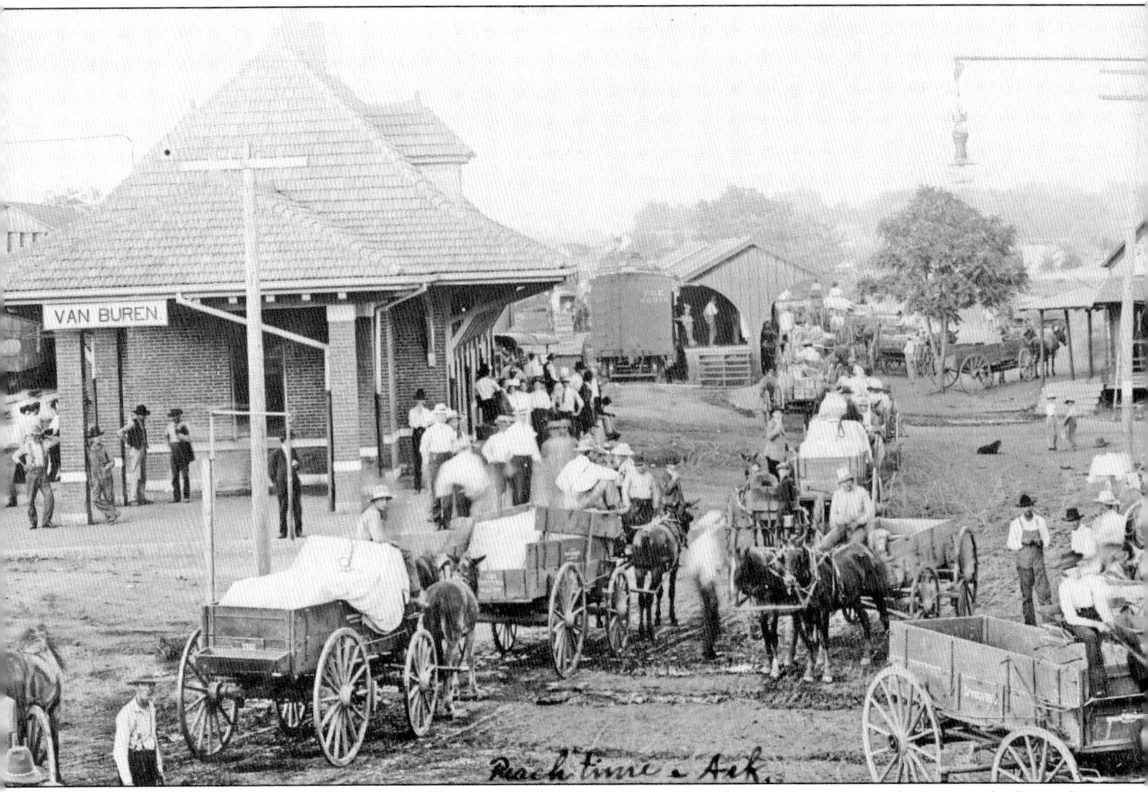

Both Van Buren and Crawford County have a rich history of agricultural products, including the peaches seen in this photograph being shipped on the Frisco in the early 1900s. (Courtesy of the UALR Center for Arkansas History and Culture.)

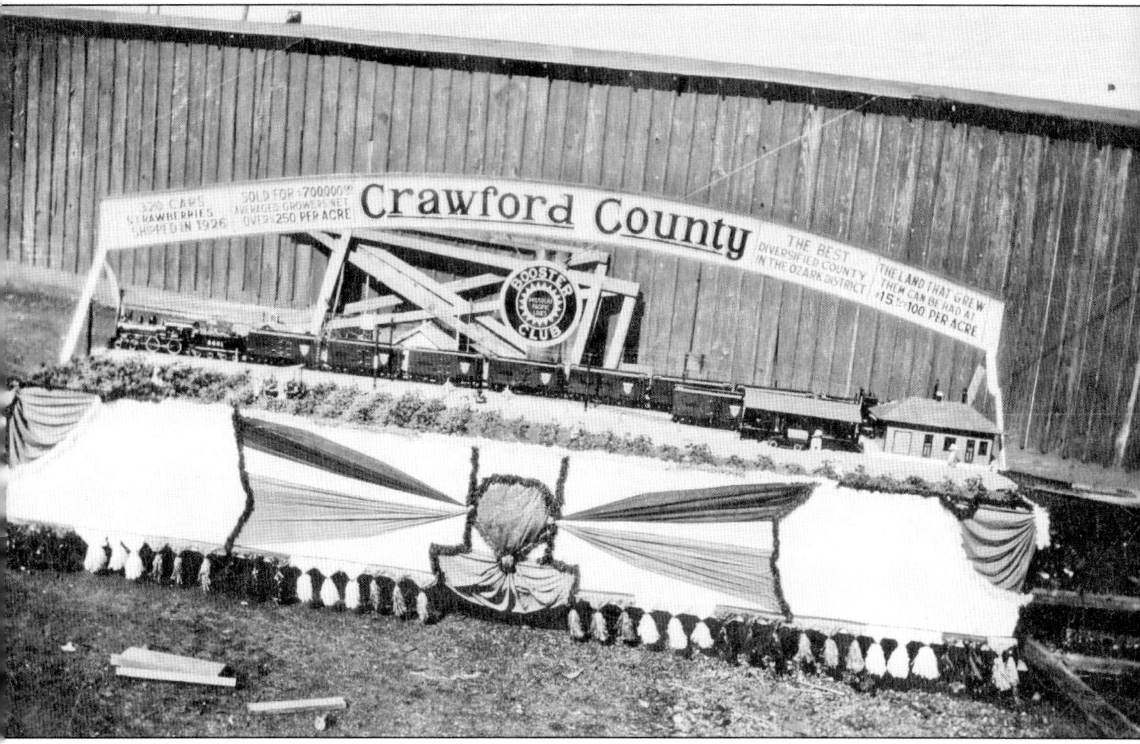

The annual strawberry harvest in Crawford County was a time of celebration that included an annual Strawberry Festival. This parade float, seen in the 1920s, testifies to Van Buren's success in producing strawberries while using facts and figures in support. (Courtesy of the UALR Center for Arkansas History and Culture.)

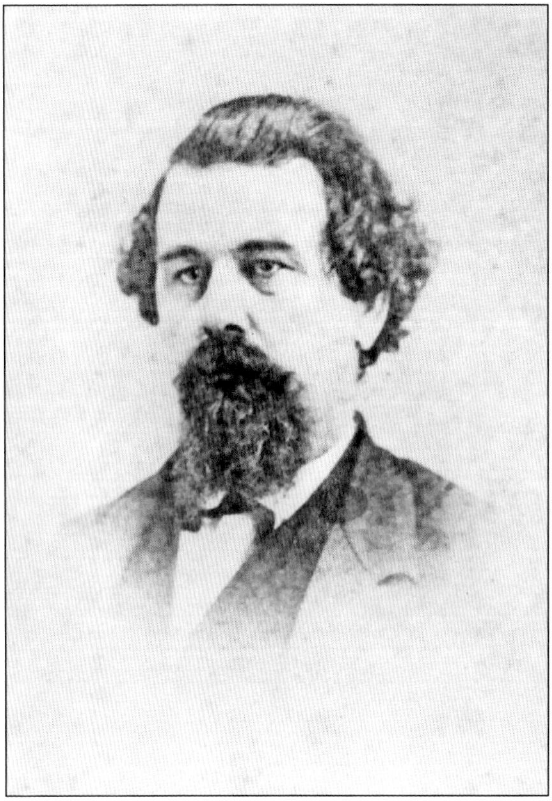

Hugh Thomason was a Van Buren resident and Crawford County delegate to the Secession Convention in 1861 and an Arkansas delegate to the Confederate Congress during the Civil War. (Courtesy of the UALR Center for Arkansas History and Culture.)

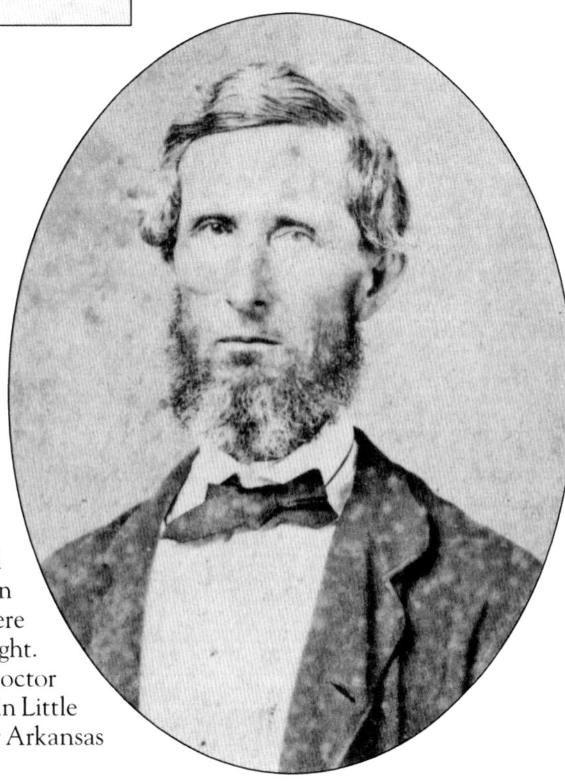

Dr. James Dibrell, pictured, was a medical doctor in Van Buren before the Civil War. Dibrell was one of the attending physicians at the famous Pike/Roan duel. Albert Pike and John Roan fought a duel on the banks of the Arkansas near Van Buren in 1846. Dr. Dibrell's services were not required as neither were hurt in the fight. Dr. Dibrell's son James Jr. was also a doctor and helped establish the medical school in Little Rock. (Courtesy of the UALR Center for Arkansas History and Culture.)

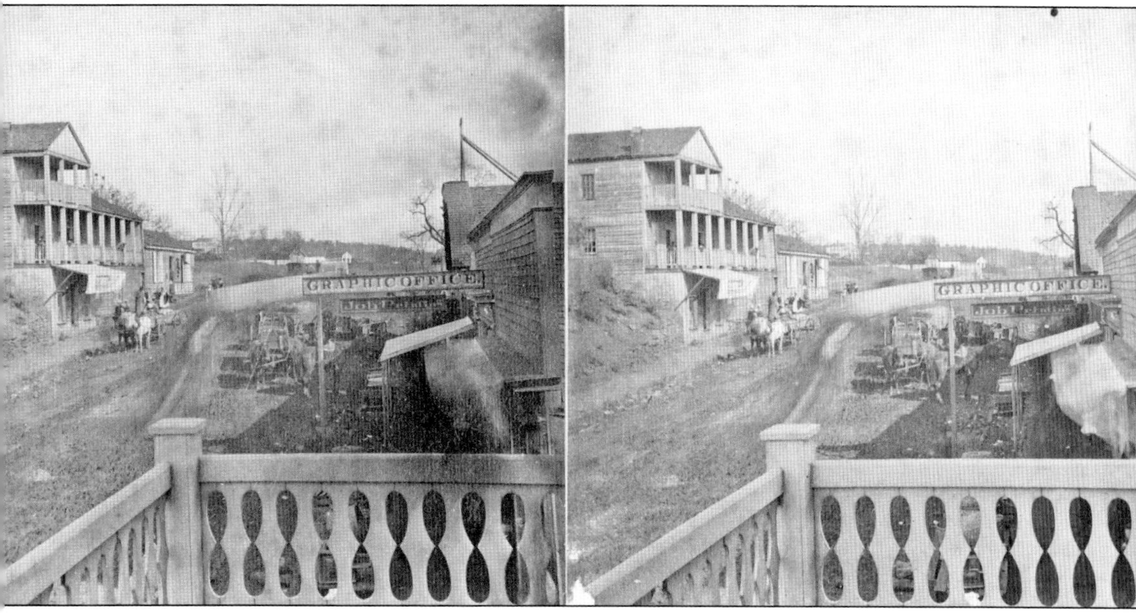

The offices of the *Van Buren Graphic* can be seen on the right in this stereo view. The newspaper was in circulation from 1881 until 1888, placing the date of this image between those years. The *Graphic* was another in a long line of papers in Van Buren, including the *Intelligencer*, the *Press*, the *Courier*, and the *Press Argus*. (Courtesy of the UALR Center for Arkansas History and Culture.)

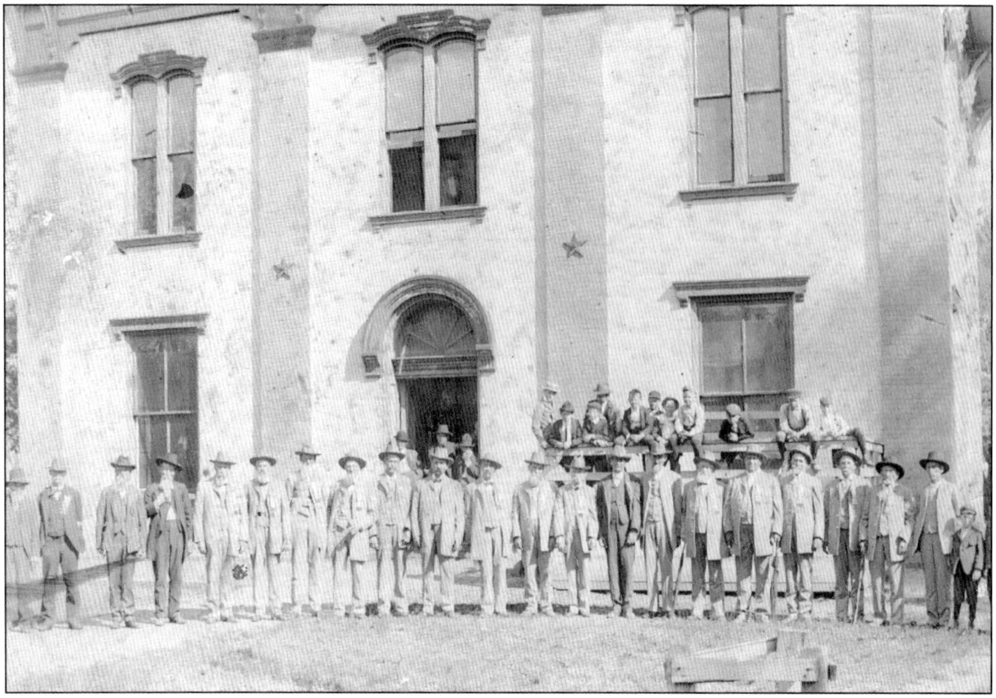

While Arkansas was officially a Confederate state, Van Buren had its share of both Confederate and Union veterans, making the town truly divided. Confederate Veterans pose here near the Crawford County Courthouse. (Courtesy of the UALR Center for Arkansas History and Culture.)

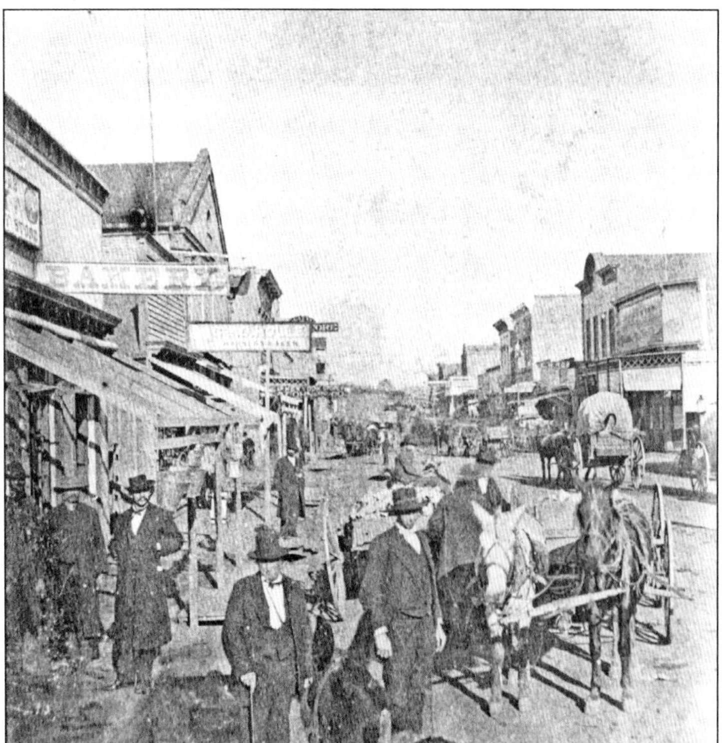

This 1870s photograph of Main Street shows an active downtown with numerous businesses and a large amount of traffic. (Courtesy of the UALR Center for Arkansas History and Culture.)

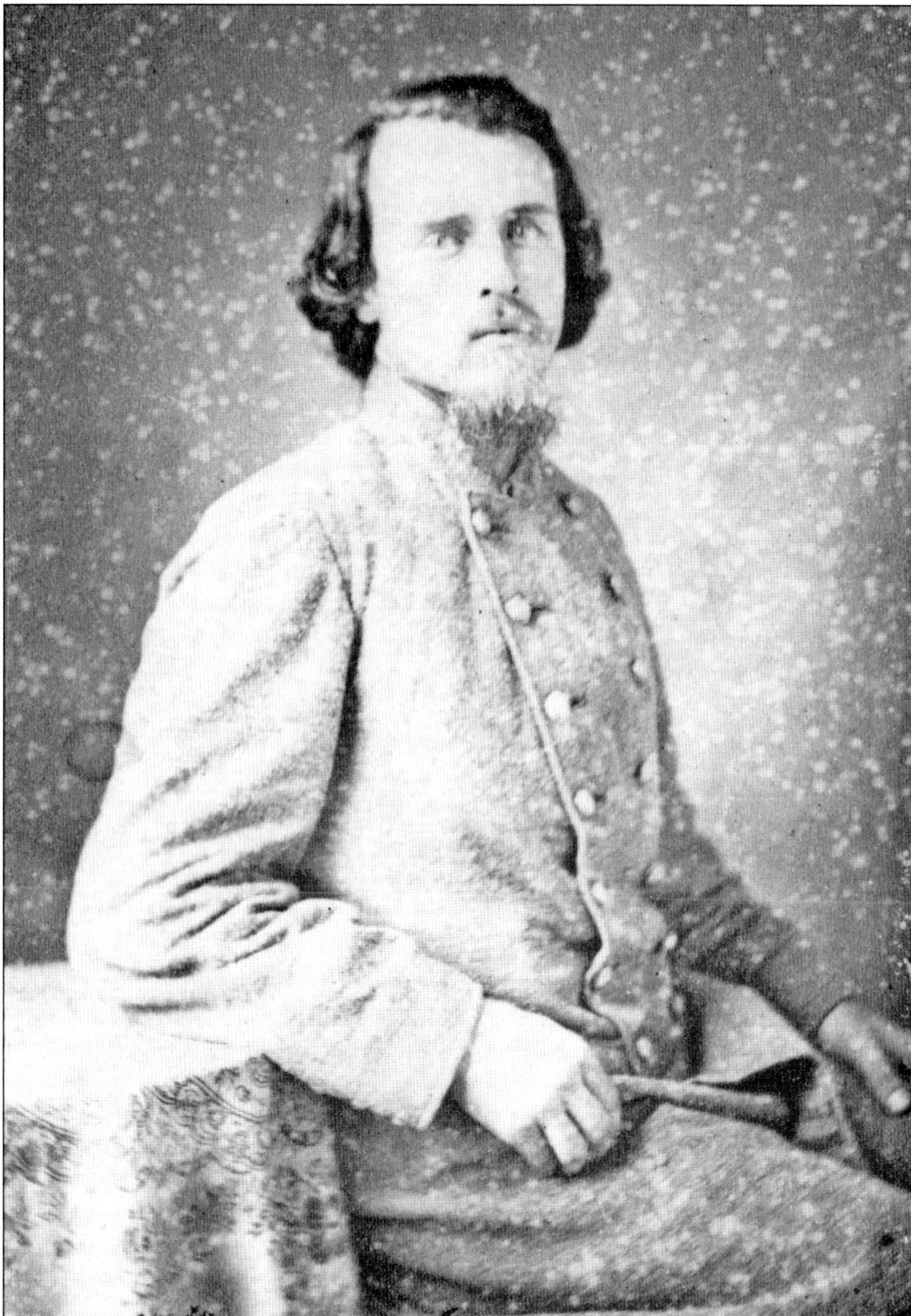

Civil War veteran Clem McColloch is pictured in the 1860s. McColloch served in the Van Buren Frontier Guards, a Confederate unit that participated in the Battle of Wilson's Creek in southwest Missouri in 1861. (Courtesy of the UALR Center for Arkansas History and Culture.)

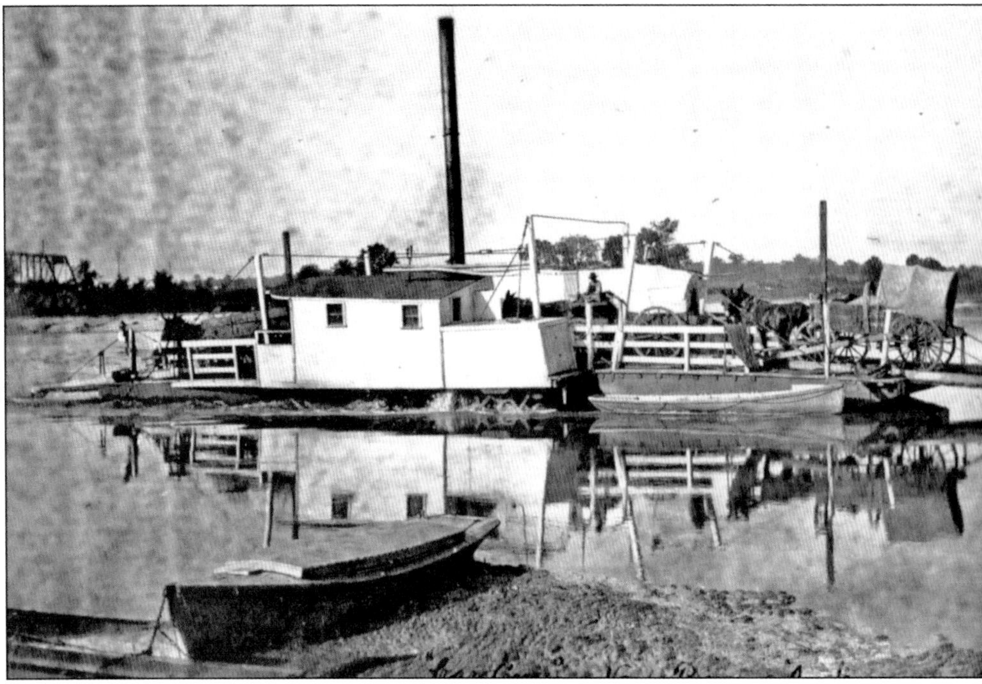

The Fort Smith-Van Buren Free Bridge was completed in 1912. Because the previous mode of crossing at Van Buren involved a ferry (pictured above) and included a fee, the "free" bridge encouraged more travel between the communities. (Both, courtesy of the UALR Center for Arkansas History and Culture.)

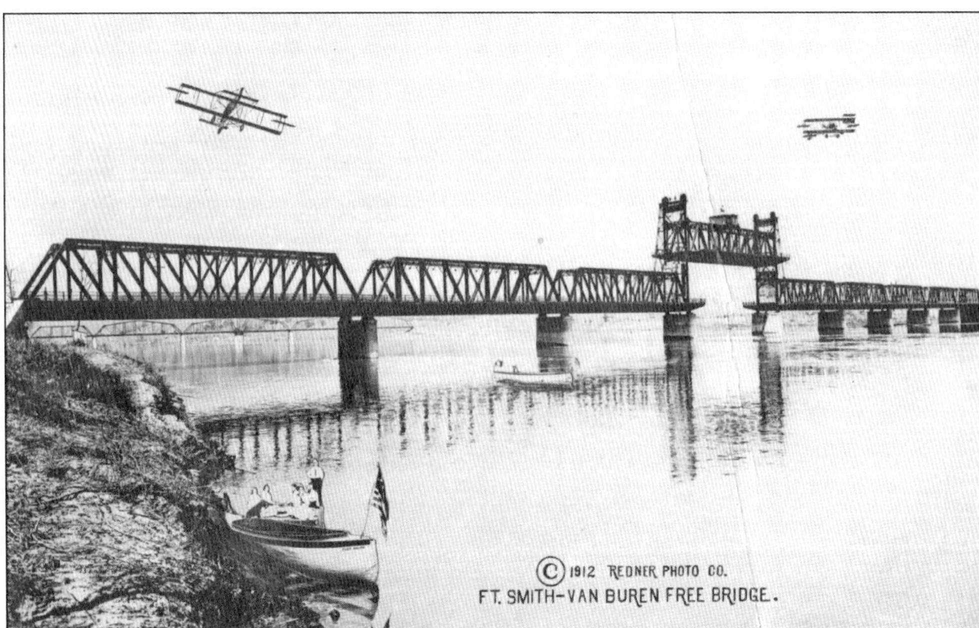

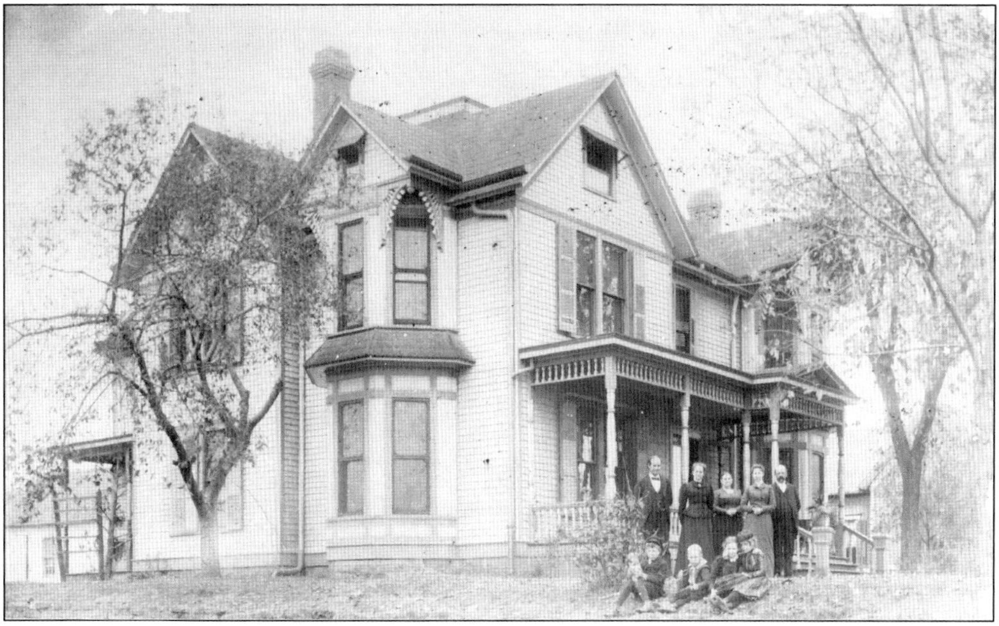

Van Buren's Lewis Bryan family poses in front of their home with their visiting cousin William Jennings Bryan. Bryan ran unsuccessfully for president in 1896, 1900, and 1908. Known for "stumping," Bryan likely came to Van Buren both to visit family and convince voters. (Courtesy of the UALR Center for Arkansas History and Culture.)

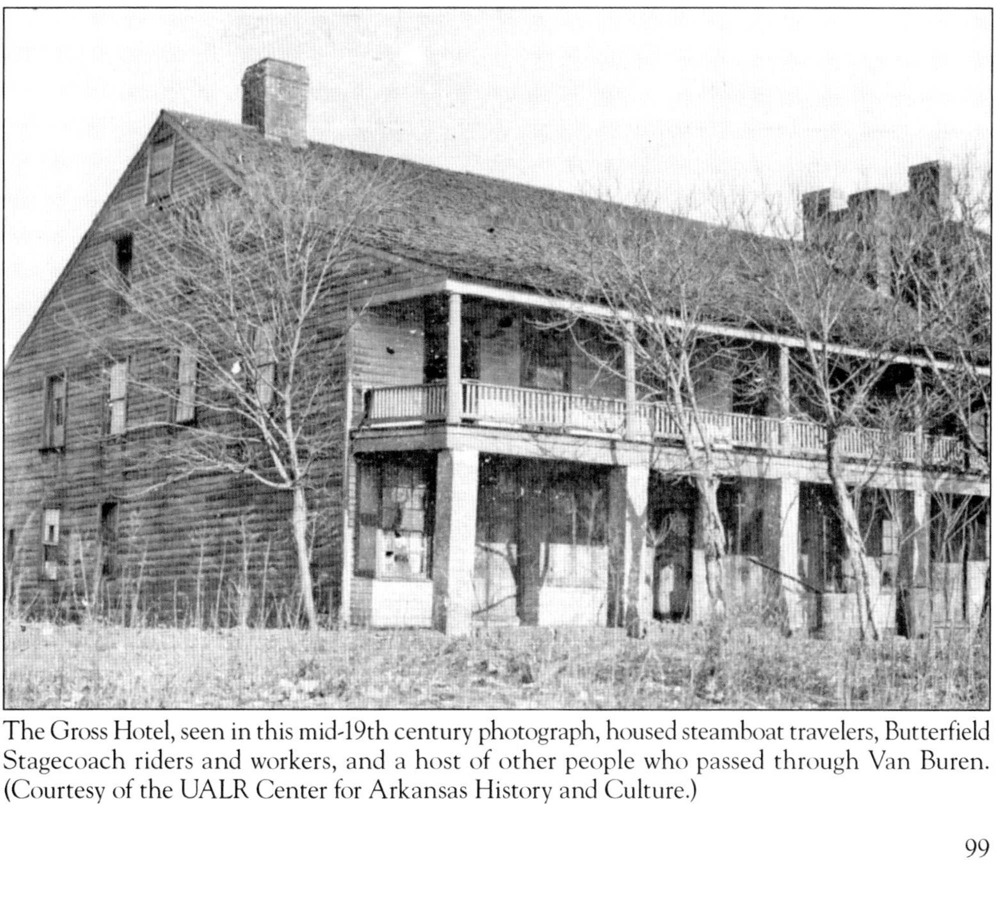

The Gross Hotel, seen in this mid-19th century photograph, housed steamboat travelers, Butterfield Stagecoach riders and workers, and a host of other people who passed through Van Buren. (Courtesy of the UALR Center for Arkansas History and Culture.)

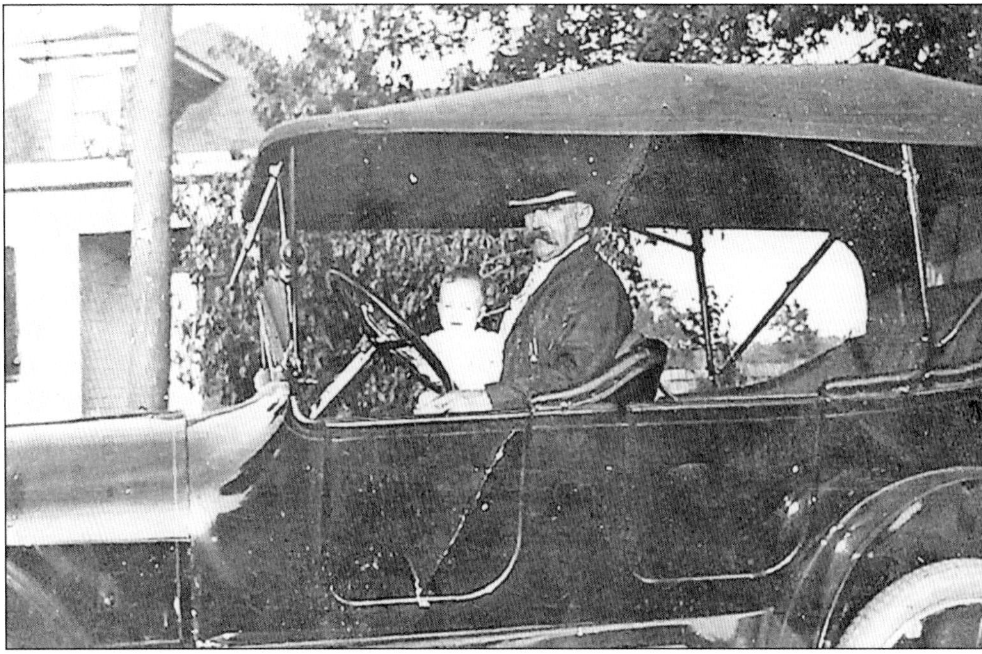

Robert Parchman Gelly sits with his grandfather Dr. Parchman in 1915. The automobile is believed to have been the first to be owned by a Van Buren resident. Dr. Parchman was acquitted of murder in the death of Charles Tolson, whom the doctor thought was involved with his daughter. (Courtesy of Joyce Gelly Patton.)

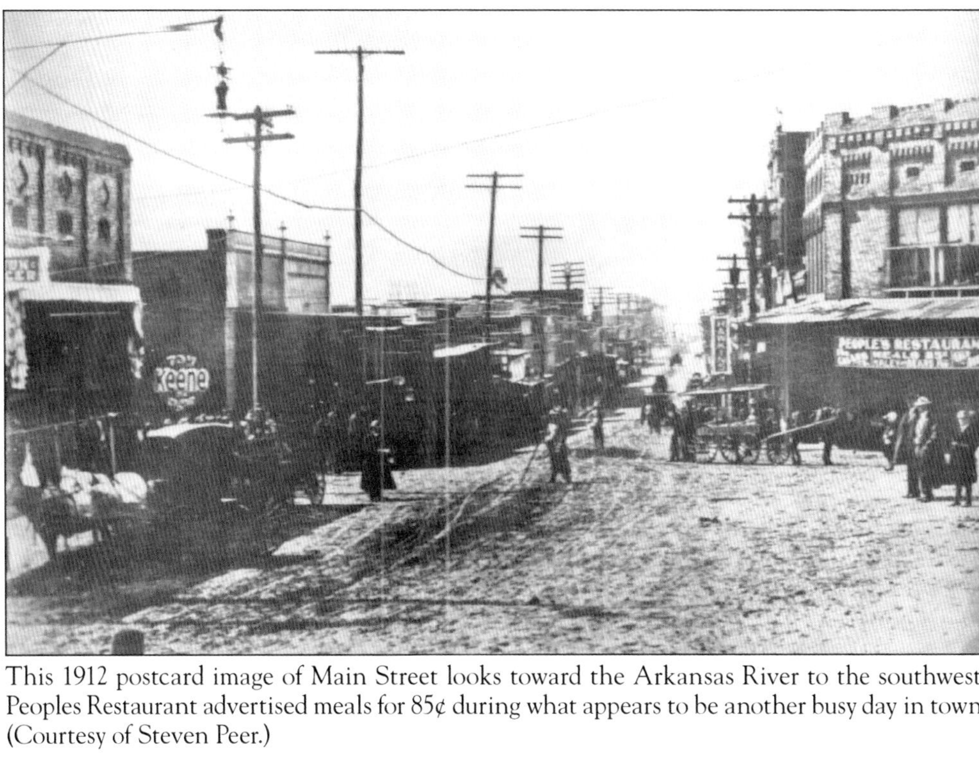

This 1912 postcard image of Main Street looks toward the Arkansas River to the southwest. Peoples Restaurant advertised meals for 85¢ during what appears to be another busy day in town. (Courtesy of Steven Peer.)

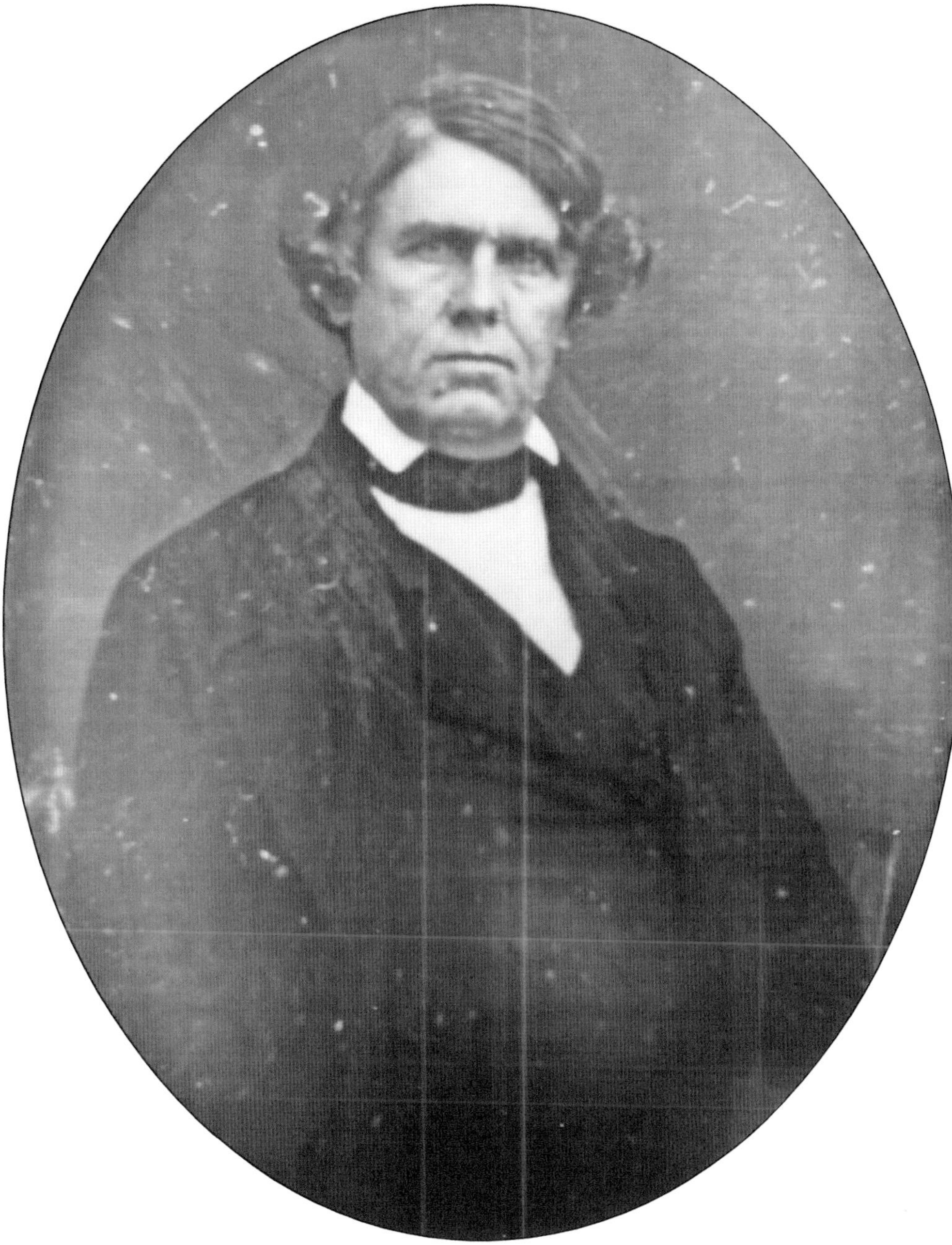

Known as the "father of steam boating in Arkansas," Phillip Pennywitt, seen in this undated photograph, was also a merchant and close friend to the Drennen-Scott family. Working closely with John Drennen and son-in-law Charles Scott, Pennywitt held partnerships with both and lived as a bachelor in the Drennen-Scott House. He is buried in the Drennen-Scott family plot and is the namesake of Charles and Caroline Scott's son, Phillip Drennen Scott. Pennywitt piloted the steamboats that took the Drennen-Scott cotton to market in New Orleans and brought back groceries and finished goods to Van Buren. He took the first steamboat up the White River in 1831 and transported Gen. Winfield Scott and territorial governor George Izard up the Arkansas to Fort Smith and Fort Gibson. (Courtesy of the Arkansas History Commission.)

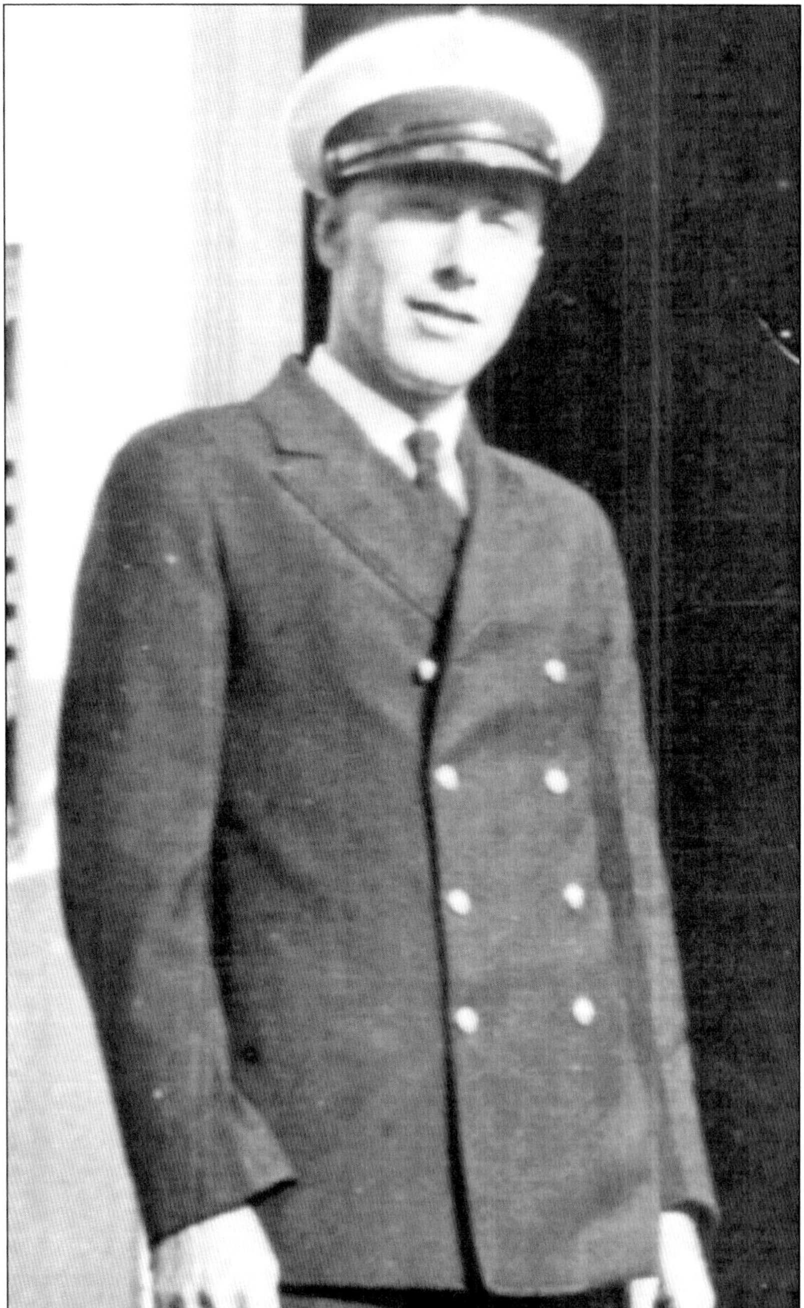

George Redmond Sagely was born in Sequoya County, Oklahoma, just west of Van Buren, but his parents were both born near Van Buren in Crawford County, Arkansas. George joined the Navy and served during World War I as a pharmacist's mate. After the war, he reenlisted and served in both the Navy and Naval Reserves until 1940. He was commended for bravery in the rescue of injured personnel in the 1935 USS *Macon* airship disaster. Sagely lived for many years in Van Buren after his service and was the uncle of former mayor Allen Ray Toothaker. (Courtesy of Norma Jean Toothaker.)

This undated postcard image of downtown Van Buren shows part of the iconic Crawford County Bank building to the right. The Gothic Revival architecture is apparent even with only part of the structure in the photograph. (Courtesy of Steven Peer.)

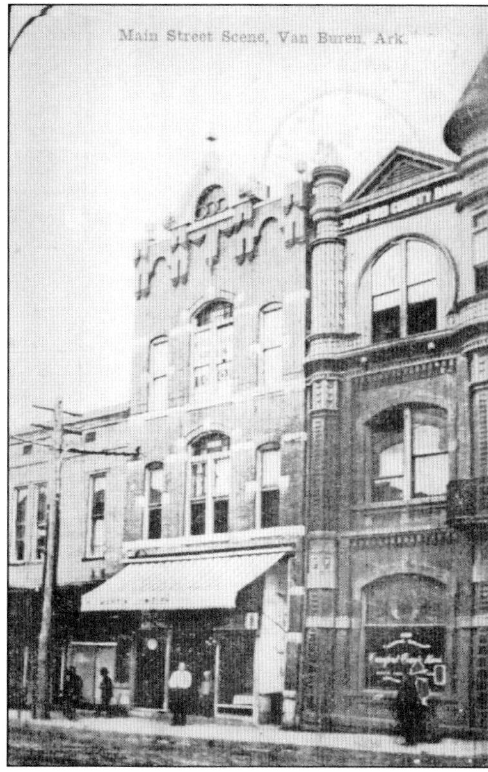

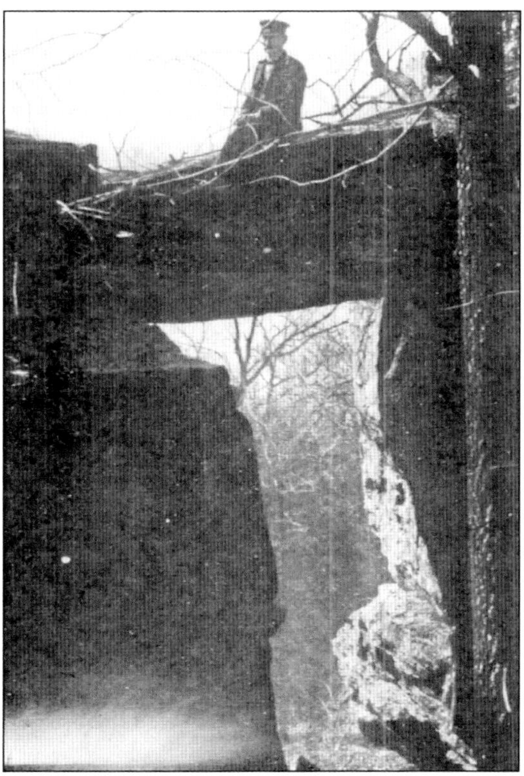

Natural Bridge, located on Lee Creek Bluff (or Mount Vista), is seen in a 1909 postcard image. The local landmark was the subject of many photographs through the years. Large rock formations are common along the bluff, which forms the boundary between the Arkansas River Valley and the Ozark Highlands. (Courtesy of Steven Peer.)

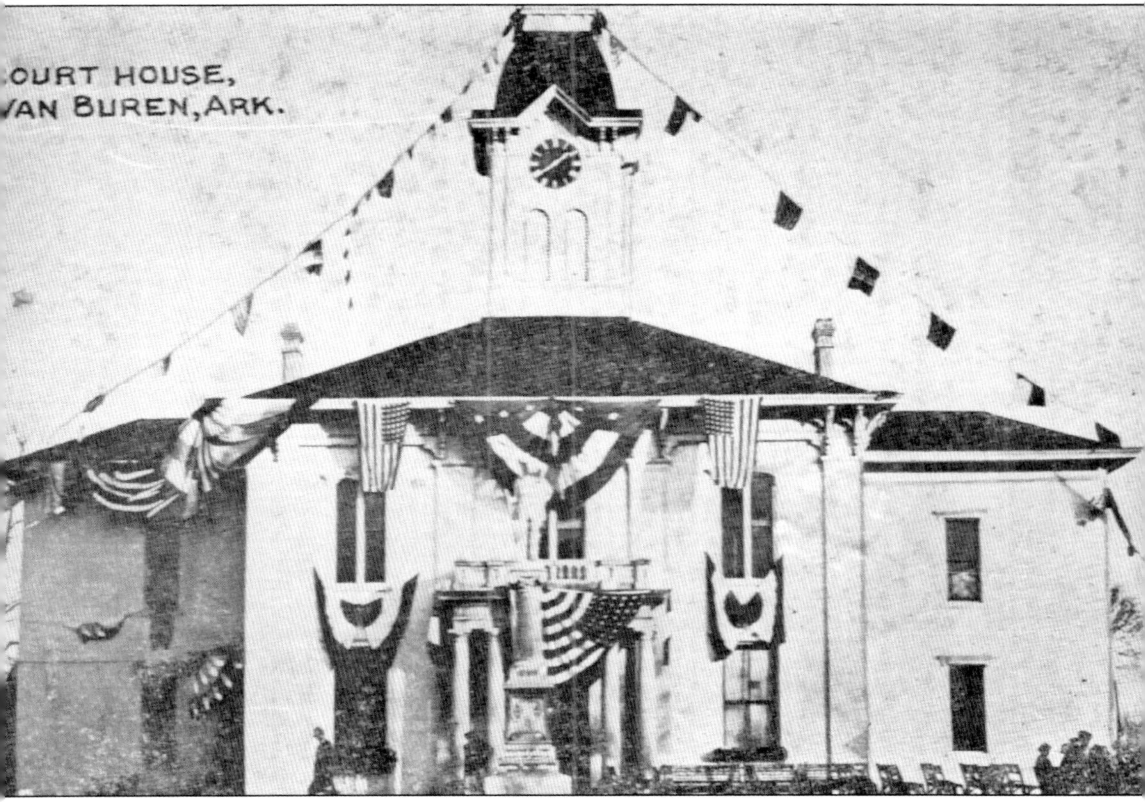

This undated postcard image of the Crawford County Courthouse includes bunting, flags, and folding chairs on the lawn. The decorations were most likely in place to celebrate Independence Day. (Courtesy of Steven Peer.)

Four

GETTING CONNECTED

The 1885 railroad bridge across the Arkansas River connected Van Buren with Fort Smith. The site for the bridge included land on both sides of the river previously owned by John Drennen for his ferry. Drennen and his family operated the ferry until the railroad sought the location for the bridge. The Butterfield Overland Stage, as well as Confederate and Union soldiers, used the ferry at Van Buren.

The railroad first came to Van Buren in 1876 with the opening of the Little Rock and Fort Smith Railroad. Transfer across the river was accomplished by the use of a double-ended side-wheeler, the *Harold B.* In 1882, the Saint Louis and San Francisco Railroad Company (the Frisco) established service through Van Buren and Fort Smith. The side-wheeler transfer across the river continued for only a short time due to increased traffic and demand.

In 1885, the Fort Smith and Van Buren Bridge Company was created to remedy the situation and completed the bridge a year later. The chief of engineers for the US Army declined the first two proposals for the bridge, citing location, bridge height, and current of the river. A compromise was eventually reached. The Union Bridge Company, which designed the bridge, recorded its construction with the photographs in this chapter. In business from 1869 until 1890, the company built many bridges in the United States, one of which crossed the Mississippi River at Memphis. These photographs were found in a bound volume with the title *Van Buren Bridge Co. New York, 1885*. The book was found and rescued by Tom Trencansky of the Cornell Railroad Historical Society. Trencansky contacted Larry Weir of Hawkins and Weir Engineers in Van Buren, who made them available for use.

The bridge has survived floods, was remodeled in 1913, and fitted with a drawbridge in 1970. Part of the bridge was replaced after being swept away by the Flood of 1943. Recently, the drop bridge cables broke but were replaced. Since construction in 1885, the bridge has served the community and remains an icon on the Arkansas River at Van Buren.

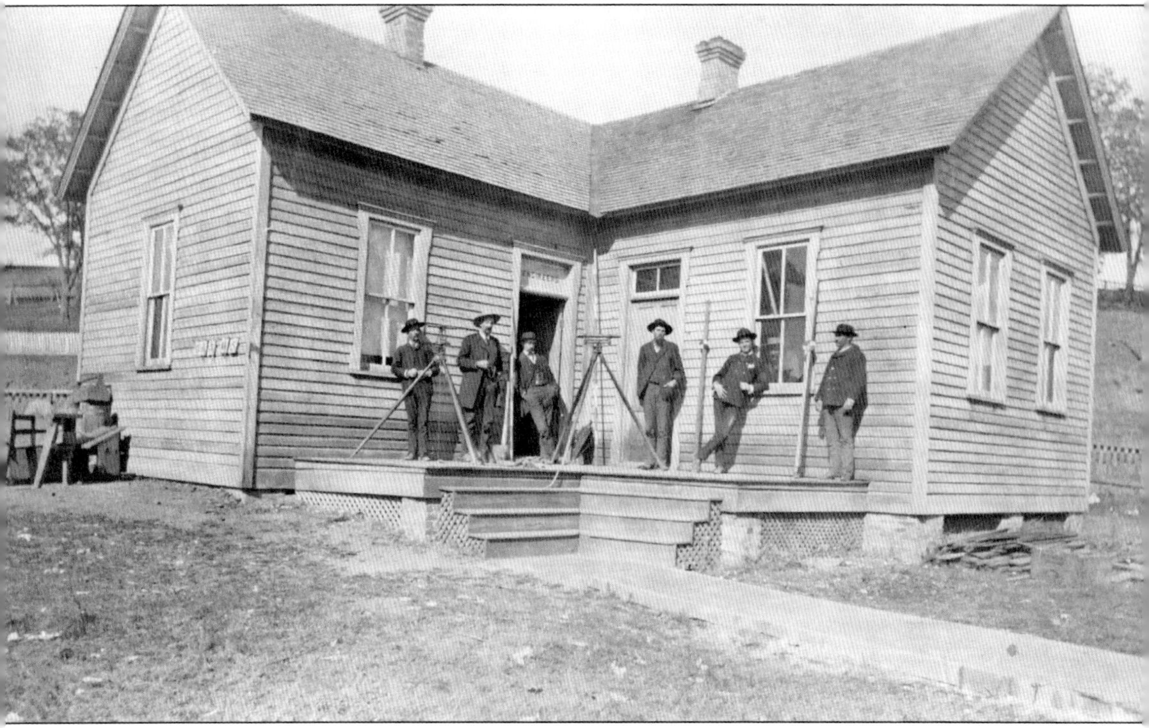

Before the bridge across the Arkansas River could be built, extensive survey and investigative work had to be done. The surveyors seen in this photograph have transits to check elevation and measure distances. The office in the background is one of many structures erected by the company on the Van Buren side of the river to facilitate construction. (Courtesy of the Cornell Railroad Historical Society.)

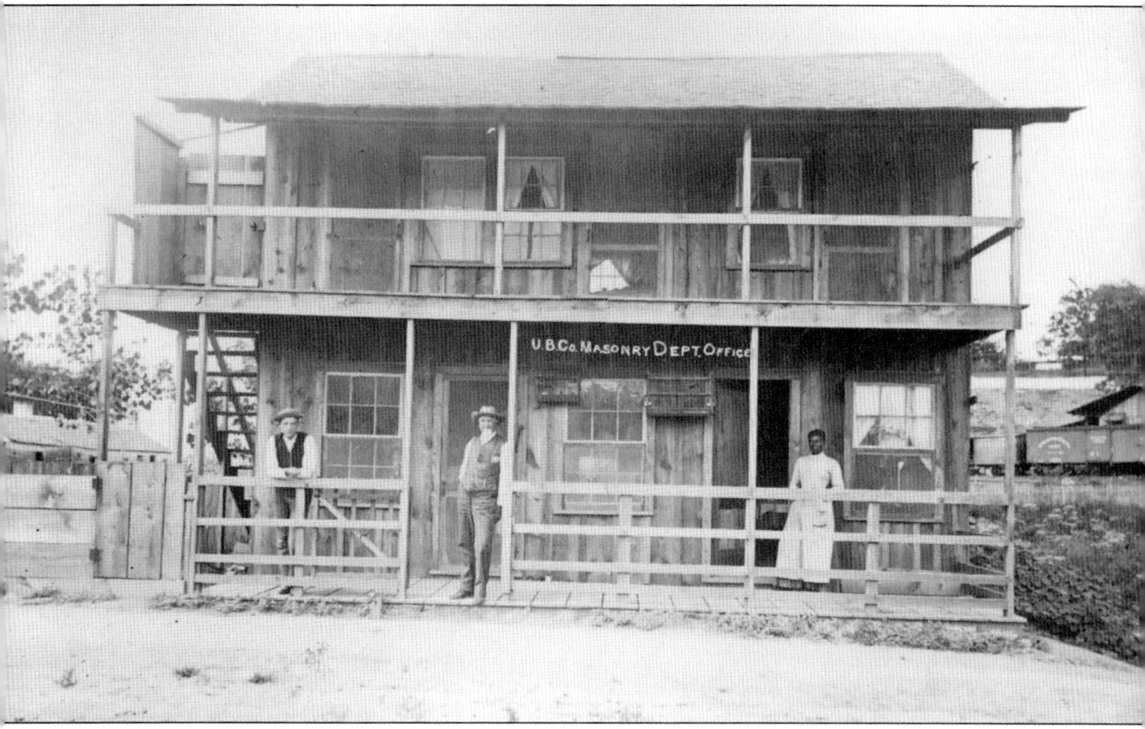

Labeled the VB Company Masonry Dept. Office, this structure on the Van Buren side of the river was used to coordinate the stone cutting and placement for the piers the bridge eventually sat upon. Stone for the piers was cut and stacked nearby, eventually placed to support the bridge. (Courtesy of the Cornell Railroad Historical Society.)

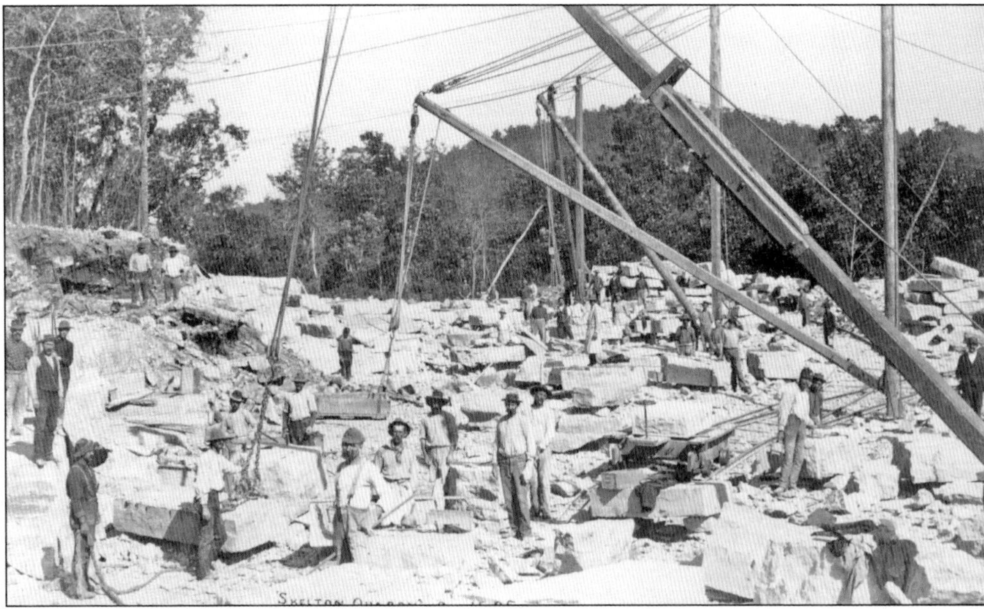

Stone for the piers came from the nearby Ozark Plateau. A geographical formation extending from the Arkansas River Valley to Missouri, its rock was convenient and reliable for bridge building. (Courtesy of the Cornell Railroad Historical Society.)

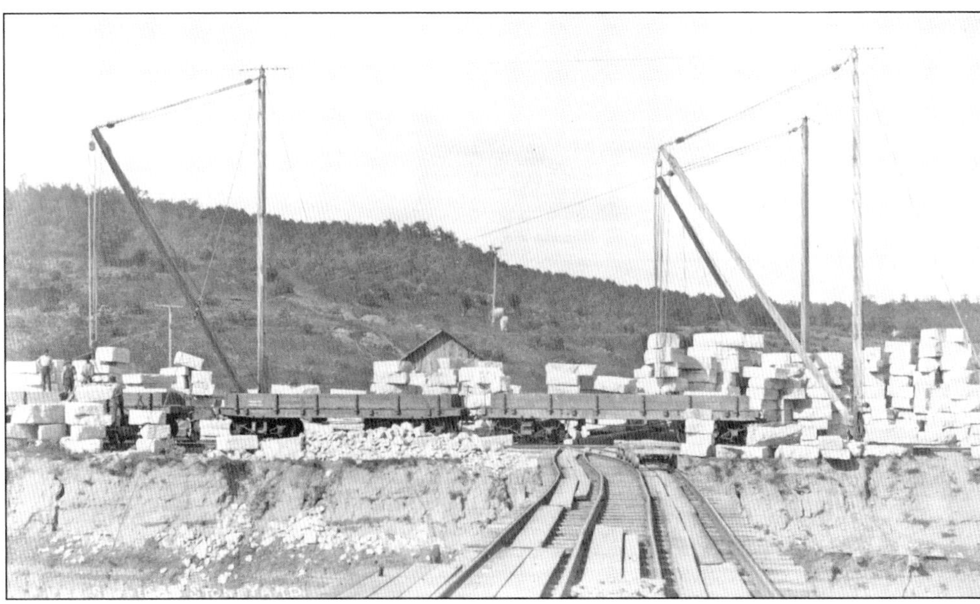

Stone was quarried, cut, and moved to an assembly point near the masonry office before being loaded onto barges and taken out to the piers. (Courtesy of the Cornell Railroad Historical Society.)

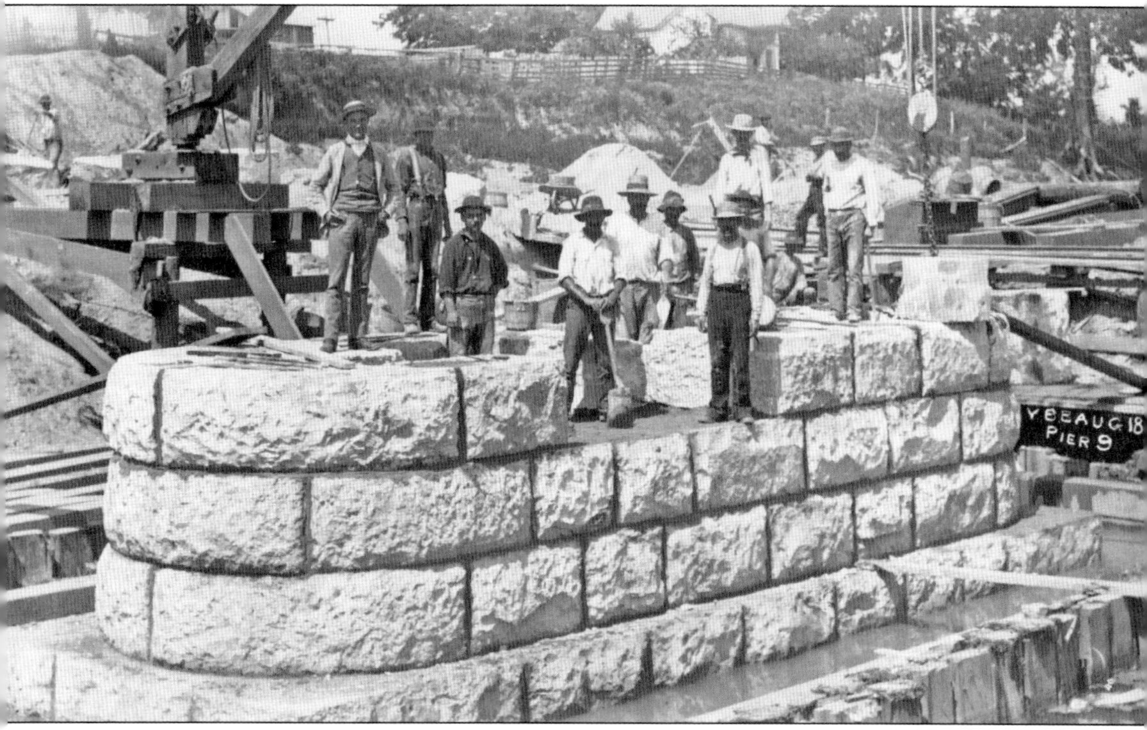

Hoists, block and tackle, and plenty of manpower were needed to place the stones into their location on each pier. The men in this photograph are about to place another stone in the dark gray mortar they have spread on top of the stones. Buckets behind and around the men were used to bring mortar to the job site. (Courtesy of the Cornell Railroad Historical Society.)

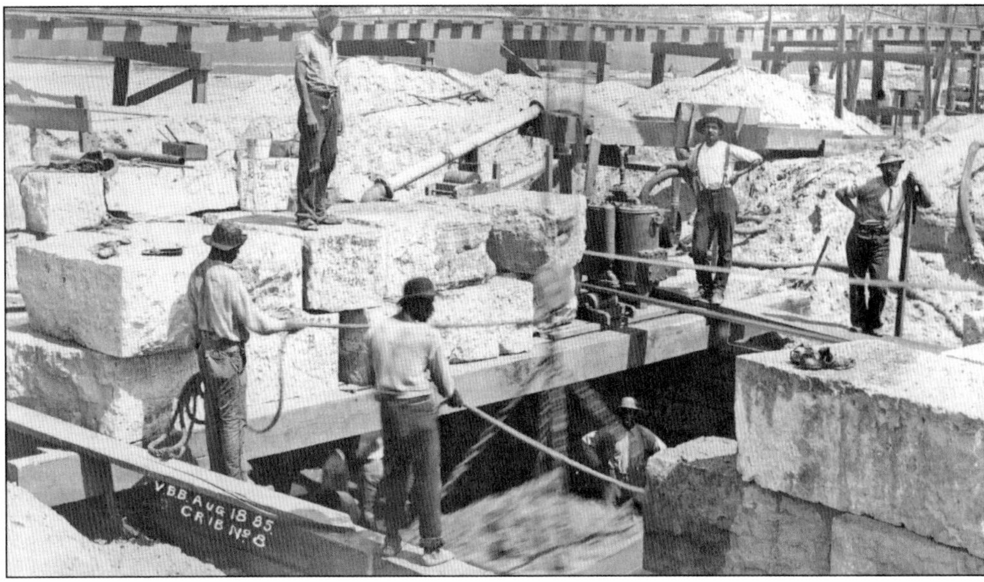

These men are placing pier stones in the temporary "crib" that will hold them in place before concrete is used to seal the structure. (Courtesy of the Cornell Railroad Historical Society.)

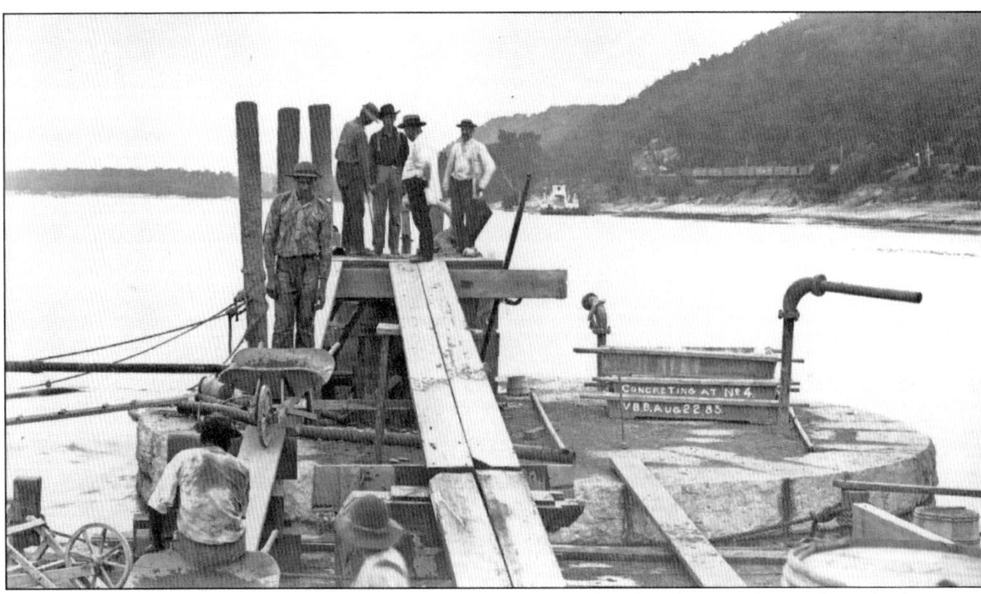

Once the stones were laid on the river bottom, held together by the wooden crib with the water displaced by the caisson, concrete was poured inside the structure for strength. (Courtesy of the Cornell Railroad Historical Society.)

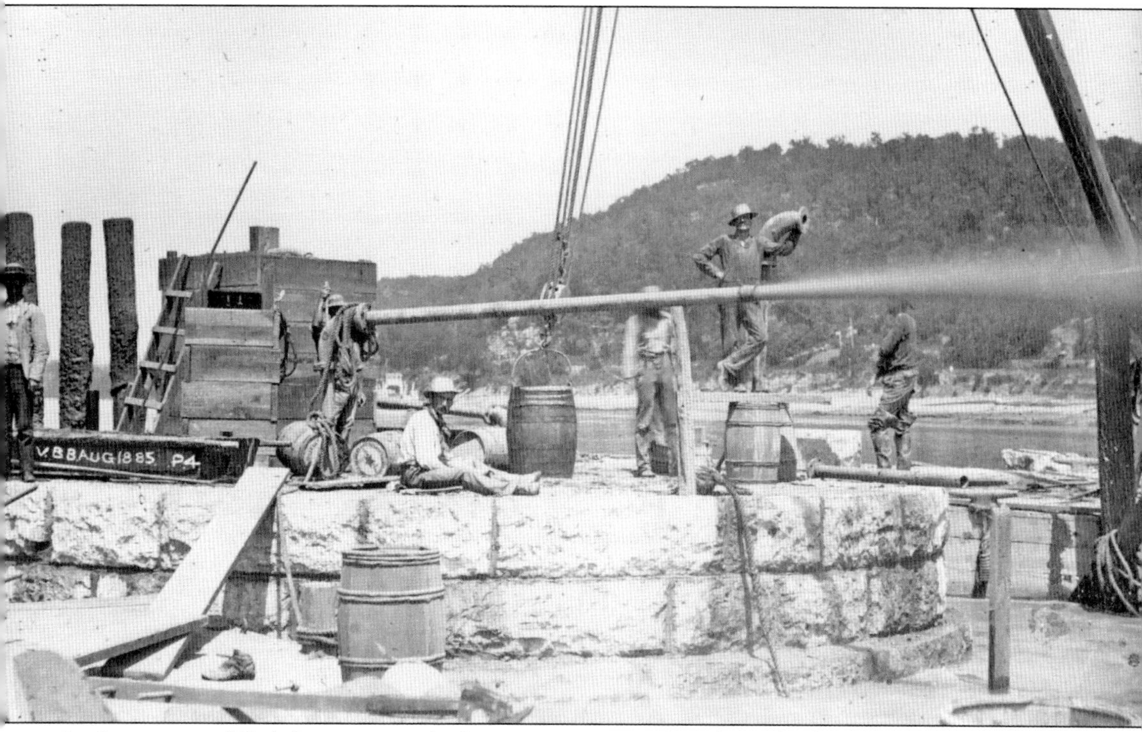

As the concrete filled the space inside the stones, water and mud was displaced through the pipe seen here. (Courtesy of the Cornell Railroad Historical Society.)

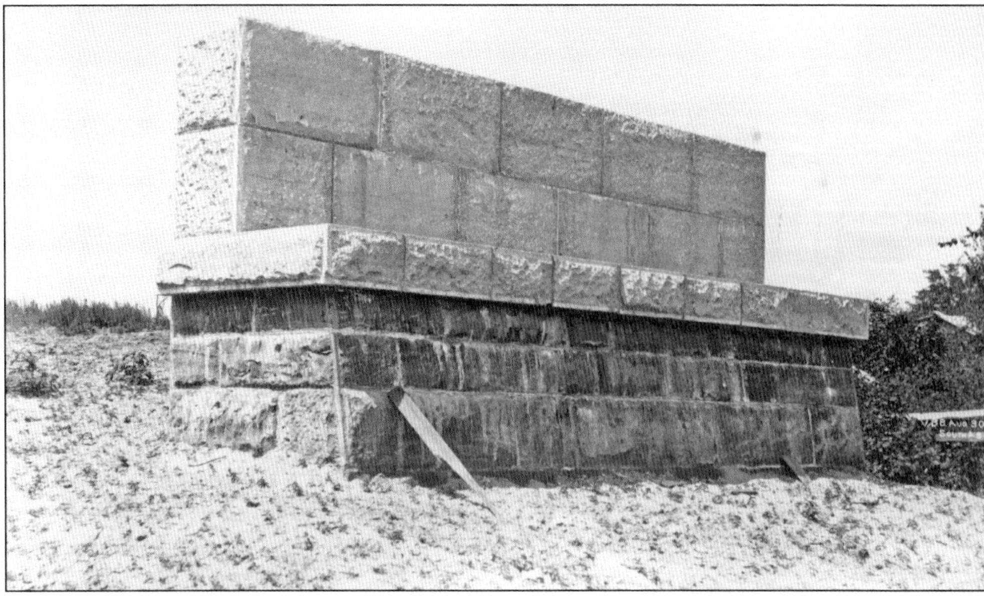

Abutments were constructed on both sides of the river where the bridge would connect to land. The south abutment, seen here on the Fort Smith side, had a matching copy on the Van Buren bank of the river. (Courtesy of the Cornell Railroad Historical Society.)

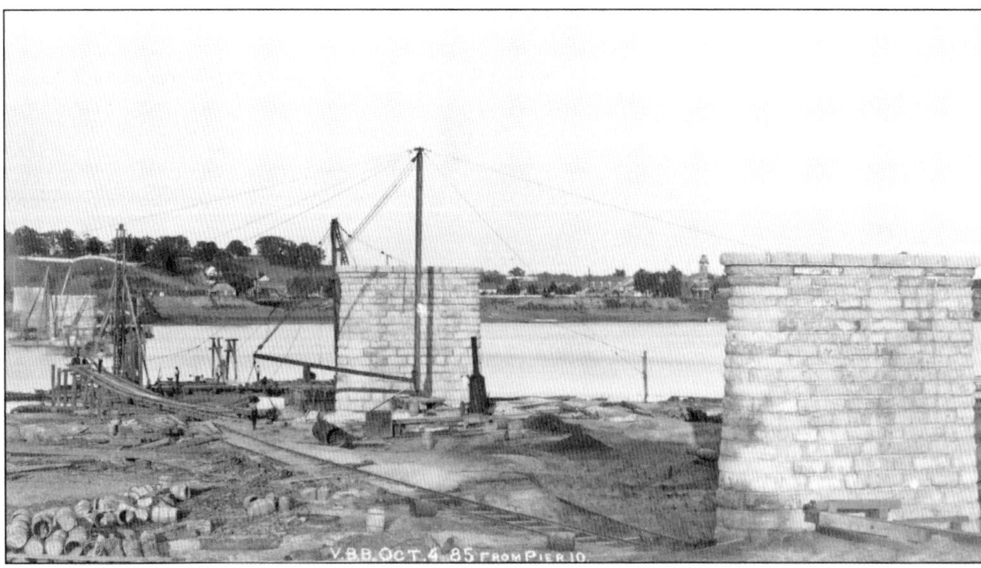

Taken from the Fort Smith side looking back at the bridge construction, a number of Van Buren landmarks are visible in the distance. To the left, white fences surrounding the Drennen-Scott estate are visible on the bluff above the bridge. Buildings along Water Street are seen from the center to the right of the photograph. Appearing almost next to the pier in the foreground is the clock tower of the Crawford County Courthouse. (Courtesy of the Cornell Railroad Historical Society.)

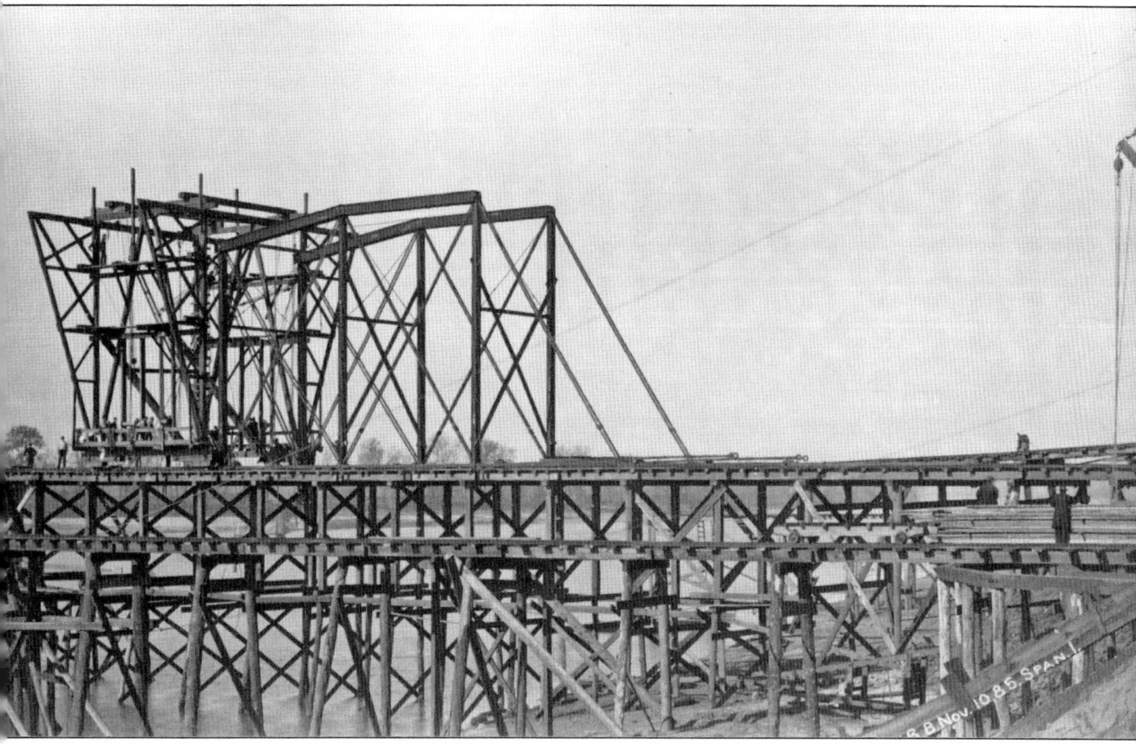

Once the piers were in place, the steel bridge girders and beams were riveted together, and the bridge began to take shape. (Courtesy of the Cornell Railroad Historical Society.)

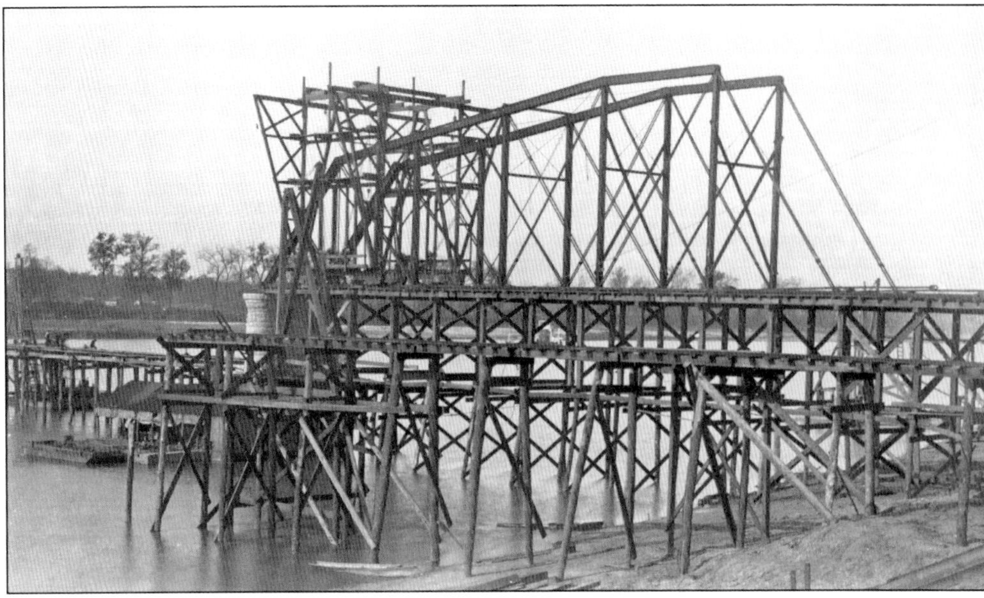

Progress is seen as workers continue to complete successive sections of the bridge. (Both, courtesy of the Cornell Railroad Historical Society.)

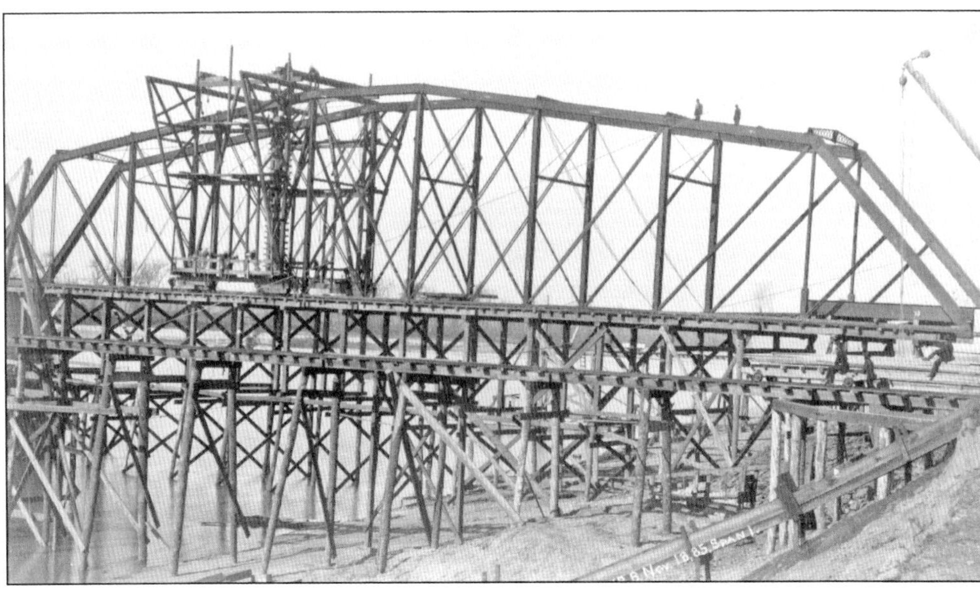

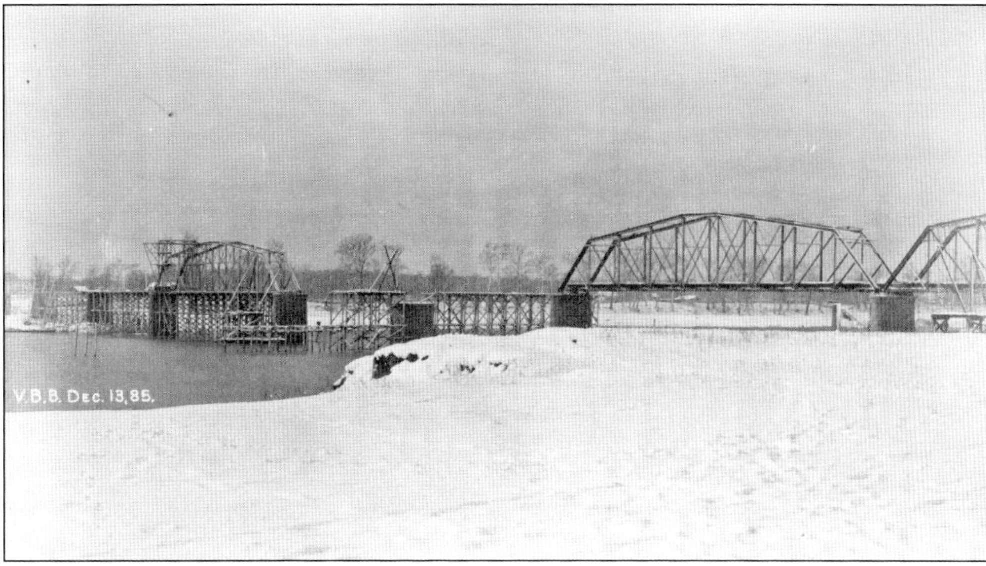

By December 1885, the bridge was nearing completion. Seen here with an early winter snow blanketing the construction site, the bridge was on schedule to open in the early spring of 1886. (Courtesy of the Cornell Railroad Historical Society.)

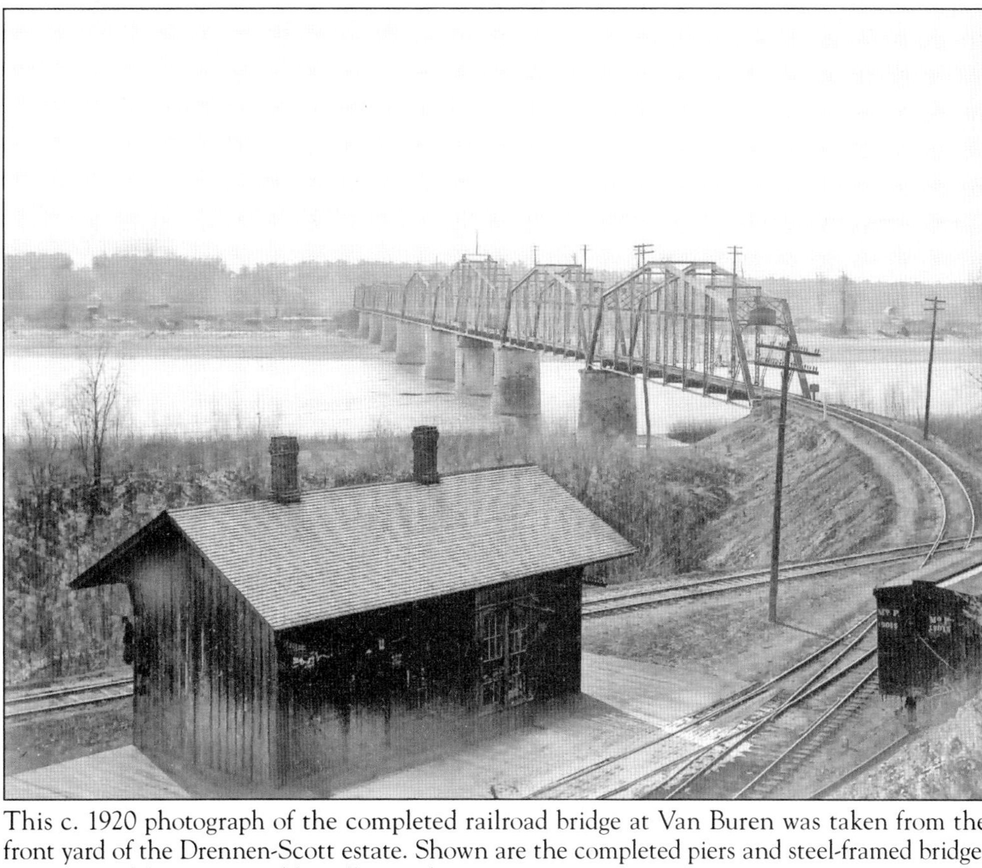

This c. 1920 photograph of the completed railroad bridge at Van Buren was taken from the front yard of the Drennen-Scott estate. Shown are the completed piers and steel-framed bridge. (Courtesy of the UAFS Cobb Collection.)

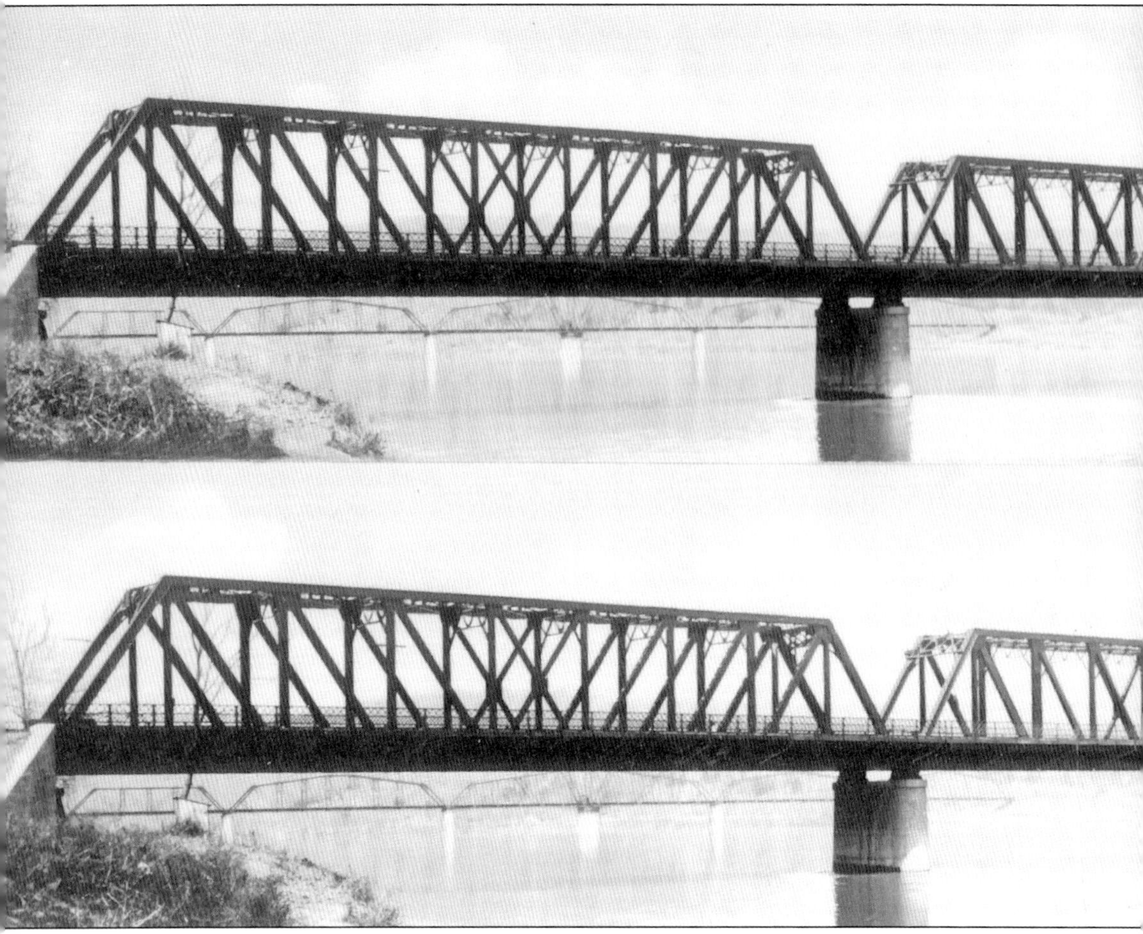

The Frisco Railroad Bridge is sometimes confused in photographs with the Fort Smith/Van Buren Free Pedestrian Bridge seen here. Built for people, wagons, autos, and the electric trolley, the

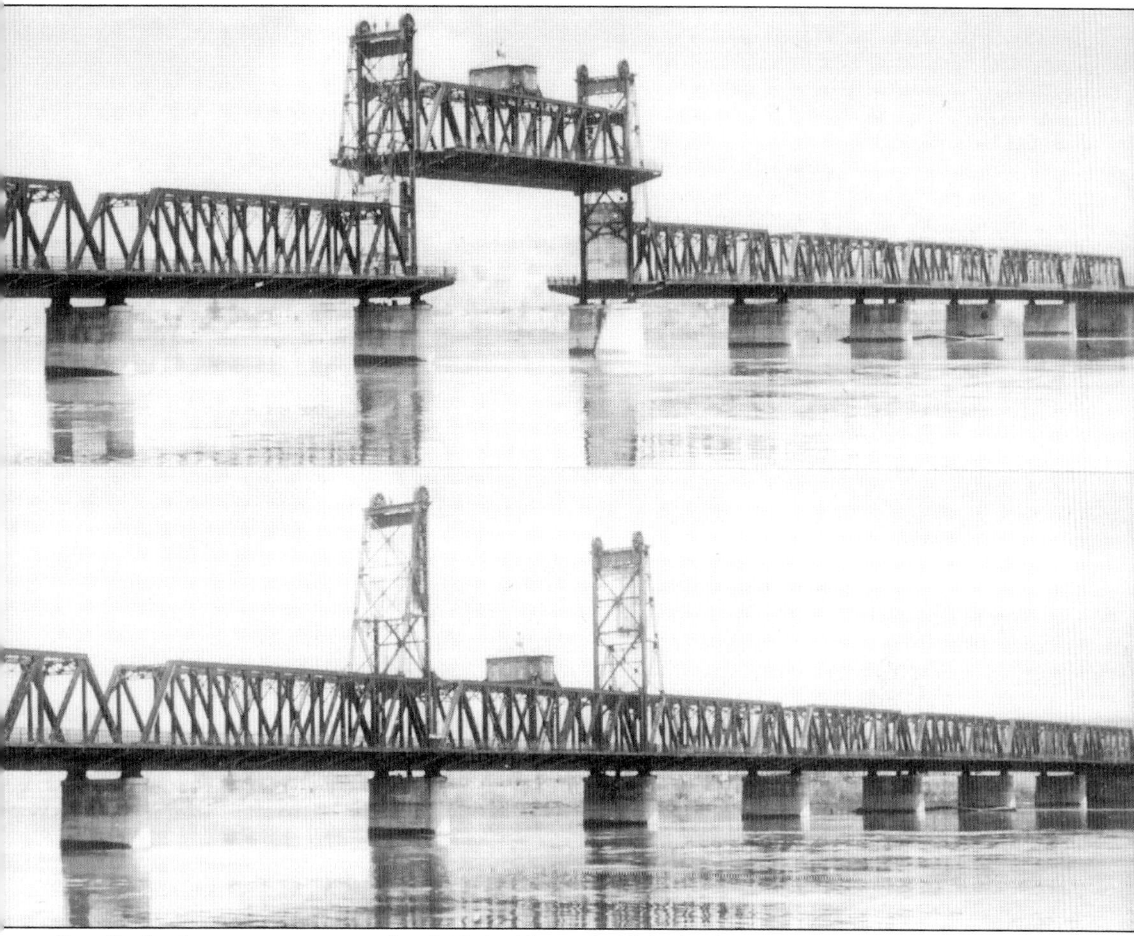

Free Bridge began operation in April 1912. Almost half the bridge was swept away in the Flood of 1943. (Courtesy of the UAFS Cobb Collection.)

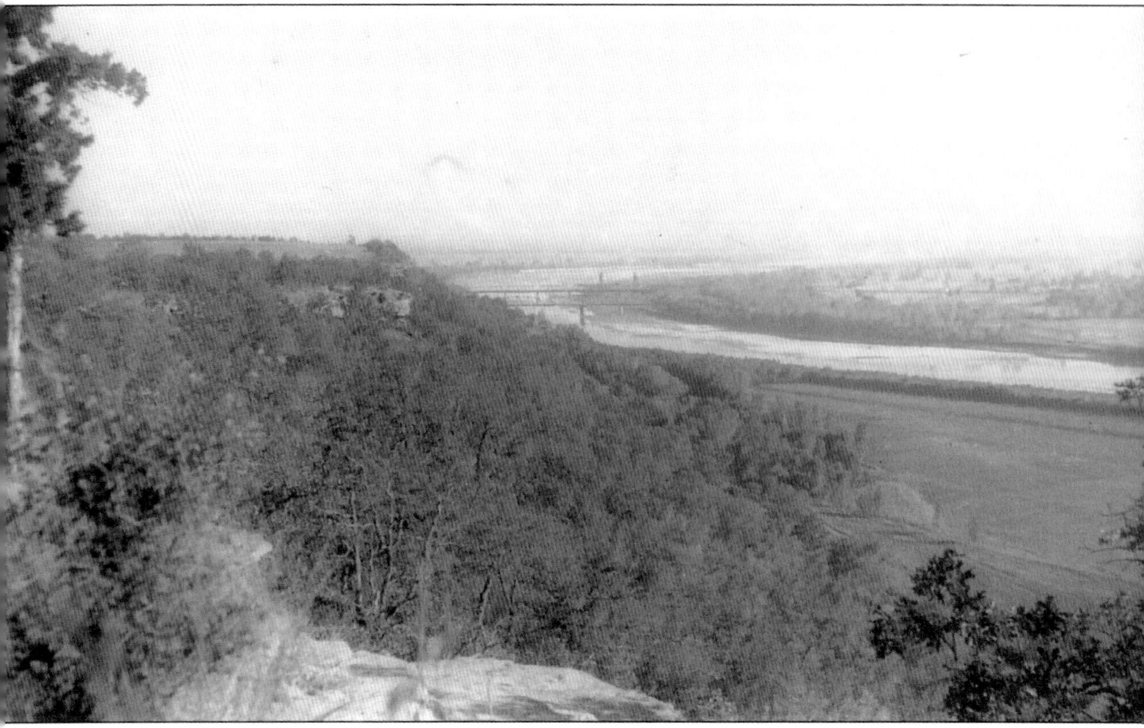

This undated photograph looking southeast from Lee Creek Bluff shows the completed bridges in the distance. The bluff obscures downtown Van Buren. The tornado of 1996 crossed the river from right to left, between the bridges and the photographer's vantage point. (Courtesy of Steven Peer.)

Five

Acts of Nature

Located on the river, Van Buren has had its share of floods over the years. In 1833, the Arkansas River crested at 38 feet and wiped out the neighboring town of Columbus. Ten years later, in 1843, the river crested at 35 feet. Clara Eno's parents arrived by steamboat during the flood and took a rowboat to the courthouse five blocks along submerged Main Street. In 1927, the river crested between 35 and 37 feet, and all levees constructed between Little Rock and Fort Smith failed. The water took an unusually long time to recede, causing dysentery, typhoid, and malaria.

In May 1943, conditions allowed for heavy rains to occur from Lake Huron to the Texas border with Mexico. Bartlesville, Oklahoma, to the northwest of Van Buren, reported 29 inches of rain from May 9 to 20. The river at Van Buren crested over flood stage twice, at a record-breaking 41 feet on May 12 and at a previous record-tying 38 feet on May 23. Upriver at Muskogee, Oklahoma, the river crested even higher at 48 feet. The discharge of the water was the main reason for the damage. During the flood stages, the river flowed between 760,000 and 850,000 cubic feet per second. As a result, the approach and a section of the Frisco Bridge at Van Buren were taken out. The Free Bridge for automobiles and pedestrians could not withstand the surging water and failed as well. The area was fortunate to have Railroad Operating Battalions of the US Army training at Camp Chaffee across the river. Some men were housed and training in the rail yards at Van Buren. Four battalions, including machinists, mechanics, operators, conductors, and medical staff, helped the relief effort. African American soldiers of the 469th Quartermaster Truck Regiment from Texas aided these troops. The soldiers erected a pontoon bridge and linked Van Buren to Fort Smith. The flood caused over $20 million in damages ($275 million in today's money).

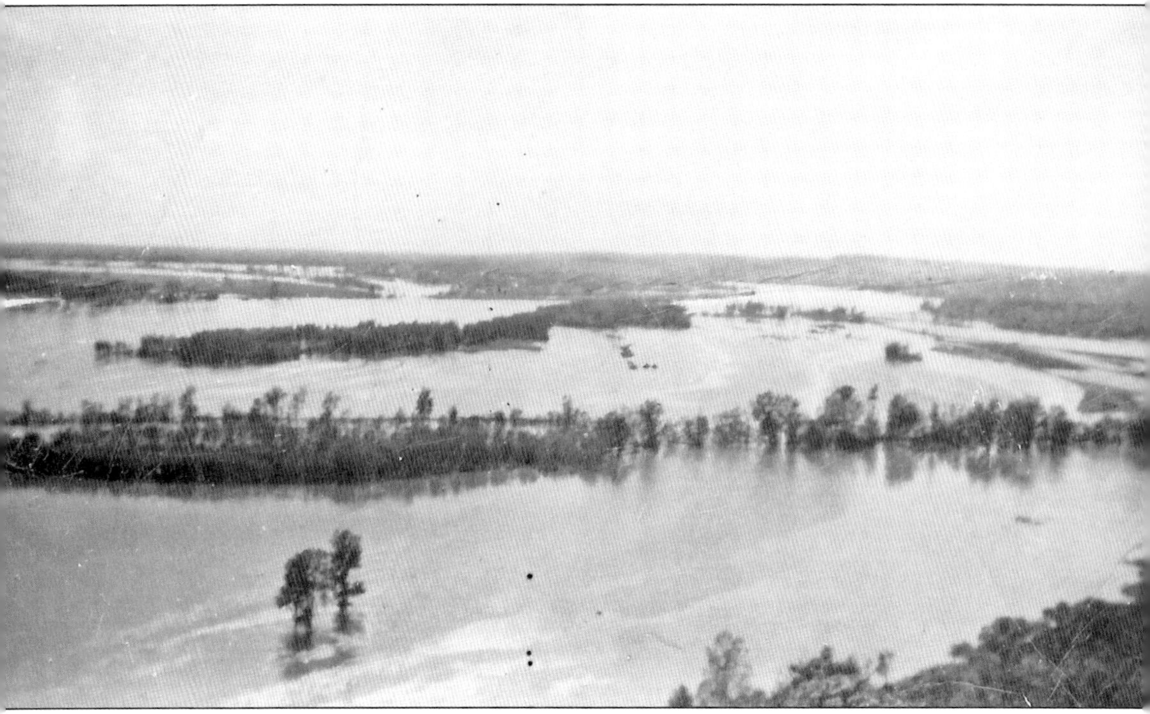

This aerial photograph shows the flooded Arkansas River Valley from the bluffs above Van Buren. Known as Mount Vista, in the 19th century the heights were called Lee Creek Bluff, named for the stream that flows into Arkansas on the western side of the hill. (Courtesy of UAFS.)

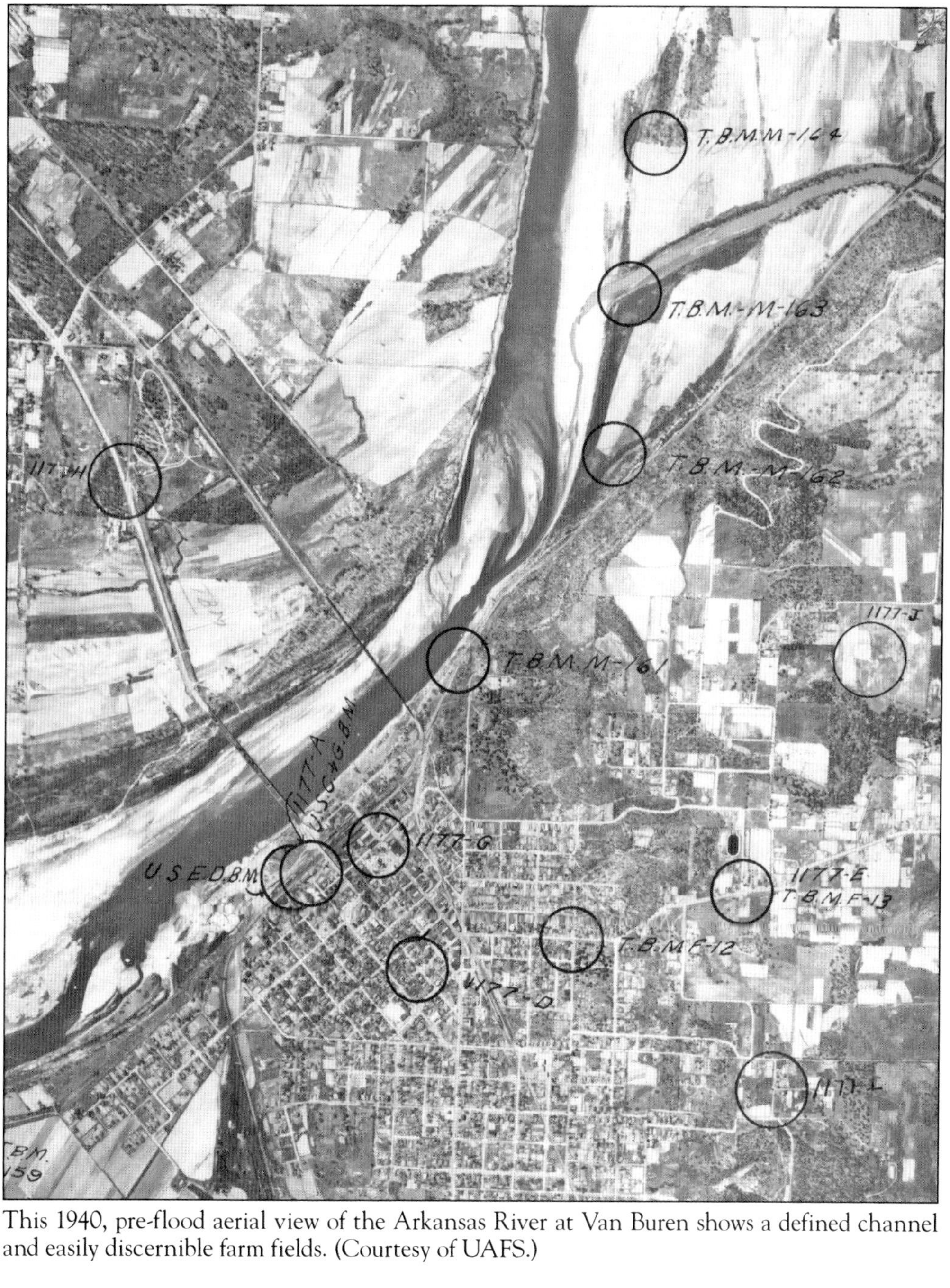

This 1940, pre-flood aerial view of the Arkansas River at Van Buren shows a defined channel and easily discernible farm fields. (Courtesy of UAFS.)

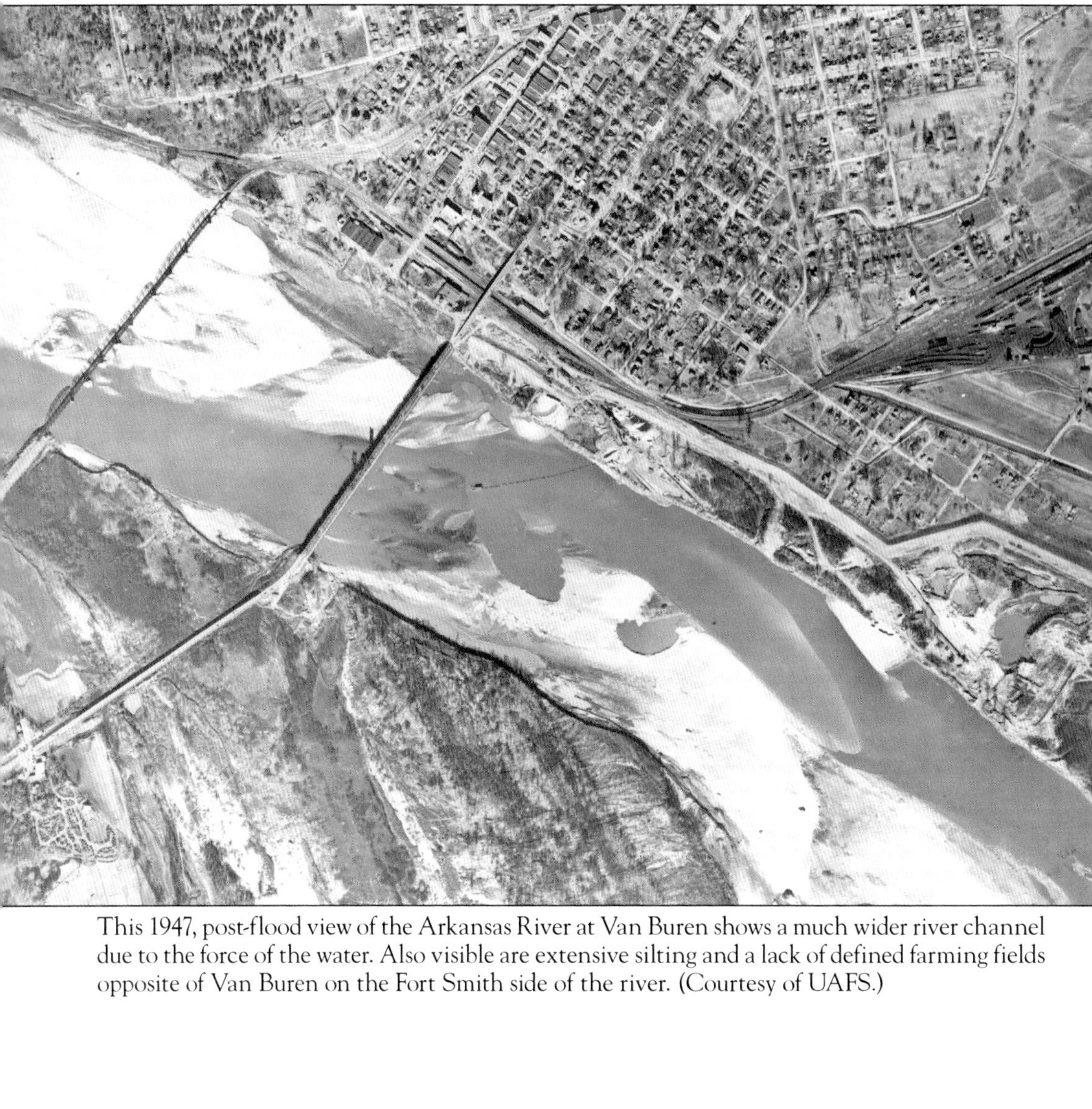

This 1947, post-flood view of the Arkansas River at Van Buren shows a much wider river channel due to the force of the water. Also visible are extensive silting and a lack of defined farming fields opposite of Van Buren on the Fort Smith side of the river. (Courtesy of UAFS.)

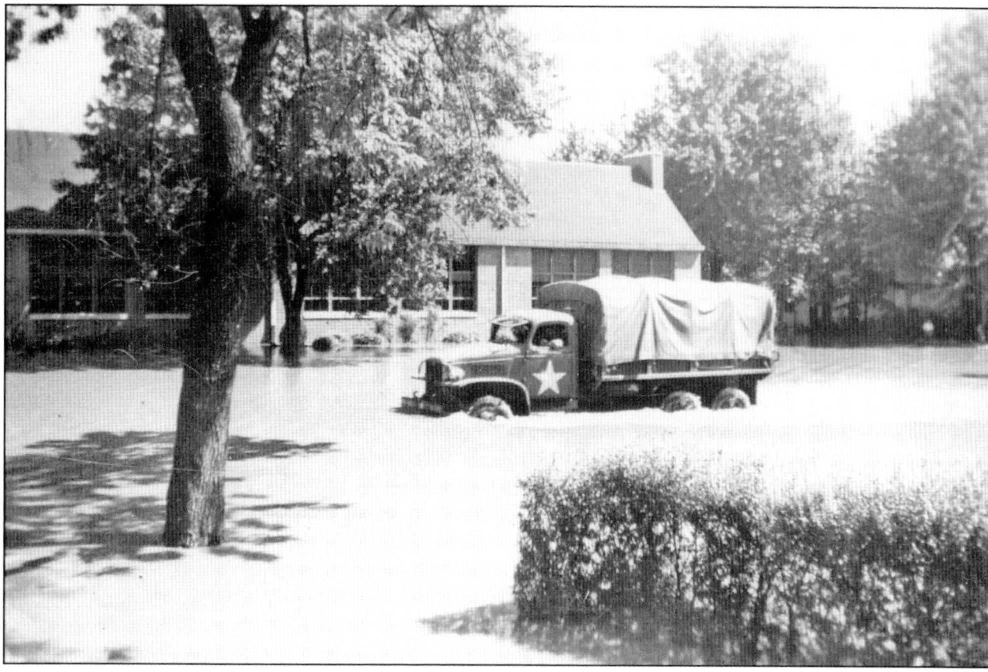

This Army truck moving through the floodwaters on Broadway was part of the military relief effort helping the citizens of Van Buren. (Courtesy of the UAFS Cobb Collection.)

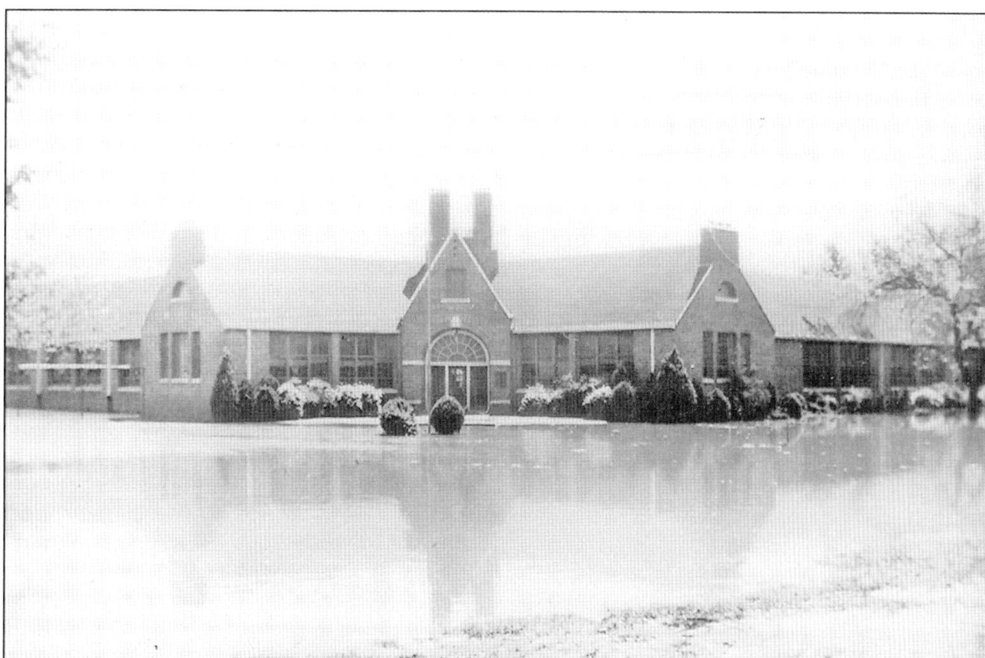

Floodwaters reached the Sophia Myer School, seen here in 1943. (Courtesy of the UAFS Cobb Collection.)

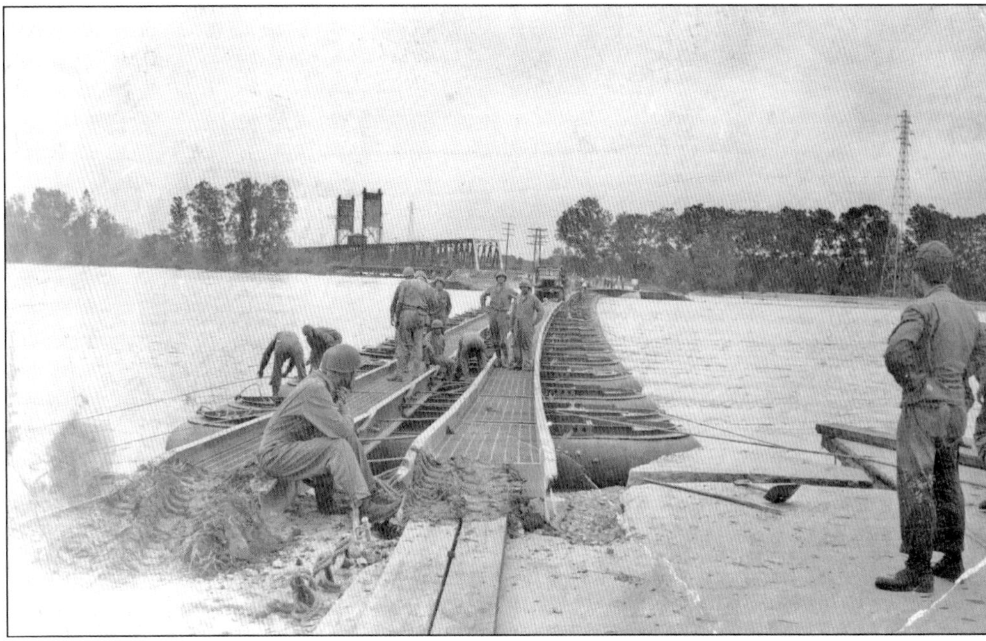

Army soldiers put the finishing touches on a pontoon bridge used to link Fort Smith and Van Buren after the Free Bridge washed away in the Flood of 1943. (Courtesy of the UAFS Cobb Collection.)

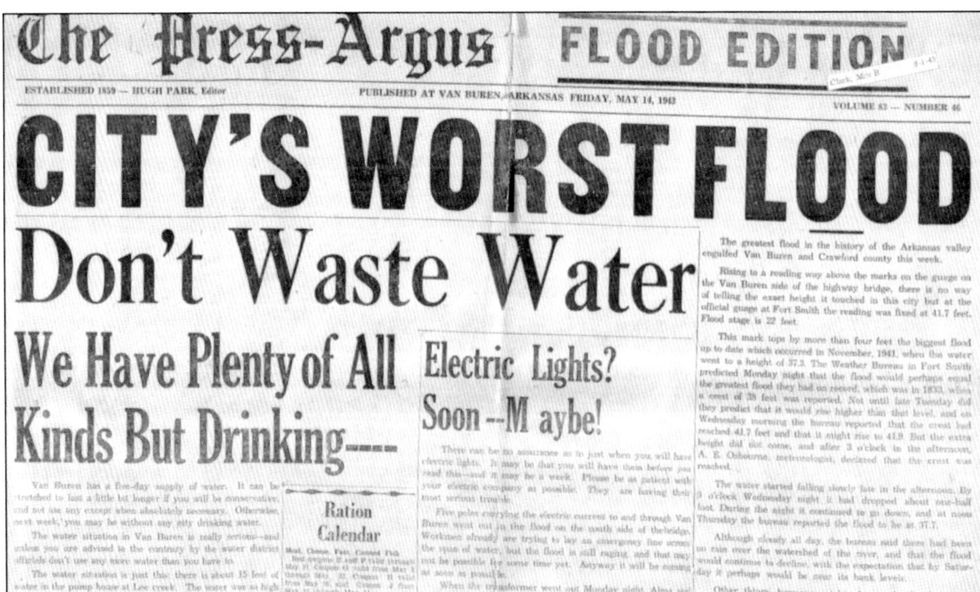

The Press-Argus FLOOD EDITION

ESTABLISHED 1859 — HUGH PARK, Editor PUBLISHED AT VAN BUREN, ARKANSAS FRIDAY, MAY 14, 1943 VOLUME 83 — NUMBER 46

CITY'S WORST FLOOD

Don't Waste Water

We Have Plenty of All Kinds But Drinking—

Van Buren has a five-day supply of water. It can be stretched to last a little bit longer if you will be conservative, and not use any except when absolutely necessary. Otherwise, next week, you may be without any city drinking water.

The water situation in Van Buren is really serious—and unless you are advised to the contrary by the water district officials don't use any more water than you have to.

The water situation is just this: there is about 15 feet of water in the pump house at Lee creek. The water was so high that the doors of the pump house could not be sandbagged,

Ration Calendar

Meat, Cheese, Fats, Canned Fish

Processed Fruits and Vegetables

Electric Lights? Soon --M aybe!

There can be no assurance as to just when you will have electric lights. It may be that you will have them before you read this—and it may be a week. Please be as patient with your electric company as possible. They are having their most serious trouble.

Five poles carrying the electric current to and through Van Buren went out in the flood on the south side of the bridge. Workmen already are trying to lay an emergency line across the span of water, but the flood is still raging, and that may not be possible for some time yet. Anyway it will be coming as soon as possible.

When the transformer went out Monday night, Alma and Mulberry and the rural lines that hook on at Alma were given

The greatest flood in the history of the Arkansas valley engulfed Van Buren and Crawford county this week.

Rising to a reading way above the marks on the guage on the Van Buren side of the highway bridge, there is no way of telling the exact height it touched in this city but at the official guage at Fort Smith the reading was fixed at 41.7 feet. Flood stage is 22 feet.

This mark tops by more than four feet the biggest flood up to date which occurred in November, 1941, when the water went to a height of 37.3. The Weather Bureau in Fort Smith predicted Monday night that the flood would perhaps equal the greatest flood they had on record, which was in 1833, when a crest of 38 feet was reported. Not until late Tuesday did they predict that it would rise higher than that level, and on Wednesday morning the bureau reported that the crest had reached 41.7 feet and that it might rise to 41.9. But the extra height did not come, and after 3 o'clock in the afternoon, A. E. Osbourne, meteorologist, declared that the crest was reached.

The water started falling slowly late in the afternoon. By 9 o'clock Wednesday night it had dropped about one-half foot. During the night it continued to go down, and at noon Thursday the bureau reported the flood to be at 37.7.

Although cloudy all day, the bureau said there had been no rain over the watershed of the river, and that the flood would continue to decline, with the expectation that by Saturday it perhaps would be near its bank levels.

Other things, however, might change the flood picture. The water which had been racing down the stream at hurri-

In a somewhat lighthearted fashion, the Van Buren *Press-Argus* reported on the worst flood in the city's history and the great amount of water available. Ten days later, when the second round of flooding hit, the humor was absent from the coverage. (Courtesy of UAFS.)

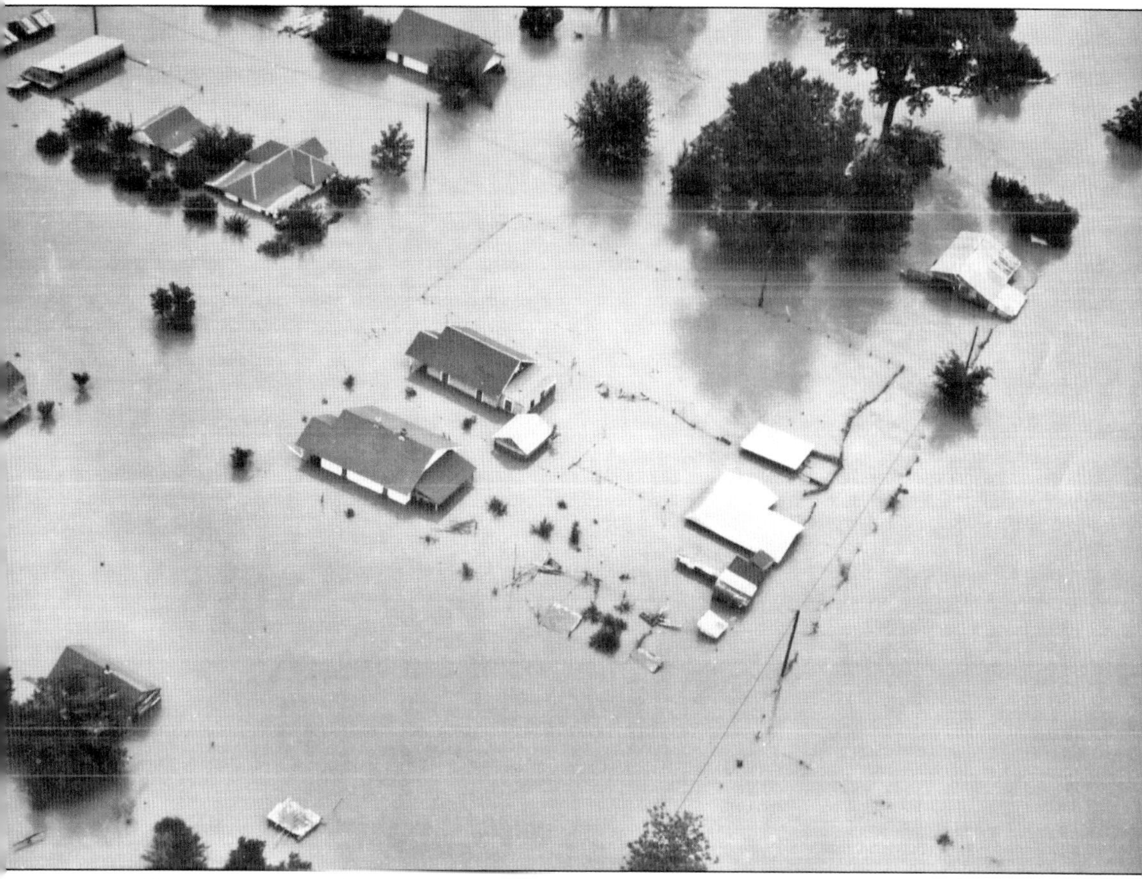

This 1943 aerial photograph shows flooded homes and property in Van Buren. Struck by two floods in May of that year, residents endured a long process of drying out and repairing the damage. (Courtesy of Steven Peer.)

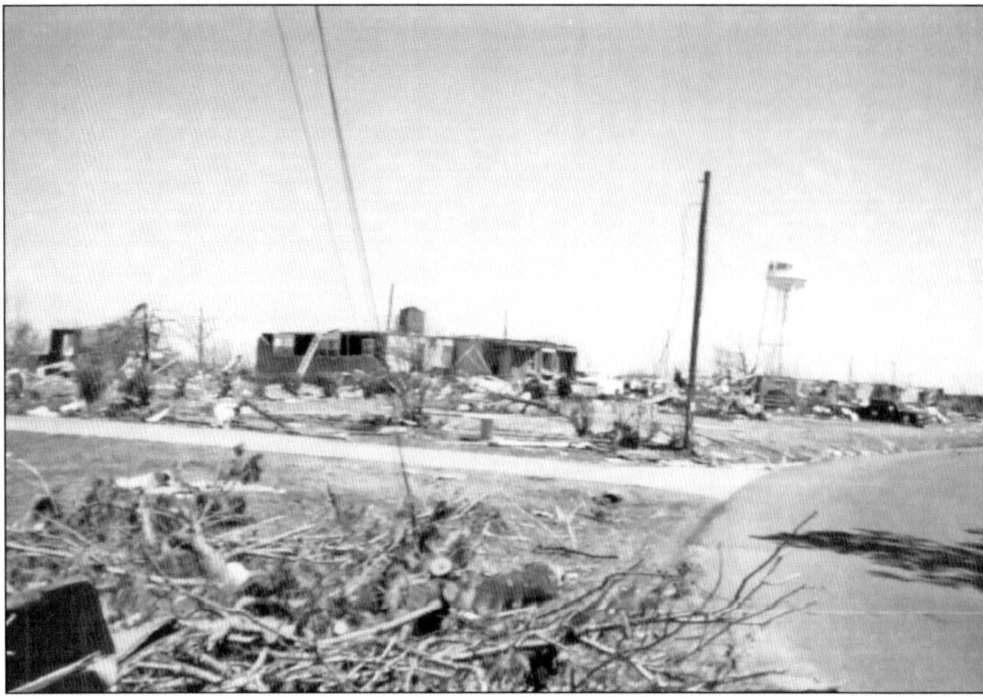

On Sunday night, April 21, 1996, an F3 tornado struck Fort Smith and then crossed the Arkansas River and caused extensive damage in Van Buren. In both towns, 1,800 homes were damaged or destroyed. Two fatalities were reported in Fort Smith, while fortunately only minor injuries occurred in Van Buren. Allen Ray and Norma Jean Toothaker took these photographs on April 22 near their home on Skyline Drive. (Both, courtesy of Norma Jean Toothaker.)

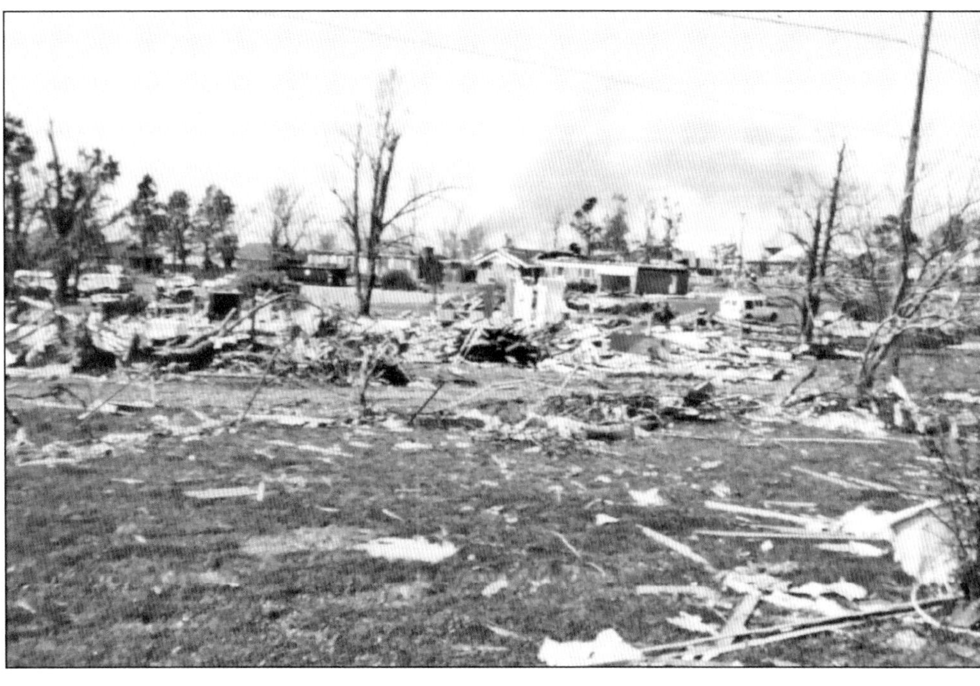

About the Drennen-Scott House

Overlooking the Arkansas River, the commanding Drennen-Scott House, initially the home of Revolutionary War descendant John Drennen and his family, is now a working laboratory for university students as they recreate the century-and-a-half-old home linked to the Trail of Tears, the Underground Railroad, and the Civil War. The house is also a museum open to the public.

Located at 222 North Third Street, the museum is open from March through November on Thursdays from 1:00 p.m. until 5:00 p.m. and also on Friday and Saturday from 10:00 a.m. to 5:00 p.m. Admission is free.

Please contact the Drennen-Scott House at 479-262-6020 for more information or visit class.uafs.edu/history/drennen-scott-house.

UNIVERSITY OF ARKANSAS - FORT SMITH
DRENNEN-SCOTT
HISTORIC SITE